Exploring Wild South Florida

Fourth Edition

A Guide to Finding the Natural Areas and Wildlife

Susan D. Jewell

Pineapple Press
Sarasota, Florida

Dedicated to my nephews, Kevyn and Michael Silverman

Inquiries should be addressed to:
Pineapple Press, Inc.
P.O. Box 3889
Sarasota, Florida 34230
www.pineapplepress.com

Library of Congress Cataloging-in-Publication Data

Jewell, Susan D. (Susan Diane)
          Exploring wild south Florida: a guide to finding the natural areas and wildlife / Susan D. Jewell — 4th ed.
                    p.   cm.
          Includes biographical references and index.
          ISBN 978-1-56164-500-8 (alk. paper)
          1.   Natural History—Florida—Everglades—Guidebooks.   2. Natural history—Florida—Florida Keys—Guidebooks.   3. Natural areas—Florida—Everglades—Guidebooks.   4. Natural areas—Florida—Florida Keys—Guidebooks.   5. Everglades (Fla.)—Guidebooks.   6. Florida Keys (Fla.)—Guidebooks.   I. Title.
          QH105.F6J49   1997
          508.759' 39—dc21   201154879

Fourth Edition
10 9 8 7 6 5 4 3 2 1

Printed in the United States of America

CONTENTS

Color section between pages 54 and 55.

VI NATURAL AREAS OF SOUTHWESTERN FLORIDA
(Collier, Hendry, Lee, and northern Monroe Counties)

ACKNOWLEDGMENTS

Numerous people contributed their knowledge and expertise for the benefit of the four editions. I would like to thank the following people for their help: Paul Allen, Steve Alvarez, Kristie Anders, Jon Andrew, Lisa Andrews, Oron (Sonny) Bass, Gary Bremen, Lois Chapman, Dan Cotter, John Curnett, Fred Davis, Sam Dorfman, Robert Ducham, Charles DuToit, Michael Duever, Michael Eng, Ted Fleming, Lynne Frazer, Frank Fusiak, Richard Haley, Roger Hammer, Wallace Hibbard, Lou Hinds, Dawn Jennings, Archie Jones, Jim Krakowski, James Laray, Andrew Mackie, Joyce Mills, Burkett Neely Jr., Mike Owen, Laura Richards, Jay Robinson Jr., James Sanders, Camille Sewell, Rob Shanks, Alexander (Sandy) Sprunt IV, Barry Stieglitz, Janet Tachi, Tony Terry, Pat Wells, Barbara Wilson, Renee Wilson, Wesley Wilson, and Andy Zavenelli.

I am especially indebted to John Ogden, formerly of Everglades National Park, for numerous helpful suggestions on the original text. Also, I thank the late Bill Robertson and Bill and Sue Smith for tackling the mountainous task of creating the original south Florida bird list.

As always, I'm grateful to my parents, Howard and Marian Jewell, and the rest of my family, whose moral support never waivers, no matter how wild my schemes may be. I also wish to acknowledge the staff at Pineapple Press for their integrity and generous assistance to me.

INTRODUCTION

A flock of roseate spoonbills sifts through the water, straining for small shrimp or fish. A zebra longwing butterfly dances vivaciously through the air and then alights on a leaf to rest. A rainbow tapes the sky together as a thunderstorm threatens to rip it open. Underwater, a bevy of dazzling parrotfish pokes around the purple sea fans, rasping the nourishing algae from a star coral. This is the south Florida you won't want to miss!

Since 1993, tourists and locals alike have been using *Exploring Wild South Florida* to find the unique flora, fauna, and habitats that define the region from Lake Okeechobee to the Florida Keys. Now in its fourth edition, *Exploring Wild South Florida* continues to reveal to readers the beauty of the Everglades, hardwood hammocks, coral reefs, and shell beaches that make south Florida a wonderful place to visit. This edition includes new locations that are now open to the public, including long-distance paddling trails. To make room for them, some locations in the previous edition that were marginally suitable for the purposes of this book were deleted.

Native Americans did not have a word for wilderness—wilderness was the normal world. There aren't many truly wild places left in south Florida. Even places that appear to be untouched have been indirectly altered, such as Everglades National Park and A.R.M. Loxahatchee National Wildlife Refuge, whose upstream waters have been tampered with outside their boundaries. What are referred to as natural areas in the following pages have not escaped the human touch.

To many people, the subconscious definition of "scenic" is a break from monotony: more topographic relief for the eye, more colors, more shapes and objects to keep the eye and brain occupied. That's why many people don't think of the Everglades region as scenic. The vast, flat expanses of mangroves or sawgrass afford little change and are often silent and monochrome. By this definition, the Keys seem slightly more scenic: the colorful exotic flowers, the bright blue and green waters, the rustling palm fronds in the breeze, and the islands dotting the bay all keep the mind busy interpreting them. Now take a closer look!

■ AN OVERVIEW

How to Use This Book

This book concentrates on Broward, Collier, Hendry, Lee, Miami-Dade, Monroe, and Palm Beach counties, the southernmost counties in Florida. From Miami, most of the places described below can be explored in a day trip. Small areas of 50 or 100 acres in urban areas, such as those associated with local nature centers, may seem too insignificant to visit. However, they are oases of natural vegetation needed by migrating and overwintering birds. Unusual concentrations of wildlife may be found in these green islands. They are especially suitable for short jaunts if you are in the neighborhood.

If this is your first trip to south Florida, you'll probably want to stick to the major attractions, such as the Anhinga Trail at Everglades National Park, Corkscrew Swamp, J.N. "Ding" Darling National Wildlife Refuge, and John Pennekamp Coral Reef State Park. If you've already been to those places or have more time, you'll be looking for other sights. Included in these pages are a variety of places from tame (barely venturing from the road) to wild (paddling 50 miles from civilization). Some will warrant only a few hours to explore and some up to a week. There should be something for everyone who wants to get outside and learn about the natural world of south Florida. This book will help the first-timer, the repeat adventurer, the high school or college ecology class, and the foreign visitor find the most interesting natural areas to explore. And for those of you who live in south Florida, have you explored your own "backyard"? Whether you're a nature photographer, a naturalist, or just tired of the city, you can discover a retreat with this book.

This fourth edition covers more than 20 new places to explore, most of which were not available to the public when the last edition was published. The sections are arranged geographically by regions: Southeastern Florida, Southwestern Florida, and the Florida Keys. After those, a new section covers the major land trails (greenways) and water trails (blueways) that are not necessarily associated with a particular park. The entries below occasionally mention other park names in **bold type** if that park has its own entry.

Some sites described in this book are also mentioned as part of the south Florida section of the *Great Florida Birding Trail* guide published by the Florida Fish and Wildlife Conservation Commission (www.floridabirdingtrail). South Florida Birding Trail locations are noted by the SFBT trail number in the information box for each park where applicable (such as South Florida Birding Trail #71 or SFBT #48).

This book is not intended as a field guide to plants and animals, and no attempt is made to be all-inclusive in the main text. Some species of special interest are discussed and illustrated, such as poisonous plants, endangered wildlife, and invasive species. However, the vertebrate checklists at the end of the book should be reasonably complete, so that you can keep track of what you see.

Distances and measurements are given in miles, feet, and acres. Temperatures are given in degrees Fahrenheit (°F). Here are some conversions that foreign travelers may find helpful:

1 mile = 1.6 kilometers	1 kilometer = 0.62 miles
1 foot = 0.3 meters	1 meter = 3.3 feet
1 acre = 0.4 hectares	1 hectare = 2.47 acres
1 pound = 0.45 kilograms	1 kilogram = 2.2 pounds
(°F-32) 5/9 = °C	(9/5 °C) + 32 = °F

Some of the natural areas described have a statement about the best time of year to visit. These are primarily based on when wildlife is present, if biting insects are a consideration, if trails may be too wet, and so on. If no preference is noted, the author finds any time of year to be suitable.

Planning Your Trip

Getting to South Florida

Public transportation to south Florida is convenient by air. The arrival point is most frequently Miami International Airport, a 45-minute drive from Homestead. Other major airports are Ft. Lauderdale International and Palm Beach International. Occasionally people fly to Marathon or Key West if they plan to tour the Keys. However, this usually requires a connecting flight from a mainland airport, which is costly and time-consuming. To visit the southwest coast, you can also fly to Fort Myers or Naples.

Buses also serve the region, and trains serve Miami. Major highways connect greater Miami from all directions, allowing a person to drive easily from elsewhere in Florida.

Public transportation to and within the Keys is poor. There are no trains, and bus service is minimal. Renting a car is usually necessary. The major car rental agencies can be found in the Miami area; smaller independent agencies are scattered throughout the Keys.

South Florida Weather

There is continual controversy over whether south Florida should be classified as tropical or subtropical. The problem is that there are several definitions for both. If only the latitudes between the Tropic of Cancer and the Tropic of Capricorn are considered tropical, then south Florida is not tropical. If the definition is an area that has historically remained frost-free, then the part of the Keys south of Key Largo would qualify. If the definition is an area where tropical plants grow, then many parts of south Florida would qualify. South Florida is at least subtropical.

Regardless of official definitions, south Florida feels tropical. Its southern latitude and maritime surroundings result in high year-round temperatures and humidity. Table 1 shows representative air temperatures for three locations.

Table 1. 30-year average temperatures (°F) of selected locations in South Florida (1971-2000)(NOAA 2010)

Month	Naples	Miami	Key West
January	64.3	68.1	70.3
April	72.5	75.7	77.0
July	82.0	83.7	84.5
October	77.2	78.8	79.2

The warmest month is usually August and the coldest month is January. Notice how much warmer the average temperature is in Key West than on the mainland. However, the three-digit temperatures that wilt other parts of the country don't occur in the Keys. The moderating influences of the Atlantic Ocean, the Gulf of Mexico, and Florida Bay are responsible for that. It doesn't seem to matter—the relative humidity makes it feel just as hot! Hence, there is the southern equivalent of the wind-chill factor, called the "heat index." The National Weather Service defines the heat index as "the temperature that a human body would feel when humidity and air temperature are factored in"—and it's frequently above 100 in the summer, meaning the air feels like it's over 100°F.

While northern Florida has four relatively distinct seasons, southern Florida has only two. South Florida's air temperature extremes range from the upper 20s to the upper 90s. A normal year would register from the lower 40s to the mid-90s. It is precipitation more than temperature, however, that gives south Florida its two seasons—wet and dry (some would claim the two seasons are "mosquito" and "non-mosquito"). The wet season extends from May to October, and the dry season is November to April. Table 2 shows the mean rainfalls for three locations in four months.

Table 2. 30-year average rainfall (inches) of selected locations in South Florida (1971-2000)(NOAA 2010)

Month	Naples	Miami	Key West
January	2.01	1.88	2.22
April	1.99	3.35	2.06
July	7.98	5.79	3.27
October	3.60	6.19	4.34
TOTAL ANNUAL	54.19	58.53	38.94

The rainfall increases in late May or June and declines in November, with peaks in June and September. The precipitation from May to August frequently falls in short, intense daily rainstorms. A visitor to south Florida during those months can expect rain (usually in the form of a thunderstorm) for 10–30 minutes almost every day. The clouds form from convection—the sun's rays evaporating water in the Everglades and ocean. The precipitation in September and October tends to fall less frequently but in larger amounts per event. This is because tropical storms and hurricanes are more frequent in the area then and often drop many inches of rain in one event.

The most reliably good weather (less chance of thunderstorms, tropical storms, cold fronts, intense heat, or mosquitoes) is in March and April. The weather is truly delightful. In fact, it's often so dry that some species of trees (such as gumbo-limbo and West Indian mahogany) lose their leaves regularly every April, and great piles of crunchy leaves can be raked from beneath barren trees. A New England "fall" is in the autumn, while south Florida's "fall" is in the spring.

The months of November and December are also good times to visit for several reasons. The rainy season has ended, but the vegetation is still lush. The weather is cooler and less humid. There is only a small chance of a cold front strong enough to discourage you from exploring. As a bonus, the lodging rates are usually the lowest until mid-December.

Pets in Parks

Information on pet regulations in the parks is included for an important reason: Florida can get quite hot even in the winter. A Florida statute prohibits leaving pets in unattended vehicles because the animals can suffer greatly or even die from the heat. Since many parks don't allow pets (except service animals), and pets usually cannot be left unattended at a park or motel, your visit may be greatly restricted if you bring Fido with you. If possible, leave your pets with a friend, relative, or kennel.

Driving

Driving around the greater Miami area (which includes Homestead and Florida City) can be simplified if you know a few tips about the layout of the roads. There are four quadrants: Northwest, Northeast, Southwest, and Southeast. Roads are numbered beginning with the lowest in downtown Miami and ascending outward. Thus, there is a NW 60th Street, a SW 60th Street, and so on. "Streets" are oriented east-west, and "Avenues" are oriented north-south. Many of these larger roads are blocked occasionally by the network of canals that laces the city. Avenues ending in the number "2" or "7" (such as 72nd Avenue or 107th Avenue) are most likely to have bridges over the canals and continue straight through. The smaller "Courts" (north-south) and "Terraces" (east-west) are rarely more than a few blocks long.

Homestead and Florida City have dual street numbering systems. The numbering system from Miami continues as far south as Florida City: the street numbers will be in the 200–300s and the avenue numbers will be in the 100–200s. Interspersed are Homestead's and Florida City's own numbering systems, which have the same pattern as Miami's, originating in the centers of the respective towns.

If you're looking for a specific address, the building's street number will give you a clue. Most addresses have long numbers that indicate their block. For example, 24850 SW 187th Avenue would be between 248th Street and 249th Street in southwest Miami.

If you're the type that gets lost easily, head for the Keys. It's almost impossible to get lost—there's only one main road. That road is US 1, also called the Overseas Highway. Beginning at the southern end of Florida City, the road is marked with small green mile marker signs placed at one-mile intervals. The numbers descend from about 126 in Florida City to 0 in Key West. Thus, you can always tell how far you are from Key West. Addresses in the Keys are given by mile marker numbers or fractions thereof, such as MM 102.5. You'll frequently hear the added qualifier of "bayside" (the place you're looking for is on the Florida Bay side of the road) or "oceanside" (on the Atlantic Ocean side). From almost anywhere in the Keys, you can easily tell which side is which.

Two roads bisect the Everglades east to west—the Tamiami Trail (US 41) between Miami and Naples, and Alligator Alley (part of I-75) between west Fort Lauderdale and Naples.

State roads will be abbreviated below as "SR" and county roads as "CR."

What to Wear

The weather information above should give you an idea of the type of clothing you'll need. Most of the year, shorts or lightweight pants are comfortable. Any time you plan to go on a trail, it's better to wear lightweight, long-sleeved shirts and long pants to prevent mosquito, chigger, poisonwood, and sunburn problems. Clothing should be loose so that it doesn't stick to you from the humidity.

It's amazing how cold it can feel during a winter cold front, when the temperature is in the 40s or 50s (°F), the wind is blowing, and it's damp. At these times (usually from late December to early March), it's good to have several lightweight layers of sweaters and jackets.

Sunglasses and a sun hat are necessary most of the year. Comfortable walking shoes or jogging shoes will be suitable for the trails, especially if you don't mind getting them wet.

Most restaurants are casual in south Florida, particularly in the Keys. Even in restaurants that serve upscale food, most people wear casual clothing. Shorts are not uncommon in restaurants.

Fishing Licenses

A state saltwater license is required for Florida residents and nonresidents, with some exceptions, such as children under 16 years of age and individuals fishing from a charter boat that has a vessel saltwater fishing license. For other exceptions, check with the Florida Fish and Wildlife Conservation Commission (www.myfwc.com/Fishing/Index.htm). Nonresidents may obtain a 3-day, 7-day, or 1-year license. Freshwater fishing licenses are also required. Licenses may be obtained from county tax collectors' offices, from sporting goods stores, on the internet, and by phone (see www.myfwc.com/Fishing/Index.htm). Be forewarned that some freshwater fish (for example, largemouth bass, gar, bowfin, warmouth, yellow catfish, redear sunfish, and oscar) in most of the Everglades are contaminated with mercury. Limited or no consumption of these species is recommended by authorities.

The State Park System

The many state parks are managed to maintain the lands as they were when the first Europeans arrived. The historic sites preserve the cultural heritage. Entrance fees are charged at most sites. Extra fees are charged for canoe and kayak rentals, campsites, firewood, launching boats, and so forth; however, ranger-led nature walks are free. If you plan to explore a number of parks, or live near a park that you visit frequently, you should consider buying an annual individual or family pass. See www.floridastateparks.org for a list of the various fees and passes.

The parks are open from 8 am to sunset every day of the year including holidays (a few open earlier). The gate may close at an odd time, such as 7:22 pm. Nature centers and visitor centers may be closed two days a week, generally Tuesday and Wednesday. Parks with campgrounds generally allow check-ins after sunset. Reservations may be made up to 11 months in advance through ReserveAmerica (www.reserveamerica.com) or call 800-326-3521 or TDD 888-433-0287. Primitive campsites have no facilities, and campers must pack out their trash.

Pets are permitted only in designated areas and must be kept on a 6-foot, hand-held leash. Pets are not allowed in swimming, beach, or concession areas and some campgrounds. Pets may not be left unattended. Service animals for the disabled are allowed in all areas. Owners must clean up after their pets. More specific information on designated areas is found within each park's entry below.

National Wildlife Refuges

The National Wildlife Refuge (NWR) system is composed of more than 550 refuges and management areas across the country. Many were established to protect habitat for migratory birds, such as waterfowl. The first refuge, Pelican Island in central Florida, was created to protect a colony of nesting water birds. Many refuges have been established to protect habitat for a single endangered species, such as Crocodile Lake National Wildlife Refuge for crocodiles, Florida Panther National Wildlife Refuge, National Key Deer Refuge, and so on.

The refuges were created solely for protecting natural resources. Only compatible activities are permitted, which may or may not include visitors. This is why few public amenities are offered. Some are closed to the public, such as Crocodile Lake, and some are managed by nearby larger refuges. Many have multifaceted educational facilities, such as Loxahatchee and J.N. "Ding" Darling. Some have concessions that rent canoes and kayaks or offer guided tours (such as J.N. "Ding" Darling). None of the south Florida refuges allows camping. When you visit a refuge, come prepared with drinking water and anything else you may need. Pets may or may not be permitted (see a specific park's entry in this book or call the refuge to confirm).

Fees are charged for many refuges (U.S. Fee Areas). If you plan to visit several national wildlife refuges and national parks over the course of a year, you should consider purchasing one of the following annual pass options:

- **National Parks and Federal Recreational Lands Pass:** Covers the entrance fee to all U.S. fee areas (federal recreational lands: national wildlife refuges, national parks, Bureau of Land Management lands, and Army Corps of Engineers lands) for a year from date of sale for $80. You can purchase a pass in person at the park or refuge; by calling 1-888-ASKUSGS, Ext. 1; or store.usgs.gov/pass/index.html. Seniors and disabled people are eligible for free passes, but those passes must be obtained in person at a national park or national wildlife refuge where an entrance fee is charged.

- **Federal Duck Stamp:** Duck Stamp holders are allowed free admission to all national wildlife refuges for one year from July 1 to June 30. The funds from the stamps are used to buy habitat for more refuges. Available at most post offices and refuges for $15.

- **Annual Pass for one refuge:** Refuges with an entrance fee usually also provide an annual pass good for that refuge for one year from the date of issue.

National Parks
Unlike the refuges, the national park system was established to protect our natural resources while also providing a way for people to enjoy them. Thus, they usually have more tourist facilities than the refuges.

Most national parks are U.S. fee areas; the remainder do not charge entrance fees. Please see previous section for information on annual National Parks and Federal Recreational Lands Pass. Parks with an entrance fee usually have an annual pass good for that park for one year from the date of issue.

When You Arrive

Conservation Tips
Good conservationists carry their habits with them wherever they go. Because of the tremendous volume of tourists coming to south Florida every year, the natural resources are stressed to the limits. You can help to ensure that your visit has a minimal environmental impact by observing a few suggestions:

1. **Conserve water.** Except during periods of heavy rainfall, south Florida often has a critical water shortage. This shortage usually occurs during the dry season, which coincides with the winter tourist season, which is also an agricultural growing season. During droughts, a county may impose water restrictions, which may include a requirement by restaurants that wait staff serve water only on request.

Other restrictions may include watering lawns and washing cars. Keep your showers short and use your ingenuity to think of other ways you can save water. The lack of water is bad enough, but a compounding problem is that it drives engineers and city planners to find new ways to retrieve water (like drilling a new well), usually at a cost to the environment.

2. **Drive carefully to avoid hitting wildlife.** Watch for snakes warming themselves on roads in the winter as the air cools in late afternoon or escaping high water after heavy rains (especially on the main Everglades National Park road to Flamingo). Drive slowly in Key deer areas (such as Big Pine Key), crocodile areas (such as the stretch of US 1 from the mainland to Key Largo), and panther areas (such as Tamiami Trail). Headlights, particularly high beams, temporarily blind animals and cause them to freeze in their tracks, so keep this in mind when driving in rural areas at night.

If you are operating a motorboat, watch the water ahead of you for ripples that might indicate a manatee is surfacing. If you are near a manatee, cut your motor to neutral until the manatee has moved away. Observe posted signs warning of manatee areas.

3. **Be a responsible angler.** Anglers should not leave monofilament line in the water or on land; a state law makes this illegal. Everyone should collect lines and hooks they find littering the water—many animals have been slowly strangled by discarded fishing lines. Don't go fishing just for sport. Catch-and-release fishing harasses fish and often causes them injury or death. Fish that are to be released should be handled carefully with wet hands and placed quickly but gently under water.

4. **Protect coral reefs.** If you snorkel or dive, don't touch the corals. Simply touching a live coral can cause the sensitive polyps to die. Don't stand on the bottom or kick up silt. Collecting of coral (even if it's dead) is illegal in Florida. Collecting of tropical fish for aquaria usually causes them to die prematurely. Do not feed the fish on the reef because it changes their natural diets and habits.

Recycling receptacle for fishing line

5. **Don't collect souvenirs from the wild.** All parks prohibit the collection of plants, animals, rocks, and so on. This is a good policy to follow everywhere. Take photographs instead.

6. **Don't feed wild animals.** Key deer, alligators, raccoons, and other wildlife learn to associate food with humans. This has caused many Key deer to wander into busy roads where they are killed by moving vehicles. Some attacks on humans by alligators looking for handouts have also occurred. The alligator usually gets shot as punishment.

7. **Recycle containers.** Recycling bins are found in most parks.

8. **Leave endangered and threatened species alone.** It is illegal to touch or disturb a protected species. This includes manatees, Key deer, and sea turtles.

9. **Don't release any animal, whether native or nonnative, into the wild**. It is illegal. Nonnative animals are particularly destructive to the environment, and many will die in the unfamiliar surroundings.

Local Precautions

There are probably no more hazards in south Florida than anywhere else in the country—some are the same and some different. Exploring wild areas is an adventurous and occasionally risky hobby. Everyone should have a safe and enjoyable trip. However, every person is different and has varying reactions to adverse conditions. While park rangers and other staff are well trained, they cannot predict the weather, wildlife–people interactions, and the experience level of each person they advise. Visitors should rely on their own common sense and recognition of their experience level to have a safe trip.

Your trip to Florida should be perfectly delightful, without any of the misfortunes mentioned below. The chance of a safe trip is increased if you are aware of the following.

Weather
Thunderstorms
The thunderstorm season begins around May and lasts until October, the duration of the wet season. The most active months are June to September. Within these months, a thunderstorm is possible almost daily. In extreme southern Florida, daily thunderstorms occur on an average of 70–80 days per year. Thunderstorms may occur at any other time of the year. They are caused by heat rising from the warming land, creating unstable air above. A cumulonimbus cloud (thunderhead) indicates a potential thunderstorm.

The major hazard of these storms is the lightning they produce. In Florida, a single day of intense thunderstorms can cause 10,000 lightning strikes. Next to being under the center of a thunderstorm, the most dangerous place is near the leading edge. Don't assume you are safe if the storm hasn't quite hit. And don't underestimate lightning—it causes about 7 deaths a year in Florida and many injuries, more than any other state.

Other hazards from thunderstorms include high winds and hail. High winds are almost always associated with thunderstorms, while hail is infrequent. High winds can be a problem for canoeists and kayakers, who should always be vigilant for thunderstorm development.

Hurricanes
The National Weather Service considers June 1 to November 30 as the official hurricane season. Hurricanes or tropical storms have occurred in the Atlantic Ocean during every month of the year except April. The height of tropical activity (tropical waves, depressions, storms, and hurricanes) is mid-August to mid-October. Therefore, you can minimize the possibility of encountering a tropical storm or hurricane by avoiding these months for your trip.

Hurricanes play a beneficial ecological role. During the summer, when the temperature of tropical waters can rise too high for marine organisms to survive, hurricanes disperse the heat. The heat rises from the water and is carried off to colder regions with the hurricane's clouds. Therefore, higher ocean temperatures increase the chance of a hurricane forming. This is nature's way of keeping the balance.

The local municipal emergency shelters may not be able to accommodate all tourists and residents during a storm. If you are in south Florida during a hurricane warning, you may be mandated to evacuate to higher ground. Only two roads link the Florida Keys to the mainland, and there is little controversy that they are inadequate to handle a major evacuation. Campers in Flamingo are also vulnerable and may be evacuated by rangers before campers in any other area. Before heading south during hurricane season, check the National Weather Service (see "Other Sources of Information") for tropical weather activity.

Tornadoes and Waterspouts

Tornadoes are common in Florida. March, April, and May are the busy months for tornadic activity. Tornadoes are not as common in the southern tip of the peninsula as in the central and northern parts. South Florida also has the aquatic version of the tornado—the waterspout. A waterspout is a tornado that forms over a large body of water, such as the ocean. Most often, a waterspout is short-lived, relatively weak, and doesn't reach land. The funnel may not even touch the surface of the water. Such a waterspout is not hazardous, but if you see a funnel cloud on land or water, seek shelter in a sturdy building.

Poisonous Plants

The initial panic an amateur botanist feels when seeing south Florida plants for the first time is that so many of them look alike. The generic morphology (form) of a tropical leaf is a shiny surface with smooth edges and a pointed tip. This facilitates water dripping off the leaf in such a humid, rainy environment. The myriad of look-alike plants presents a problem to the careful naturalist who won't touch any plant that he or she can't identify. Some plants in this region have parts that are caustic if ingested or touched by a sensitive person. Only three are likely to give the average person a rash if merely touched, and those three are described below. Two of those (manchineel and poisonwood) fall into the category of having a tropical-looking leaf, and they are considered tropical trees.

The three described below are not the only poisonous plants in the area. To be safe from an irritating rash or worse, always identify a plant before touching it. If you find you have brushed against one of the three species mentioned, wash your skin with soap and cold water as soon as possible.

Manchineel

The most infamous of our native poisonous plants is manchineel in the spurge family. This small tree (up to 30 feet) has shiny alternate leaves 2–4 inches long, with faintly round-toothed margins and pointed tips. Manchineels are known for their caustic sap (which is very irritating if it contacts human skin or internal tissues), and the fatally poisonous fruit (which is 1–1.5 inches and looks like a crab apple). Manchineels can be found in coastal forests along the southern edge of Everglades National Park and the Keys. They are common around Flamingo, Whitewater Bay, and on Cape Sable (particularly in the buttonwood hammocks along the coast), but it is unlikely that you will encounter one. They are less common in the Keys, where public pressure to remove these "undesirable" trees has caused most of them near houses, trails, or roads to be destroyed. The tree is also sensitive to frost. It is on the state's protected list and is classified as endangered.

Poisonwood

The second of the three poisonous plants is another tree, known as poisonwood or Florida poisontree. This relative of poison ivy shares the characteristic caustic sap. Touching the leaves yields a blistering skin rash similar to poison ivy. Poisonwood has alternate compound leaves with five shiny leaflets that are smooth-edged and pointy-tipped. Unlike manchineel, there is a good chance that you will encounter a poisonwood tree in extreme southern Florida. The tree grows in wet and dry habitats, near roadsides and in unspoiled wilderness, in hammocks, in pinelands, and in coastal regions—in other words, just about anywhere. But it is becoming increasingly scarce, suffering the same fate as the manchineel. Because of its irritating sap, many homeowners destroy such trees in their yards. This causes problems for wildlife, since the fruits are a valuable food. The state-threatened white-crowned pigeon, a tropical fruit-eating bird found in the Keys, is especially dependent on poisonwood fruits. Biologists from the National Audubon Society's Research Department in Tavernier, who recognized the value of poisonwood to the pigeons, have been trying to educate the public to save poisonwood trees.

Poison ivy

The third poisonous plant is the familiar three-leaved poison ivy. Since this plant is so common elsewhere in the country, it's not necessary to describe it here, but you should expect to encounter it just about anywhere around south Florida, including the Keys.

Vertebrate Animals
Venomous Snakes

South Florida is home to four kinds of native venomous snakes: the eastern diamondback rattler, the dusky pygmy rattler, the Florida cottonmouth (also known as the water moccasin), and the eastern coral snake. Encounters with these snakes are rare. The nonvenomous Florida water snake is often mistaken for the less common cottonmouth, and the nonvenomous scarlet snake and scarlet kingsnake can be confused with the coral snake. Coral snakes are primarily nocturnal and burrow under loose litter, so it is not likely you will encounter one by accident. If you see a brightly colored snake whose identity you are unsure of, recall the adage "Red touch yellow kills a fellow" to remind you that if the red and yellow bands are touching each other, you are looking at a venomous snake. Pygmy rattlesnakes are the most likely venomous snakes you will see. They often warm themselves on paved roads. They are usually less than two feet long, with a dusty appearance and round, dark blotches. Their rattles are so tiny they often go unnoticed. Even if you can identify snakes, all should be left alone.

Sharks

Sharks are common in the warm Florida waters. The majority are small, nonaggressive, and nonthreatening to humans. Swimmers and waders in shallow, murky water are at risk because the sharks can smell something swimming nearby, but they can't see what it is. Spear-fishermen have had fish they just caught snatched from their

Nurse shark (bottom) and blacktip shark (top) are common reef sharks—harmless unless provoked.

hands. One diver lost her hand this way. Some sharks eat lobsters, so sport lobsterers also should be cautious.

To decrease your chances of getting bitten by a shark, avoid standing or swimming in shallow, murky water and don't hold fish or lobsters in your hand underwater. This is also a good reason for divers and snorkelers to refrain from attracting reef fish by feeding them.

Alligators
Although they appear lethargic and slow-moving, these giant reptiles can react with blinding speed when provoked. Normally, alligators that have never seen a human are no threat to people. The problem arises when an alligator that lives near houses or a park becomes accustomed to people feeding it. Thereafter, that alligator recognizes humans as a source of food. Since an alligator has little intelligence, it doesn't distinguish that the food does not include the whole package. A state regulation prohibits people from feeding alligators. Observing this regulation is important for everyone's safety.

In the wild, female alligators are protective of their young. Since females may guard the young for more than a year, no time of year is without defensive females. Therefore, if you are walking in an area where alligators are present, look and listen carefully, and be ready to back off if you hear the babies' squeaky whimpering defense calls.

Insects

Most people deal with insects by applying repellents. While this works, repellents are not without hazards sometimes worse than the original problem. The active ingredient in most repellents, called DEET (N,N-diethyl-m-toluamide), has been linked to seizures and several deaths in the United States (MMWR 1989). DEET is absorbed through the skin and into the circulatory system. About 10–15 percent of the amount applied to the skin passes into the urine. Insect repellents with DEET can melt vinyl and plastic. Watchbands and car seats can be damaged if your DEET-covered skin contacts them. Here is a summary of some precautions to take when using repellents with DEET:

- wear long sleeves and pants and apply repellent only to exposed skin or to clothing
- use low concentrations of DEET
- never apply repellent to wounds
- apply once every 4–8 hours; over-application will not improve effectiveness
- do not inhale or ingest DEET
- wash skin after returning indoors

Certain people, such as children, are more sensitive to repellent than others. Be courteous by not spraying repellent near other people. Never spray it indoors—some people don't dare venture outside without first saturating their skin and clothes, leaving others inside to breathe the DEET.

Mosquitoes

More than 40 species of mosquitoes inhabit southern Florida. From June to November, coinciding with the wet season, the mosquitoes can be unbelievably numerous. It's been suggested (tongue in cheek?) that Everglades National Park should be closed for the summer because of mosquitoes, analogous to northern parks closing for the winter due to heavy snow. Too many foreigners have had miserable trips to the southern Everglades in the summer because they didn't know about the mosquitoes.

Now that you have been sufficiently warned of the worst, you'll be happy to know that many months of the year can be devoid of mosquitoes. The months of December to May usually are dry enough to prevent mosquitoes from hatching, and cold fronts kill the adults.

Mosquitoes need water to hatch their eggs. The eggs hatch 5–10 days after flooding by rains or high tides. Standing water, such as accumulates in old tires, flower pots, and gutters, is perfect for the proliferation of mosquitoes. Therefore, many residents contribute to their own mosquito problems by allowing mosquito breeding places in their yards.

You are more likely to encounter mosquitoes in the coastal mangrove areas and hammocks than in the freshwater marshes. The common saltmarsh mosquito shuns strong sunlight, so you are better off in the open than in the shade and better off in the daytime than at night.

The female mosquito needs the protein from blood to form her eggs, thus it is only the female that bites. The males feed on nectar; they do for marsh flowers what bees do for meadow flowers—they pollinate them. We need mosquitoes.

County mosquito control commissions spray insecticides daily in developed areas during the peak of the mosquito season. Spraying is not allowed over mangroves, national parks, and national wildlife refuges.

Scorpions

The scorpions in Florida are not the same as the ones found in the southwestern United States. Ours are not fatally venomous, but their stings can make a person ill. Scorpions are found throughout south Florida, including the Keys, but you will not be likely to see one unless you are searching for it. Scorpions prefer to hide under wood (such as fallen trees or lumber) rather than rocks. If you turn over a piece of wood, do not use your bare hands—use a walking staff or tripod leg instead. Always put the wood back exactly as you found it, so unseen creatures are not left homeless.

Fire ants

People can ignore swarms of mosquitoes, listlessly swat at horseflies, and calmly step around rattlesnakes. But no one can respond to fire ant attacks any other way than to explode in a frenzy of motion. The subject ants are the red imported fire ants (*Solenopsis invicta*), which were accidentally introduced into Alabama from Brazil in the 1920s. Since then, they have spread throughout the southeastern United States, eventually reaching south Florida in the early 1970s.

Fire ants are red and less than an eighth of an inch long. They are not often seen unless their mound is stepped on. Fire ants react faster to nest agitation than almost all ant species, and it's usually too quick for the agitator. These ants leave itchy, raised pustules that persist for weeks. The nest mounds are piles of dirt about 6–12 inches high and are most often found in disturbed areas, such as the side of a road.

Other insects

No-see-ums or "sand-gnats" (*Culicoides furens*) are minuscule midges that take painful bites that leave welts. No-see-ums are so small and quick that most people don't even see what bit them, hence the colloquial name. They appear at dawn and dusk, usually near mangroves and salt water, and stay for a brief but uncomfortable hour. Because of these tiny insects, camping tents must have the fine-meshed no-see-um-proof netting, not just mosquito netting.

Conversely, deerflies (*Tabanus* spp.), which resemble giant house flies, are large and slow enough so that it's hard to miss them even before they bite. This is lucky, because their bites take more than their fair share. They are active in open sunlight, usually in the summer.

Chiggers are almost microscopic orange larval mites (not true insects) that burrow under the skin, causing itchy welts that can last for weeks. The best prevention for chiggers is wearing long pants tucked into your socks, not sitting on rocks or logs, and showering immediately after hiking.

Diving and Snorkeling

Scuba diving and snorkeling are two of the most popular outdoor activities in south Florida, especially in the Keys. Both can be extremely hazardous because of the number of motorboats and personal watercraft also in Florida waters. To assist motorboat operators with locating people in the water in adequate time, all divers and snorkelers must by law display a "diver down" flag—a square red flag with a white diagonal stripe. The flags are sold at sporting good stores and dive shops. This will warn boaters that someone is in the water. Even if you are snorkeling from shore, you must tow a float with a "diver down" flag. The exception is if you are snorkeling at a roped-off, designated area at a park.

Humidity

Photographers beware! The south Florida humidity and salt spray can wreak havoc on your delicate equipment. Binoculars and spotting scopes are often victims, too. Wipe moisture and salt spray off the exterior surfaces frequently. Carry a plastic bag with you in case of a sudden downpour.

Sunburn

Locals can usually tell who the tourists are—they have the peeling sunburns or the dark tans. People who have lived a long time in Florida have learned how harmful the sun's rays can be. They protect their skin and consequently look pale compared to visitors. Skin cancer is prevalent in the South and getting more common every year as the protective ozone layer in the atmosphere is depleted. No time of the year is safe. In winter, although the Earth's axis is tilted away from the sun, the Earth is closer to the sun, so the rays are very strong. In summer, the Earth is farther from the sun but the rays are more direct. If you are swimming, boating, or just wading through water, you'll get a double whammy, because the rays will reflect off the water. Use sunblock or wear a hat and long sleeves to keep the sun off your skin. Prolonged exposure to strong ultra-violet (UV) rays can damage the retinas of your eyes, so wear glasses that block UV rays.

Crime

Regrettably, the greater Miami-Ft. Lauderdale area has suffered a high crime rate, some of which is aimed at tourists. Thieves watch people for signs of vulnerability, such as being lost or in unfamiliar surroundings. Crime is not common in most of the places mentioned in this book, but disguising yourself as a local and using common sense will go a long way toward deterring it.

A Brief Human History of South Florida

The first Europeans to gaze upon the shores of Florida were the Spanish explorers, lead by Juan Ponce de León in 1513. Ponce de León, who was seeking riches and natives to capture as slaves, bestowed the name *Florida*, after the Spanish for "Feast of the Flowers," and claimed the area for Spain.

The native Tequesta inhabited southeast Florida and the Calusa inhabited southwest Florida until they were annihilated by Europeans or fled to West Indian islands. The Seminoles and Miccosukees, the two Native American tribes currently residing in southern Florida, were not original inhabitants. These two tribes were descended from Creeks who settled there after being chased from their ancestral lands in present-day north Florida, Georgia, and Alabama by intolerant Europeans. Both tribes preferred to live quietly without interference from Europeans. They retreated farther and farther south until they ended up in the Everglades, a vast wetland scorned by the Europeans. Still, the federal government, supported by wealthy white landowners eager to acquire more land, wanted all the native people expelled. The Indian Removal Act of 1830 forced the southeastern Indians, including the Seminoles, to march on foot more than 800 miles to a reservation in what is now Oklahoma. The forced exodus is known today as the "Trail of Tears" because so many died of hunger, exhaustion, cold, heat, and disease. Some Seminoles resisted the removal, including the Seminole leader Osceola. Osceola led his people in this struggle against the federal government, which became known as the Second Seminole War (1835–42). The Seminoles never surrendered, but the war wound down after the federal government lost 1,500 men and $30 million.

The Seminoles and the Miccosukees are recognized as separate tribes by the federal government. The Seminoles' Big Cypress Reservation (one of six reservations in Florida) is in Hendry County, near the northern side of Big Cypress National Preserve. Miccosukees have three reservations in south Florida, the largest being in western Broward County. Both tribes try to keep their cultures flourishing by hunting and selling crafts.

Spain and Britain alternated ownership of the Florida peninsula until 1821, when Florida was ceded to the United States. John James Audubon, the famous artist and naturalist, first visited the Florida Keys in 1832 and lived in a house on Whitehead Street in Key West for a few months. The house has been preserved as a museum and is open to the public.

Until the late 1800s, few nonnative people lived in south Florida. Much of the area was marsh and swamp. Only a narrow strip of coastal ridge from Miami northward and the islands of the Keys were dry enough for development. Few roads existed, and most people traveled by boat.

In the late 1800s, Miami became a boomtown for several reasons. The area grew into a popular winter vacation spot for wealthy people from northern states. The Florida Keys were attractive to farmers for the year-round growing season. The fashion industry in New York, London, and Paris dictated that egret plumes were a must for stylish women's hats, and milliners looked to the Everglades as the source of plumes.

By the early 1900s, large-scale developers had devised schemes to drain the

Everglades and provide more land for development. It was a multipronged assault on the irreplaceable wetland: they dug canals from Lake Okeechobee to divert water to the ocean, built levees to keep water out of developed areas, and planted thirsty, nonnative trees to soak up water. The methods worked over much of the Everglades. Little did they realize their near-sighted actions would ruin a perfect system created by nature.

Another self-appointed savior was Henry Flagler, who dreamed of creating a quick passage for travel from the mainland to Havana, Cuba. His idea was to extend the Florida East Coast Railroad from Miami to Key West, where a ferry would deliver the passengers across the short watery stretch to Havana. Flagler was an old man with plenty of money to finance the construction and a desire to do something sensational with his last years.

Originally, Flagler planned the route to go overland from Miami to Cape Sable and then mostly over water across Florida Bay to Key West. His engineers tried for two years to find a route through the Everglades to Cape Sable. But the land was too mucky to support a railroad. Then Flagler sent his engineers to test the Florida Keys. They reported that the route was possible, so Flagler approved it.

Spend a minute now contemplating what the Everglades would be like today if Flagler had succeeded in his initial route. The railroad tracks would cut across what is now Everglades National Park. Houses, hotels, stores, roads, and farms would probably line the entire route, and more of the Everglades would have been drained to prevent flooding. Flamingo would be a bustling port like Key West. The Everglades would not exist as we know it today, even in its current sorry state. It's a small consolation that the Everglades was spared at the expense of the Keys.

Seven-Mile Bridge stretches into the distance connecting Knight's Key and Little Duck Key in Marathon, a distance of 6.8 miles.

The railroad construction was begun in 1904 and completed in Key West in 1912. Because Key West was the most populated town in Florida at the turn of the century, there was not enough land for the terminal station. So 134 acres were created by pumping mud and marl from the Gulf of Mexico.

The engineers originally wanted to connect all the Keys with ramparts (causeways), with no more than six miles of bridges. But the local people protested, claiming it would prevent the flow of seawater between the islands during storms and cause the water to flood over the islands instead. They were proven right during the 1909 and 1935 hurricanes, and that is why there are so many bridges on the Overseas Highway. The longest one, the Seven-Mile Bridge in Marathon, is the longest bridge of its kind in the world.

The railroad was short-lived. The big hurricane of 1935 destroyed so much of the railroad that the cost to rebuild was too great. The railroad had already been losing money, and it had facilitated a loss of population in the Keys (the impoverished locals had a way to leave, and many never returned). In 1938, the railroad bed was converted into a road, which is still the only road that goes to Key West. Portions of the old track are still visible along the middle and lower Keys.

A Quick View of the Mainland

The two outstanding topographic features of southern Florida are the amount of surface water and the flatness of the terrain. Combined, they make the tip of the peninsula look like a giant, shallow lake at certain times of the year. Actually, it's a giant, shallow, and very slowly moving river. Marjory Stoneman Douglas recognized this and coined the name "River of Grass" for the Everglades in the 1940s. Historically, the Everglades began at the southern end of Lake Okeechobee, where the water overflowed the banks and gradually drifted south to Florida Bay and the Gulf of Mexico. The topographical gradient is so small—only one or two inches per mile—that early white settlers didn't even know the water flowed.

West of the Everglades basin is Big Cypress Swamp, one of the largest remaining wilderness areas in Florida. The swamp has a slightly higher elevation than the Everglades basin. Although it contains marshes, it is predominantly forested with cypress and pines. It is underlain by the fossiliferous Tamiami limestone. The hydroperiod (the amount of time the area is covered by water) is shorter than in the Everglades, leaving marl instead of peat for the soil type. Old growth pine stands contain small populations of the endangered red-cockaded woodpecker. Because of limited accessibility in the Big Cypress, less exploration has been done here than in the Everglades, and less is known about the flora and fauna.

A rock ridge composed of limestone outcroppings extends from Miami southwest to Long Pine Key in Everglades National Park. This region of higher elevation between the coast and the interior marshes was preferred for development and farms because of the lack of flooding. The highest elevations in Homestead are about 13 feet above sea level and in Miami about 23 feet above sea level. The latter can clearly be seen by driving along South Bayshore Drive in the Silver Bluff area of Miami (between Coconut Grove and the Rickenbacker Causeway). The old shoreline, which abutted the limestone bluffs, can be seen in the yards of the houses on the west side of the road.

The Atlantic coastal ridge, which punctuates Palm Beach, Broward, and Miami-Dade counties, prevents most of the Everglades water from flowing east into the Atlantic. A few rivers, such as the Hillsboro, Miami-Dade, and New Rivers, historically penetrated the ridge and allowed some water to pass. But the remaining water backs up against the western side of the ridge. Formerly, the water pressure pushed through the limestone in some places, creating high volume springs that emerged east of the ridge (for example, in Miami Springs). The decrease in water level over the past 90 years has caused the springs to cease flowing. The rivers are now entirely channelized.

The huge pool of water that collects west of the ridge—the real Everglades—not only flows southward but also downward. By percolating through the porous limestone, it recharges the underlying Biscayne Aquifer. Most of south Florida's residents, farmers, and industries depend on this aquifer, and therefore the Everglades, for their water.

The colonization by Europeans caused some development to begin in south Florida, but it wasn't until the 1900s that serious environmental degradation began. Huge dredges dug canals to drain the water from the Everglades, creating more farmland. The fill from the canals was used to build levees for flood protection and roads. The series of canals, levees, and pumping stations that now criss-cross the southern Florida peninsula—totaling some 1,400 miles—have changed the face of the Everglades. In some places the water no longer flows. In others, the hydroperiod

The walking dredge changed the way water flows across south Florida. This dredge is at Koreshan State Historic Site.

has decreased so much by draining that the peat is exposed and fires ravage the fertile soil. Complications too numerous to elaborate on here have arisen because of the juxtaposition of a sensitive wetland with a burgeoning metropolis.

In the 1970s, an insidious enemy began to reveal itself. Observant land managers in the Everglades noticed dense stands of cattails growing where sawgrass formerly grew. The problem was traced to excess nutrients (primarily phosphorus) in agricultural runoff, exacerbated by the artificial manipulation of water flow. The canals were carrying the phosphorus far downstream from the farms into the Everglades. This "overfertilized" the natural system, which was adapted to very small amounts of nutrients. Plants started growing too tall and too dense. The wrong plants, such as native cattails, started taking over the sawgrass. This is just one of the easy ways of seeing the problem, although much more is not readily visible.

In 1988, U.S. Attorney Dexter Lehtinen filed a suit against the State on behalf of A.R.M. Loxahatchee National Wildlife Refuge and Everglades National Park to protect them from this polluted water. In 1991, the State conceded that it had not enforced its water quality standards for the Everglades. Since then, A.R.M. Loxahatchee NWR, Everglades National Park, the South Florida Water Management District, Florida Department of Environment Protection, U.S. Environmental Protection Agency, U.S. Army Corps of Engineers, the agricultural community, and others have been implementing a major cleanup of the water.

The water quality improvements are just part of the $8 billion ecosystem restoration project that is under way from Kissimmee River to Florida Bay. Other aspects include restoration of the quantity, pattern, and timing of the water flow as well as invasive species control, land acquisition for habitat protection, and endangered species recovery. For example, water flow is being restored by culverts under US 41 (Tamiami Trail) into Everglades National Park, and lands were added to the park to protect more of Taylor Slough. The restoration includes the construction of wetlands to filter pollutants from the agricultural area upstream of the Everglades; see **Stormwater Treatment Areas** (STAs) below for new wildlife observation locations at the STAs. For more information on the Everglades restoration, see www.sfrestore.org.

Aerial view of Key West

A Quick View of the Florida Keys

The word "key" as it relates geographically to south Florida originated from the Spanish word *cayo* for "little island" or "island reef." All small marine islands in south Florida are called keys. The group of islands that comprise the archipelago that stretches about 125 miles from Key Largo to Key West is known collectively as the Florida Keys. Most are linked by roads and 42 bridges, but there are undeveloped and unconnected islands on both ends.

The Florida Keys are composed of several forms of limestone. Exposed very recently geologically, these 5,000-year-old islands are barely separate from the sea. They rise an average of 2 to 4 feet above sea level, with the highest islands (Key Largo, Plantation, Windley, Lignumvitae, and Big Pine) rising only to 18 feet. Actually, the landfills create the highest land now in the Keys.

From Soldier Key in the north to part of Big Pine Key in the south, the substrate rock is Key Largo limestone, an old coral reef. Fossilized remnants of coral skeletons can be easily seen on surface rocks in many places on the Upper Keys. Look for a place, even a parking lot on US 1 in Key Largo, that has rocks on the ground and you will probably see striations from former coral colonies. The more serious geology students will want to visit Windley Key Quarry (see entry for **Windley Key Fossil Reef Geological State Park**) to get the real picture.

From Big Pine south to Key West, the rock is called Miami oolite, named for the tiny calcareous spheres that look like eggs or ooids. The difference in shape between the two groups of islands is obvious on a map.

The difference in substrate between the Upper and Lower Keys determines the availability of fresh water on the islands. In the Upper Keys, the Key Largo limestone is permeable and rain water quickly soaks through to mix with the brackish groundwater. There are few freshwater wells or ponds in the Upper Keys. In the Lower Keys, the dense Miami Oolite retains water that sits in pools or "lenses" above the denser salt water. The pinelands of the Lower Keys exist because of the availability of fresh water. Many mammals, reptiles, and amphibians not found in the Upper Keys can survive in the Lower Keys because of the fresh water. The Key deer and Key mud turtle are examples.

You may notice that it rains less in the Keys than on the mainland. Frequently in the summer, you can drive from earth-shaking thunderstorms in Florida City south across the "18-Mile Stretch" (a colloquial name for the section of US 1 south of Florida City to the drawbridge at Jewfish Creek near Key Largo), and when you arrive in Key Largo the sun is shining. Because the air and ground are both drier, there are few natural sources of fresh water on the Keys. The public water supply is piped 135 miles from Navy Wells (see **Navy Wells Pineland Preserve**) in Florida City to Key West. Virtually every person on the islands is dependent on this one aqueduct. The aqueduct is mostly buried, but you can see it along the bridges. Now you can understand why fresh water is expensive and precious in the Keys.

The vegetation of the Keys is distinctly West Indian. Since the Keys are islands, the most likely way for seeds to reach them would be by drifting on the ocean or the wind. Most of the West Indian plants are adapted to those forms of dispersal, but most of the mainland ones are not. Furthermore, the most likely species to survive would be ones adapted to island features, like salty air. The climate resembles that of the West Indies more than that of the mainland. One's overall impression of the Keys is that one is on a Caribbean island.

As a group, the most distinctive trees are the graceful palms. Some botanists would argue that palms aren't trees since they are monocots and lack a true woody structure. But they are tree-like in form and function and are considered trees by most people. Only eight species are native to south Florida. The coconut palm, so common in this area, is not one of them. Many species of palms have been introduced and thrive in the mild climate.

The animal life, however, brings a northerner back to reality. You will recognize many species from the mainland of Florida: opossums, raccoons, rat snakes, green treefrogs, spadefoot toads, ospreys, and mockingbirds, to name a few. Aside from the birds and insects, which could fly to the islands from far away, other animals were restricted to shorter distances and perhaps less intentional methods of transportation. Mammals, except bats, either swam island-hopping fashion or drifted on flotsam. Some of them may have walked during extremely low tides and sea levels. Most reptiles probably also arrived this way. Small mammals, reptiles, amphibians, and flightless insects probably hitched rides on floating logs or were carried by hurricanes. More recently, humans have aided dispersal (intentionally and unintentionally) with roads, ships, and other methods. Through the pet trade, humans have brought species from all over the world that subsequently escaped and established themselves. The wildlife present now is a blend of three parts continental, two parts West Indian, and one part totally bizarre.

Key limes, a local specialty, are actually of Mexican origin. The lime trees were imported to the Keys by botanist Henry Perrine in the 1800s and have become commercially important. The small, round yellow fruits are used for the famous Key lime pie.

On a drive down the "18-Mile Stretch" from November to March you are likely to pass roseate spoonbills and other wading birds. Another road, called the Card Sound Road (SR 905A), leads from Florida City to North Key Largo. This was the original road and is less traveled and more picturesque than US 1. The southern end, near where Card Sound Road intersects with SR 905, may harbor a well-concealed crocodile in the shallow water around the mangroves (Crocodile Lake National Wildlife Refuge).

Camping under the slash pines at Long Pine Key in Everglades National Park

▌▌ HABITATS

Coral Reefs

Coral reefs are extremely diverse and complex marine ecosystems existing only in the warmer oceans of the world. Coral reefs recycle nutrients and provide food, shelter, and nursery habitat for other marine organisms. They buffer the adjacent shorelines from storm waves, giving stability to the soil and vegetation.

The only coral reefs in the continental United States are off the south Florida coast. Although occasional corals may be found north to about latitude 30° (St. Augustine), reef development reaches its peak in the Florida Keys archipelago, where the warm Florida Current flows. The reef in the Keys is the third largest barrier reef in the world. In 1990, the Florida Keys National Marine Sanctuary was created, encompassing all marine waters from the Upper Keys to the Dry Tortugas.

Corals flourish on the eastern sides of continents because the water is usually warmer from ocean currents. Clear water with salinities about 35 parts per thousand, temperatures between 68 and 86°F, and a good food supply are the controlling environmental factors. Water clarity is essential because an integral part of the reef-building coral organism is the one-celled alga known as zooxanthella, which requires

Coral reefs contain a variety of forms of corals, such as sea fans (lower left) and sea rods (upper right). Both are examples of soft corals.

sunlight to be able to photosynthesize. Thus, the clearer the water, the deeper the corals can live.

Corals are animals belonging to a group known as the coelenterates, along with jellyfish, anemones, and hydroids; they are radially symmetrical. They have two life stages: asexual sessile polyps and sexual free-swimming medusae. The stony corals that form the backbone of the coral reef have hard, calcareous skeletons of calcium carbonate secreted by the soft polyp. Each polyp resembles a small sea anemone, with its base attached to a small limy cup that it hides in during the day. Unless you go snorkeling or diving at night, all you'll see is the rocklike limestone skeleton.

The coral reefs gained notoriety with the early European explorers and traders (particularly the Spaniards visiting Mexico) because of the danger of wrecking on the shallow "rocks." Many lives and cargoes were lost. Some early Keys residents supported themselves by salvaging shipments of gold, silver, and other valuables. Today, treasure hunters spend fortunes and lifetimes searching for the wrecks. While this may seem harmless, rarely can they sift and rake through the sediment without agitating and destroying the sea-bottom life.

The Florida Keys reefs are the number one diving destination in the world. Not even the Great Barrier Reef in Australia garners as many underwater explorers. The Florida reefs are home to about 400–500 species of fish and numerous invertebrates, many of them extremely colorful, and all worth at least a glassbottom boat or snorkel trip. Along with the benign-sounding names of angelfish, trumpetfish, butterflyfish, and rock beauties, a few names conjure up apprehension: barracuda, moray eel, southern stingray, and tiger shark.

Barracudas always look as if they are about to strike, but in reality they must swim with their mouths open to breathe. Barracudas have rarely been reported to attack humans, and incidents usually occurred when the water was murky or the person was wearing something shiny. Moray eels are dangerous only if you stick your hand in their hiding holes or crevices. Stingrays are a problem only if you step on them, so watch where you walk in shallow water. They camouflage beautifully, so you must be observant. Sharks are also maligned. The rare attacks by sharks generally occur in murky water, when the victim is wearing contrasting tones, when there is blood or chum present, or when the victim is splashing around. In general, with a little common sense, the reef is a safe and enjoyable place to be.

On the other side of the coin, are the reefs safe from humans? Divers and snorkelers often don't realize how easily they can kill coral. Touching the surface of a coral can injure the protective mucous membrane. Because water clarity is so essential, kicking up silt is also extremely destructive to coral. In heavily visited areas, whole patches of coral have been killed, often by people trying to be considerate but bumping or kicking corals accidentally.

All corals are protected by law from collecting. The coral souvenirs found in the local gift shops are imported from other countries, such as the Philippines. However, these protections are not enough. Coral reefs are fragile ecosystems, and the combination of water pollution, rising global water temperatures, disturbance from watercraft, commercial and recreational fishing, and the introduction of invasive species (such as lionfish) is causing the gradual death of the Florida Keys coral reefs.

You can see the coral reefs by visiting Biscayne National Park, Dry Tortugas National Park, Bahia Honda State Park, John Pennekamp Coral Reef State Park, and Looe Key.

Mangroves

Four tree species in Florida are collectively considered mangroves: red mangrove, black mangrove, white mangrove, and buttonwood. Only the red mangrove, however, is in the mangrove family (Rhizophoraceae). The northernmost mangroves are found around St. Augustine on the Atlantic coast and Cedar Key on the Gulf coast.

All four species share the common traits of being highly tolerant of salinity and water level changes; thus, they thrive in tidal zones and represent the transition between the sawgrass marshes and the ocean. Black and white mangroves have mechanisms to excrete salt (you can see these salt glands at the base of each white mangrove leaf), while red mangroves don't allow salt to enter their tissues. Because they do not need salt water, mangroves can thrive in freshwater habitats, though they are rarely found there because they are outcompeted by freshwater-adapted trees.

Ospreys nesting on red mangroves

Red, black, and white mangroves have seeds called propagules that begin germination while still on the tree. Mangrove propagules and roots can anchor well only on low-energy shorelines—that is, shorelines with such shallow slopes that the waves and tides are barely noticeable. Much of Florida, especially the southwest coast, is like that. Another environmental requirement is a warm climate. Together, these reasons make south Florida home to the most extensive mangrove swamps in the United States.

Mangrove systems are vital as rich nursery grounds for fish and invertebrates, such as snook, tarpon, mullet, mangrove snapper, spiny lobster, pink shrimp, oyster, and blue crab. Many birds, such as wood storks, roseate spoonbills, brown pelicans, and white-crowned pigeons, nest on mangrove trees. As the tide recedes, the exposed mud flats draw shorebirds and wading birds to feed on crustaceans, stranded fish, and other marine life.

Red mangrove trees are easily recognized by their arching prop roots, which resemble a spider's legs. Black mangroves (and occasionally white mangroves) have pencil-like root appendages called pneumatophores that grow above ground like new shoots of asparagus. Buttonwoods have no distinguishing root structures.

Mangrove trees are protected from human destruction by Florida law because of their vital roles as nursery grounds and coastal stabilizers. Good places to see mangroves are Everglades National Park, Biscayne National Park, John Pennekamp Coral Reef State Park, Rookery Bay, Long Key State Park, J.N. "Ding" Darling National Wildlife Refuge, Collier-Seminole State Park, John U. Lloyd Beach State Park, and John D. MacArthur Beach State Park.

Cypresses

Scattered throughout the freshwater wetlands of southern Florida (particularly in Big Cypress National Preserve, Corkscrew Swamp Sanctuary, Fakahatchee Strand Preserve State Park, A.R.M. Loxahatchee National Wildlife Refuge, and Everglades National Park) are vast stands of bald-cypress trees known locally as cypresses. The name "Big Bald-Cypress National Preserve" just wouldn't have the same ring. Although they are conifers, cypresses (as they will be called in this book) shed their needles around November each year (hence look bald) and sprout new ones in February or March. Cypresses are related to the redwoods of the Pacific coast. Taxonomists argue whether the pond-cypress is a separate species or a variety of bald-cypress. They grow side-by-side at the main entrance of A.R.M. Loxahatchee NWR.

Cypresses grow best with their roots in water and are the most flood-tolerant freshwater trees in Florida. Two of their most recognizable characteristics, the swelling buttresses and spindly "knees," are adaptations to their watery environment. The knees are projections of the roots that emerge from the water, probably to assist with respiration when the oxygen levels surrounding the roots are low. The buttressed bases of the trunks provide stability in the soft substrate. Although the seeds need to soak in water, they won't germinate under water.

Cypresses in south Florida are often found growing in one of two types of arrangements: domes and strands. Cypress domes are small, circular concentrations

Cypress dome in Everglades National Park

of cypress trees in a pond-like situation. The tallest trees are in the center where the water and soil are deepest, and the shortest trees are around the edges, giving a dome-like silhouette. This may be seen along the road to Flamingo. Cypress strands are long and narrow, sometimes many miles in length. Their alignment generally indicates the direction of water flow during high-water periods. Fakahatchee Strand is an excellent example. Another excellent example is the strand that formerly stretched 70 miles from Lake Okeechobee to Ft. Lauderdale. The largest intact remaining section is along the east side of A.R.M. Loxahatchee NWR and the current terminus is at Fern Forest Nature Center in Coconut Creek.

Vast cypress swamps across the southeastern United States were logged for their rot-resistant lumber. Cypress lumbering is still big business in some areas. The largest and oldest trees left are in Corkscrew Swamp, fortunately protected in perpetuity by the National Audubon Society. Some animals that use cypress habitats are swallow-tailed kites, turkeys, deer, otters, panthers, and bobcats. Cypress trees should be protected everywhere, because they are slow-growing, stabilize wetlands, and provide food and shelter for wildlife.

Slash pines in Everglades National Park and nearby areas are also known as Dade County pines. The lumber is famed for resistance to rotting and insect damage.

Pinelands

Much of central and northern Florida is covered by pine flatwoods, but the pinelands of extreme south Florida are different. They are associated with the south Florida rocklands and are restricted to outcroppings of limestone. These limestone ridges have the highest elevations in the area.

Three main areas have pine rocklands: the Miami Ridge, the lower Florida Keys, and Big Cypress Swamp. The Miami Ridge (from Miami to Long Pine Key in

Everglades National Park), composed of Miami limestone, is the largest outcropping. The Lower Keys (from Big Pine to Key West) are also on Miami limestone. In Big Cypress, the older Tamiami limestone is exposed. The bedrock in these pinelands is often exposed, and the soils are shallow. Numerous pits, pinnacles, and solution holes are formed when the acidic leaf litter, mixing with rain water, dissolves the limestone. This is a characteristic feature. The early settlers had to plant their crops in the solution holes—the only places with deep enough soil. Pine rocklands can be seen in Everglades National Park, Big Cypress National Preserve, Navy Wells Pineland Preserve, and National Key Deer Refuge.

Pine flatwoods are found from Palm Beach County northward and occur on level, often low-lying, poorly drained terrain. The main overstory species comprising the south Florida flatwoods is slash pine. The canopy is rather open, with a well-developed low shrub layer and an often sparse herbaceous layer. The plants are fire-adapted and able to withstand months of drought in the dry season and months of flooding in the wet season. Typical shrubs found in the flatwoods are staggerbush, wax myrtle, and saw palmetto. Some reptiles that are common in pine flatwoods are the pine woods treefrog, pine woods snake, eastern diamondback rattlesnake, eastern glass lizard, and Florida box turtle. Typical mammals are fox squirrels, eastern moles, black bears, gray foxes, and bobcats. Brown-headed nuthatches, red-cockaded woodpeckers, Bachman's sparrows, and pine warblers typify the bird life. Pine flatwoods can be found at Corbett Wildlife Management Area, Dupuis Reserve State Forest, and Corkscrew Marsh.

Essential to the continual regeneration and success of the slash pines is fire. Without the lightning-caused fires that swept through the pines over the centuries, the pinelands would have reverted to hardwoods. Much of the original pinelands have been lost that way, since we newcomers have suppressed fires. The suppression has been direct in many cases and indirect in many others. The networks of roads, canals, and farms throughout the area have served as effective firebreaks. Natural resource managers in parks containing pinelands (such as Everglades and Big Cypress) practice prescribed burning to keep the pines regenerating.

The understory vegetation of the pinelands must have fire-resistant roots or seeds to be able to regenerate quickly after fire. Saw palmetto, velvetseed, willow bustic, tetrazygia, varnish leaf, and myrsine are common. Coontie was formerly more common. Much of the vegetation is West Indian.

Another major destroyer of pinelands has been lumbering. The local variety of slash pine has virtually insect- and rot-resistant wood, making it a blessed building material. So much of early Miami and Homestead depended on this tree for construction that it is known locally as "Dade County pine."

Sawgrass Marshes

The Everglades is a vast freshwater marsh generally known as a sawgrass marsh. Some of it is characterized by deep organic soils (peat) and hydroperiods greater than nine months. Where hydroperiods are slightly shorter, marl substrates may form instead of peat. Sawgrass is the most common plant, but many other plants grow also. The name sawgrass is both accurate and misleading. The blades do indeed have

Sawgrass marsh at A.R.M. Loxahatchee National Wildlife Refuge

serrated edges, but the plant is a sedge, not a grass. Sawgrasses may grow ten feet tall.

Periphyton is vital to the Everglades freshwater marshes. Periphyton is an assemblage of small plant organisms (mostly algae) that either float or are attached to surfaces under water. They may form a spongy mat insulating the ground from total dehydration during the dry season.

Mixed in with the sawgrass are spike rush, bladderwort, pickerelweed, muhly grass, and many other wetland plants. Another species, the cattail, is becoming a scourge in the sawgrass marshes. Thriving on the added nutrients released upstream by the agricultural practices around Lake Okeechobee, cattails are outcompeting the sawgrasses. This is devastating to the natural community because cattails deplete dissolved oxygen and can form such dense stands that wildlife movement and usage is impaired. A major multi-agency conservation effort is under way to change farming practices to reduce the added nutrient load to the Everglades.

Sawgrass marshes can be seen in many places, including Everglades National Park, Big Cypress National Preserve, A.R.M. Loxahatchee NWR, Southern Glades Wildlife and Environmental Area, the Water Conservation Areas, and Fakahatchee Strand Preserve State Park.

Hammocks

Hammocks are "islands" of trees generally growing on higher elevations than the surrounding landscape or on lower elevations in pines where greater moisture reduces fire threats. They have evolved from lack of fire exposure and are the upland climax community. They grow on rich organic soils and are generally densely canopied and diverse in flora. Hammocks occur as bay heads, rock reefs, or tropical hardwood hammocks.

Bayheads, small clumps of hardwoods in the freshwater marshes, consist of such trees as redbay, sweet bay, wax myrtle, and coco-plum. Bayheads are found in the sloughs of Everglades National Park, A.R.M. Loxahatchee NWR, and Big Cypress National Preserve. From the air, their characteristic teardrop shape is apparent. The teardrop forms when water flowing down the slough washes detritus from the upstream end and deposits it at the downstream end.

Rock reefs are ridges of limestone that create higher elevations that allow hardwood trees to flourish. From a bird's-eye view, a rock reef looks like a giant snake of trees crawling through the marsh. Rock Reef Pass in Everglades National Park is a good example.

Tropical hardwood hammocks, which exist from Miami south to the Keys, are dense stands of primarily West Indian trees. They are the only tropical hardwood forests in the continental United States and are probably the most endangered habitat in the country. Their demise began in the 1500s when early Spaniards

Hammock or tree island

began leveling the giant mahogany trees for shipment back to Europe. West Indian mahoganies, native to south Florida, have valuable wood. They are now on the state's threatened plants list. The current land-grab and development boom in this resort area is destroying what's left of this geographically limited habitat. Conservation groups must work hard to save the remaining tropical hardwood hammocks. Everglades National Park, Castellow Hammock, Crane Point Hammock, Matheson Hammock, Biscayne National Park, Dagny Johnson Key Largo Hammock State Park, and Lignumvitae Key all have tropical hardwood hammocks.

Lakes and Rivers

One lacustrine (lake) feature in the region—Lake Okeechobee—is so large at 730 square miles that it is identifiable from space. Lake Okeechobee was formed in a depression in the bedrock. The lake is fed primarily by rainfall and inflowing rivers like the Kissimmee and Fisheating Creek. The lake has no natural outflowing rivers. Before the Hoover Dike and outflow canals were built, the water would slowly spill over the natural bank at the south end and flow imperceptibly through the Everglades. The lake is so shallow that the average maximum depth is less than 16 feet. Historically, the lake had a broad littoral zone in the northwest section—a zone with water only a few inches to 2 feet deep, where aquatic plants flourished and much of the animal life was concentrated. The artificial manipulation of water levels by humans, aided by pumping structures and a massive dike built around the entire lake, has destroyed much of this rich nursery, where many species of fish reproduce. The man-made connections from the lake to the Gulf Coast by way of the Caloosahatchee River and to the Atlantic Ocean by the St. Lucie Canal have greatly altered the lake's ecological components. Fishermen lament that the sport and commercial fisheries have suffered substantially from these alterations. The South Florida Water Management District, U.S. Army Corps of Engineers, and numerous other agencies are working to restore the ecological functions of the lake, but it is a monumental project.

The rivers of south Florida are generally sluggish because of the shallow grade. Whitewater exists only where a rock breaks the surface and causes a ripple. This flatness made many rivers ideal for travel in the early days of Florida's history. The color of the water is usually brownish, caused by tannins from oaks and other leaves. The major rivers of south Florida are the Caloosahatchee, Loxahatchee, and Fisheating Creek. The 75-mile-long Caloosahatchee was named for the Calusa Indians that once cherished it as their larder and highway. The river was channelized and connected to Lake Okeechobee by the famous swamp-drainer Hamilton Disston in the 1800s. Loxahatchee River and Fisheating Creek have been left nearly undeveloped and natural. During many months of the year, manatees feed in the rivers, sometimes swimming many miles inland.

Estuaries and Bays

Where the rivers meet the oceans is a nebulous area of half land, half water. This is where the estuaries lie—those rich nurseries where many species of fish, crustaceans, and mollusks start their lives. Wading birds, dolphins, sea turtles, and small sharks

Aerial view of mangrove estuary in Naples

are attracted to the bonanza of prey that thrives in the brackish water. Oysters, conchs, blue crabs, shrimp, mullet, and snook are some of the prey that humans are attracted to. The high productivity of commercially valuable fish and shellfish cannot be disputed or ignored. The estuaries include salt marshes, lagoons, seagrasses, and mangroves.

Salt marshes are one of the most highly productive habitats in the world. They are periodically flooded, treeless coastal areas at the landward edge that depend on the tides to wash in nutrients and flush out detritus regularly. Salt marshes act as filters by keeping pollution caused by upland development from entering the ocean. They stabilize the shore so that sediment isn't continually eroding. Cordgrass, saltwort, and glasswort are three plants common to Florida salt marshes.

A lagoon is a confined body of water located near the ocean but with few openings to it. Water doesn't flush well from a lagoon and may remain for months or years until an extremely high tide occurs.

Some estuaries support seagrasses, which are flowering plants that grow completely submerged and are rooted to the bottom. Seagrasses provide the forage for such grazing animals as manatees, sea turtles, and some ducks. Turtle grass and widgeon grass are two examples. Many small fish, seahorses, crabs, and shrimp forage in the dense cover of seagrasses. Large seagrass beds may be seen by snorkeling in Florida Bay and Biscayne Bay.

Some of the larger estuaries in south Florida are in Florida Bay, Whitewater Bay, and the rest of western Everglades National Park; Matlacha Pass, Estero Bay, Rookery Bay, and Biscayne Bay. They are exciting places to paddle because of the variety and abundance of wildlife, although novice paddlers should not attempt unguided trips due to the winds, tides, and risk of getting lost.

Beaches and Dunes

Along the coasts without barrier islands and on the seaward sides of the barrier islands, the beaches and dunes lie restlessly. They shift with the winds, the tides, and the currents. One storm alone can remove 6 to 8 feet of sand from a beach. When left unaltered by humans, however, beaches and dunes have a way of equilibrating—that is, where the sand is removed from one place, it is deposited somewhere else. The salt-tolerant dune plants (such as sea oats, sea purslane, and bay-cedar) are the main stabilizers. This is why it is so important for them to be left undisturbed. Sea oats, which can have 5-foot-deep roots and rhizomes that ably bind the sand, are protected by state law. Nesting sea turtles and oldfield beach mice depend on the sandy beaches and dunes.

Beaches and dunes can be seen at John D. MacArthur Beach State Park, Hugh Taylor Birch State Park, John U. Lloyd Beach State Park, Bill Baggs Cape Florida State Park, Cayo Costa State Park, and Lovers Key State Park.

▌▌▌ A PEEK AT THE SPECIAL WILDLIFE

Tree Snails

Bejeweling our south Florida tropical hardwood hammocks are the colorful tree snails. The Stock Island tree snail (*Orthalicus reses*) is federally listed as threatened. Its range is limited to a few small islands of the Lower Keys and individuals have been transplanted to National Key Deer Refuge. The Florida tree snail (*Liguus fasciatus*) has 58 named color forms, some of which have vanished forever. The *Liguus* were once found from Collier and Broward counties southward through the Florida Keys.

General habitat destruction has eliminated many hammocks and the tree snails that depend on them. Development has destroyed hammocks outside protected park boundaries. In undeveloped areas, hammocks have burned because poor water management practices artificially simulate droughts that cause hotter and more widespread fires than the hammocks can withstand.

Tree snails grow during the wet season, mainly from May to September, adding more spirals of bright color. They feed on fungi, lichens, and mold growing on the bark of wild-tamarind, Jamaica dogwood, gumbo-limbo, and other smooth-barked trees. Their role in the ecosystem is to clean mold and algae from trees. Courtship and

Tree snails, about 1.5–2.5 inches, are white or cream-colored with streaks or bands of yellow, brown, pink, or green.

mating occur from late June to September, and since tree snails are hermaphroditic (individuals possess both male and female sex organs), they need only find another tree snail to reproduce. Eggs are laid in the leaf mould in early fall and hatch at the beginning of the next rainy season.

During the dry winter months, the snails seal their shells tightly to a tree and aestivate (go dormant) to protect their bodies from moisture loss. That is why they need smooth-barked trees. Removing a snail at this time will break the protective seal and may cause the snail to die. Unless you see a tree snail actively crawling around, do not touch it. Occasionally a warm winter rain will reactivate a snail temporarily. Tree snails are protected by law.

Spiny Lobsters

Unlike their northern cousins, spiny lobsters (*Panulirus argus*) have no large claws. Spiny lobsters are just as tasty, but the meat lies mainly in the tails. The name comes from the spines on the antennas and carapace.

Harvesting by commercial and sport lobsterers is permitted. The harvesting season runs from early August to March 31, when any person possessing a Florida saltwater fishing license and a lobster stamp may collect lobsters. Sport lobsterers can use nooses, nets, or other noninjurious devices except traps. Traps are used only by commercial lobsterers and may be seen during the off-season (April–July) stacked along the roadside in the Keys. Since egg-bearing and undersized lobsters must be released, such injurious methods of capture as spearing are not permitted.

Lobsters may be caught by snorkelers and scuba divers. While most people are ecologically conscientious when they capture lobsters, some are careless or destructive. During the day, these nocturnal creatures hide under ledges with their sensory feelers exposed. At the first sign of trouble, a lobster will withdraw as completely as possible into the rocks, making it difficult to extricate it. Impatient humans have torn the rocks apart to free a lobster. Sometimes the rocks destroyed are actually living coral. People have even poured bleach into the rocks to drive lobsters out. Repeated poking and prodding at a group of lobsters may drive them out of hiding to walk across exposed sea bottom to find a safer place. This harassment makes them easy prey for sharks and other large predators.

The most conscientious way to capture a lobster is to: 1) learn to judge the relative size of a lobster by its antenna length, so you leave undersized ones alone; 2) try only two or three times to catch a lobster (after that, your chances of success decrease and you will only be harassing it); and 3) leave the area if you see that the lobsters are becoming agitated and may try to flee for other cover. Check for egg clusters on the abdomens and immediately release any egg-bearing females.

Until 1992, the last full weekend in July every year was the opening weekend of the state's sport lobstering season. The mania that surrounded it was phenomenal. It was traditionally the busiest weekend of the year in the Keys. Local merchants planned for it months in advance. Diving equipment and motel rooms were all taken. Travel on US 1 slowed to a crawl. In 1992, the state changed the season to begin in midweek, hoping to avoid the insanity of that intense two-day harvest. But the federal season (in waters three miles or more offshore) still begins that last weekend, so the situation is not much improved.

Conchs

Queen conchs (*Strombus gigas*) are large marine snails, sometimes weighing as much as five pounds, found in shallow seagrass beds and sandy bottoms from southern Florida to the West Indies. You'll hear the word conch (pronounced "conk") frequently in the Keys.

For centuries before Europeans arrived, conchs were harvested for food by the native people. The shells were used for tools, bowls, and ornaments. With the influx of immigrants to the southern end of the peninsula, conch harvesting reached exorbitant levels. Conchs were a staple diet for the early settlers to the Keys. In fact, a person who was born and raised in the Keys is often referred to as a "conch."

Queen conchs were also collected as souvenirs for tourists. Since 1985, conchs have been completely protected in Florida, because the conch population had reached critically low numbers. They are still harvested in the Bahamas and West Indies, which is the current source of conchs sold in Florida.

Conchs are a Keys culinary specialty. Conch meat is tough and rather bland. It has to be pounded into oblivion (or "cracked" as the locals call it) and spiced to the hilt to be tender and tasty enough to qualify as a delicacy. Cracked conch (pounded and breaded), conch fritters, and conch chowder (usually spicy) are the three most frequent conch items on local menus.

Florida Panthers

While settlers from the 1600s to 1900s were systematically destroying the wilderness haunts of the panthers and hunting the cats almost to extinction (they were hunted for bounty until 1950), a small population survived in the untamed Everglades and Big Cypress. The Florida panther is a subspecies of the mountain lion (or cougar), which once roamed almost every habitat in North America. In 1958, the panther became protected by the state of Florida, and in 1967, the U.S. Fish and Wildlife Service listed it as endangered. Today, only 100 or so panthers roam Florida, most from Lake Okeechobee south to Long Pine Key in Everglades National Park. The number is only slowly increasing from fewer than 30 in 1994 in spite of intensive cooperative efforts by the U.S. Fish and Wildlife Service, Florida Fish and Wildlife Conservation Commission (FWC), National Park Service at Everglades National Park and Big Cypress National Preserve, and other entities. Radio-tagged panthers are being tracked by National Park Service staff in Big Cypress and Everglades National Park and by the FWC elsewhere. A captive breeding program has been established by the agencies listed above and is being conducted by zoos in Florida.

The primary known causes of mortality are collisions with automobiles and malnutrition. The reason the nighttime speed limit on Alligator Alley and Tamiami Trail was lowered to 10 mph less than the daytime limit in the 1990s was to prevent vehicles from hitting the nocturnally active panthers. Nevertheless, a record 17 panthers died in 2009 as a result of motor vehicle hits. Panther vehicle mortality was also the reason the wildlife underpasses were added as part of the conversion of Alligator Alley into I-75 and on several other roads. Since the underpasses and the accompanying chain link fences that line both sides of I-75 were completed in 1995, no panthers were killed on this road. Evidence from video cameras and tracks shows that panthers, deer, and other wild animals are using the underpasses.

A decrease in the number of white-tailed deer (the panthers' preferred diet) has caused the panthers to feed on smaller prey (such as raccoons and young alligators) in some areas. Panthers may survive on small prey items, but they are not likely to bear young. Studies have shown that a female panther needs large prey items like deer to reproduce and raise her cubs. Another problem is arising with the switch from large to small prey. The fresh waters of the Everglades are contaminated with mercury, which becomes concentrated in aquatic animals, such as raccoons, otters, and alligators. Panthers that feed on such animals will acquire the poisonous mercury themselves, and some have died from it.

Florida panthers resemble western mountain lions with a few minor differences. Panthers are redder than the tawny mountain lions, have a "cowlick" in the middle of their backs, and have a sharp bend in the distal end of their tails. They also are slightly smaller, weighing about 70–150 lbs. Other subspecies introduced or escaped into Florida have intergraded with the native cats, so some individuals do not carry these traits.

Dolphins

Anyone who spends some time in a boat in the warm, shallow waters of Florida Bay, Whitewater Bay, Biscayne Bay, or the Gulf Coast is likely to catch a glimpse of these graceful creatures. Many people are treated to an even grander spectacle when the

Atlantic bottlenose dolphins often race alongside motorboats in nearshore waters.

dolphins approach their boat. Such dolphins are either engrossed in feeding or are curious about the boat. Dolphins will occasionally drive fish into the shallow water around the tiny mangrove islands in Florida Bay, trapping the fish for easy feeding.

The Atlantic bottlenose dolphin is the most frequently seen species of cetacean (whale relative) in these waters. This is the dolphin made famous by the television show "Flipper" that was filmed partly in the Keys in the 1960s. They are extremely intelligent animals; some scientists believe they are even more intelligent than humans. Sometimes they are known as porpoises, although they are not true porpoises.

Don't be alarmed if you find yourself staring at a menu in a seafood restaurant in south Florida and see "dolphin" as the catch of the day. That dolphin is a common fish harvested locally for human consumption. The bottlenose dolphin is a mammal that receives protection from intentional commercial harvesting.

Dolphins are common in Florida Bay and the Ten Thousand Islands all year. If you camp on a beach, such as at Cape Sable, Flamingo's walk-in tent sites, or the Everglades National Park island campsites, you may hear a dolphin spouting at night when it surfaces to breathe.

Manatees

One of the most treasured experiences a naturalist can have in Florida is to see a West Indian manatee. Only around 3,800 of these endangered sea mammals remain. Manatees may be visible in south Florida any month of the year. The colder the winter, the more likely it is to find them. They are sensitive to cold water, and a prolonged cold spell may drive them south from northern Florida.

Manatees are nicknamed "sea cows" because they are large marine mammals that graze on underwater vegetation. They are even more harmless than cattle, because they have no hooves or horns to inflict injury. In fact, manatees are so defenseless and nonaggressive that they fall easy prey to humans. They lack defensive mechanisms because, as adults, they have no natural predators; most of the large sharks remain off-shore in deeper water than the manatees.

The greatest danger to manatees in the last hundred years is from humans. The early settlers in the Keys depended on manatees for fresh meat, since there was little land for raising cattle. A waterway through a patch of mangroves near Plantation Key is known as "Cowpens Cut," because (before refrigeration became a part of Keys life) the local people would trap manatees in the waterway by blocking the ends. The manatees would survive in this "cow pen" until their captors needed fresh meat.

Manatees are protected from hunting now, but they face more modern dangers. One is from motorboats. Since manatees are mammals and must breathe air, they forage in shallow water where they can surface easily. This puts them squarely in the path of motorboats, whose deadly propellers and hulls killed a record 97 (or more) manatees in 2009, and 83 in 2010. State and federal conservation agencies are working on laws to add more slow-speed zones and manatee sanctuaries. Total manatee deaths in the state were at least 429 for 2009. Cold weather contributed to an annual record of 767 manatee deaths in 2010.

Finding a manatee will be a challenge. Most manatees in Everglades National Park dwell along the mangrove-lined rivers and creeks between Flamingo and Everglades City. Thus, paddling the Wilderness Waterway may provide some encounters. Try asking the rangers at Everglades or Biscayne National Parks if any have been seen recently. Occasionally manatees loll around the Flamingo Marina. Manatees utilize the Intracoastal Waterway from Miami-Dade County north. Lovers Key State Park often has manatees. They also frequent the canals in the Keys where the residents treat them to fresh water from garden hoses. Because we humans have restricted the flow of fresh water coming down from the Everglades into Florida Bay and have destroyed the natural springs that once poured fresh water into nearshore seawater, manatees can sometimes be stressed for fresh drinking water. Although it is tempting to attract a manatee by feeding or watering it, it is illegal and should not be done. Feeding and watering causes them to lose fear of humans and linger around canals and docks. This places them dangerously close to boats.

If you are fortunate enough to encounter manatees while you are paddling, don't panic. They are docile and will swim sluggishly around you. If you make a sudden move that startles them, you'll be amazed at the energy they will display when they turn tail and flee. It is legal to swim with these gentle giants as long as you do not alter their behavior; for example, you can't cause them to swim in a direction other than that in which they were headed, so just float and watch them. If you find an injured or dead manatee, call the Florida Marine Patrol at 1-800-DIAL-FMP.

Alligators and Crocodiles

Few creatures in North America evoke as much fear and curiosity as the two largest native reptiles, the American alligator and the American crocodile. Much myth and mystery surrounds them.

Alligators are found from North Carolina to Florida and west across the Gulf states to Texas. They number in the millions. Alligators prefer fresh water, although occasionally they'll be found swimming in salt water around the Ten Thousand Islands, Flamingo, and so on. Crocodiles, which number 600–1,000 and are federally threatened, have a limited U.S. range of southern Florida. Never venturing far from the sea, they prefer salt water but will occasionally wander into fresh water.

Differences in appearance are subtle. An alligator's skin color is black (although it often appears and is depicted as green), while a crocodile's skin is gray. An alligator has a wide snout, while a crocodile has a narrow one with the large fourth tooth from the lower jaw protruding when the mouth is closed.

Neither species is especially dangerous to humans. The local crocodiles are not the same species as the so-called man-eaters of Australia, Africa, and India. Our crocodiles and alligators are generally nonaggressive to humans (see "Alligators" on pages 12–13).

Alligators disperse during the wet season and may be difficult to locate. During the dry season, they are easily seen at the Anhinga Trail and Shark Valley Tram Road in Everglades National Park, as well as A.R.M. Loxahatchee National Wildlife Refuge,

American alligators in south Florida range in total length up to 13 feet for males and 10 feet for females.

Big Cypress Bend, and Corkscrew Swamp Sanctuary. Crocodiles are rare and always difficult to find. Your best, but not necessarily reliable, bet is to drive down Card Sound Road (the road from Florida City to North Key Largo) and stop just before the intersection with SR 905. A group of mangrove ponds known as the Crocodile Lakes are part of the Crocodile Lake National Wildlife Refuge (no visitor services, contact National Key Deer Refuge for information). Look from the road with binoculars for a crocodile head, preferably on a sunny day when the reptiles are basking. Also try the Buttonwood Canal by the Flamingo Marina or West Lake in Everglades National Park.

Gopher Tortoises

The gopher tortoise is the only species of land tortoise in the eastern United States. The reptiles are found throughout the drier parts of Florida. They are known by ecologists as a "keystone species" because so many other types of animals depend on tortoise burrows for survival. More than 100 species of vertebrates and invertebrates, including indigo snakes, gopher frogs, Florida mice, burrowing owls, lizards, and many insects, regularly retreat to the burrows or at least seek refuge during fires. As many as 250 more species have been found to use the burrows at least occasionally. If gopher tortoises and their burrows disappeared from the area, hundreds of associated animals would eventually perish without shelter.

A tortoise digs its burrow with its shovel-like front feet. The burrow may be 10 feet deep and as much as 40 feet long. It provides cooling shade during the heat of the day and insulating warmth during cold fronts. The soil must be well-drained and loose, which is just the type of substrate that developers seek. This competition for scrub habitats has caused the tortoise to lose substantial habitat, such as the coastal ridges along the Atlantic seaboard. A distinguishing feature of the tortoise burrow is that the entrance is oblong, unlike the armadillo's and pocket gopher's round burrows. This shape accommodates the tortoise's shell, which is wider than it is high. A large sandy mound a foot or more in diameter next to the hole (called the "apron") makes it easy to spot gopher tortoise burrows.

An additional assault on gopher tortoises is a respiratory disease that can be passed from one tortoise to another. The disease may have been spread by the

Adult gopher tortoises grow to a length of a foot or more.

release of tortoises at Sanibel Island. The relocation of gopher tortoises from areas slated for development was a standard mitigation method until this disease was discovered. This is a clear example of what wildlife biologists have been trying to convince people of for years—that releasing an animal anywhere besides its own territory can have serious repercussions. Relocations of most species of animals by the U.S. Fish and Wildlife Service and state agencies are usually preceded by quarantines and veterinary examinations.

Gopher tortoises and their burrows may be seen at John D. MacArthur Beach State Park, Koreshan State Park, Picayune Strand State Forest, on Sanibel Island, on Cape Sable in Everglades National Park, and other places with higher, sandy elevations. Anywhere you see prickly-pear cactus growing, you may see a gopher tortoise, since that's a favored food. Another favored food is gopher apple. Gopher tortoises are listed as a threatened species by the state.

Sea Turtles

Florida is well-known to tourists for its thousand miles of white, sandy beaches with warm waters and gentle tides that make them perfect for sunbathing and swimming. For these same reasons, sea turtles also think Florida beaches are the greatest and flock by the tens of thousands to lay their eggs every summer. The densities of nests along Florida's eastern coast are among the highest in the world. Sea turtles spend most of the year at sea or feeding along a coast. When the nesting urge overtakes the females, they head for their own birth place, even if it's thousands of miles away. No one knows for sure how they navigate, but it is probably a combination of methods that include using the sun, landmarks on the ocean floor, currents, and scents. If they do use olfactory cues to guide them to ancestral beaches, imagine how confused they are when we dump our sewage into the water.

Sea turtles have suffered directly from drowning in shrimp nets. The nets are dragged along the ocean floor, scooping up the scavenging shrimp. An entangled turtle drowns because it can't escape to the surface to breathe. Special devices that attach to shrimp nets and allow turtles to escape (called Turtle Excluder Devices or "TEDs"), are now mandatory for most shrimp boats.

Plastic bags and deflated party balloons are another nemesis of sea turtles that prey on jellyfish. Floating plastic bags and balloons so resemble jellyfish to the nearsighted turtles that they eat them and die from blocked digestive systems.

Nesting has declined in Florida from human interference. One cause is the presence of garbage on the beach, which interferes with the turtles' ability to crawl on the sand and dig their nests. Another major culprit is fishing line, which entangles the turtles. The roots of the invasive Australian-pine trees prevent turtles from digging their nests. Hatching turtles become disoriented from artificial light cast onto the beach at night by adjacent hotels, condominiums, and parking lots. The hatchlings are instinctively drawn toward the lightest horizon, which is normally the ocean reflecting the stars and moon. The lights turn them inland where they die or are killed by cars, raccoons, snakes, opossums, and so on. Laws now prohibit such lighting in some places, but more towns need to abide.

Four species of sea turtles found in Florida are federally endangered (green, hawksbill, leatherback, and Ridley), and one is threatened (loggerhead). The loggerhead is the most common nesting species and may weigh up to 350 pounds (although historically they reached 1,000 pounds). The reddish-brown carapace color is the easiest way to distinguish the species. Loggerheads lay their eggs from May through August on both the Atlantic and Gulf coasts.

Green turtles nest from June to September and only on the Atlantic coast. They are common in the Caribbean, where they were hunted for food for centuries. They have green carapaces and can weigh up to 450 pounds. Leatherback turtles are the largest of all living turtles; they can grow to 1,200 pounds. Their carapaces don't have bony scutes (thus no hard shell) but are covered instead by dark, leather-like skin. Although they are not hunted for their meat, their eggs are sought for food. The Atlantic hawksbill rarely nests in Florida but may be seen in Florida waters. The Atlantic Ridley does not nest in Florida but does feed offshore.

The following places have sea turtle nesting beaches: Atlantic coast—John D. MacArthur Beach State Park and other public beaches along Palm Beach and Broward County coasts; Gulf coast—Sanibel Island, sandy beaches from Ten Thousand Islands to Cape Sable, and Cayo Costa State Park.

Raptors

Many of the local raptors are familiar to people from other parts of North America because the birds have migrated from those parts. Red-shouldered hawks, kestrels, and ospreys are three examples. South Florida's resident red-shouldered hawks, however, differ slightly in appearance by having pale gray heads.

Many raptors pass by the region as they migrate farther south to Central and South America. The peninsula of Cape Florida and the string of Florida Keys create the typical bottleneck that concentrates raptors before they set off across the Straits of Florida. Reluctant to leave the thermals, resting places, and prey that the land provides, the migrating raptors often linger around Bill Baggs Cape Florida State Park and Boot Key in Marathon during September and October. A few species of special interest and where to find them are highlighted here.

Everglade snail kites are medium-sized hawks that require shallow fresh water where their staple food, the native apple snail (*Pomacea paludosa*), dwells on sawgrass, spike rush, and other aquatic plant stems. The kites are present in south Florida throughout the year, although they may concentrate at Lake Okeechobee and the Kissimmee region during periods of extended drought in the Everglades. It may take several years of suitable water levels after a marsh dries out to restore the snail populations and attract the kites again. A 2000 statewide survey revealed an estimated 2,800 kites, higher than any previous year. A decade later, the population has plunged to barely 700 because habitat alteration and invasive species. The snail kite has been listed as federally endangered since 1967. The primary threat facing snail kites is the loss of habitat, both by development of wetlands and artificial manipulation of the remaining wetlands. Another problem is the presence of invasive plants such as water lettuce and water hyacinth. These cover the water and prevent the kites from seeing the snails. A third increasing problem is an invasive species of snail (the island apple snail) that was introduced from South America for the food and pet trade. This nonnative snail is larger than any other freshwater snail and outcompetes the native apple snail that sustains snail kites. This snail is threatening to devastate the kite's main food source. The snail kite's bill size and shape is adapted for the native snail, not the larger nonnative snail. Look for the kites along the Tamiami Trail, especially near the Miccosukee restaurant by the Shark Valley entrance to Everglades National Park and along the Shark Valley Tram Road. They may occasionally be seen at the Headquarters area of A.R.M. Loxahatchee NWR. Also check the Solid Waste Authority Greenway Trail System in West Palm Beach at dawn or dusk (45th Street and North Jog Road). Look around there or north on Jog Road. Kites roost there year-round (mostly June–October) and nest in the summer.

Swallow-tailed kites are fairly common between March and August over pinelands and cypress and mangrove swamps. They may be seen gliding gracefully over the treetops, ready to seize a lizard or snake from a branch. Look for them around the pinelands of Everglades National Park.

Peregrine falcons may be seen in winter from the Observation Deck at Flamingo hunting over the mud flats or around concentrations of shorebirds on Cape Sable. Peregrines, merlins, and kestrels are often seen on Cape Florida and in the Keys during October.

Burrowing owls prefer open, well-drained short grass fields, including fallow farm land, college campuses, and airports all over south Florida. The owls nest from February to August. A drive along a rural mainland road, such as SR 80, may produce the owls if you watch for levees or small mounds of dirt on which they like to stand. Burrowing owls may be seen in the Cape Coral area of Fort Myers, Sombrero Beach in Marathon, Florida Atlantic University Campus in Boca Raton, and Brian Piccolo Park in Ft. Lauderdale.

Ospreys have recovered since their perilous decline from the pesticide DDT in the 1950s and 1960s. They may be seen anywhere along the coast, Florida Bay, canals, lakes, and ponds. They often build their sturdy large stick nests atop utility poles; nests can be seen along US 1 in the Keys and US A1A on the east coast, although the nests are active only from December to May.

Bald eagles also have recovered since suffering the same fate as the ospreys and brown pelicans in the 1950s. The U.S. Fish and Wildlife Service declared bald eagles as "recovered" and removed them from the threatened and endangered species list in 2007. Bald eagles can be seen year-round near large bodies of water where they hunt for fish or filch them from ospreys. Eagles nest on the larger islands in Florida Bay and the coastal prairies of Everglades National Park. Bald eagles may be seen around Mahogany Hammock because they roost near there (see Mahogany Hammock under Everglades National Park) and Lake Okeechobee.

Short-tailed hawks are a Florida specialty, although they are not common. They are usually found in central Florida in the summer and south of Lake Okeechobee in the winter. Birds of both light and dark color phases may occasionally be seen soaring in thermals with vultures, and they may be found in pinelands or grasslands, such as the various stops along the road to Flamingo.

Crested caracaras are vulturelike members of the falcon family, with a range in the southeastern United States that is restricted to central Florida (they are also found in Texas and Mexico). Specifically, most are found north and west of Lake Okeechobee; they may occasionally be seen southwest of the lake. Caracaras prefer open grassland where they feed on carrion, especially if cabbage palms are present for them to nest on. Only about 400 caracaras are left in Florida because of habitat loss—citrus groves are taking over. As you drive along such roads as SR 80 or US 27, watch the utility poles and fence posts for a perching caracara.

Wading Birds

One of the great attractions the Everglades holds for many people is the promise of seeing large flocks of graceful and colorful egrets, ibises, herons, spoonbills, and storks painting the sky at dusk. The protection of such flocks was one reason part of the region was set aside as a national park.

Before human intervention, approximately 100,000 pairs of wading birds nested in the southern Everglades. Now it may be only 10,000 pairs in a good year, a reduction of 90 percent. Part of the decrease was caused by the practice, in the late 1800s and early 1900s, of killing the birds during the breeding season to collect plumes for sale to the fashion moguls. Some species recovered, but some (like the reddish egret) have maintained low populations. The rest of the decrease has been

White ibises at Eco Pond in Everglades National Park. White ibises forage in shallow waters and mud flats, where they feed on crabs and other small organisms.

attributed to water management practices that altered the quality, quantity, and timing of water that flowed through the Everglades. Those practices still continue and still affect wading birds.

Enough wading birds remain in the Everglades to make a thrilling sight. Species you are most likely to see are great blue heron, great white heron, great egret, snowy egret, little blue heron, tricolored heron, green heron, black-crowned night-heron, white ibis, roseate spoonbill, and wood stork. A small group of flamingos occasionally feeds in the mud flats off Snake Bight and Sandy Key in northwest Florida Bay, but this is the northern edge of their range and their occurrences here are sporadic. Debate exists over the origin of the flamingos in Everglades National Park; they may be escapees from a tourist attraction or wanderers from Cuba or the Bahamas.

One of the hardest-hit species is the white ibis, the most numerous wading bird in the state. Populations have plummeted so sharply from loss of habitat that the species was listed by the state in 1994 as a "species of special concern." This is an example of a wildlife agency trying to prevent a populous species from becoming endangered, when it is clear from the signs that it will. Remember the passenger pigeon, which numbered in the billions more than a hundred years ago and is now extinct? It could happen with the white ibis.

Another suffering species is the endangered wood stork, whose populations have declined primarily because of loss of wetlands. Historically, the stronghold for wood stork nesting was south Florida. In the 1980s and 1990s, a new trend began emerging. Storks were shifting their nesting sites farther and farther north. Central Florida now holds the greatest concentration of stork colonies. Wood storks usually nest at Corkscrew Swamp Sanctuary from January to June. Even if local foraging or water conditions prevent nesting, they should still be visible in the area. Stork populations are slowly increasing.

Add the snowy egret to the list of declining populations—it never recovered from the slaughter for its plumes in the early 1900s. Snowy egrets do not seem as resilient as tricolored and little blue herons, with which they share feeding and nesting habitats.

Roseate spoonbills nest primarily in Florida Bay. After the nesting season, they disperse northward along the coasts (May through August). Then they may be seen at John D. MacArthur Beach State Park, J.N. "Ding" Darling National Wildlife Refuge, Flamingo, and other coastal areas.

The best time to see wading birds is from November to June, when the decreasing water levels concentrate the birds around their aquatic prey, and winter migrants may also be present. The best places to look in Everglades National Park are the mud flats at Flamingo, the Anhinga Trail, and the Shark Valley Tram Road. Also check the Ten Thousand Islands at Everglades City, the "18-Mile Stretch" of US 1 between MM 108 and MM 111, "J.N. Ding" Darling NWR, and A.R.M. Loxahatchee NWR.

Red-Cockaded Woodpeckers

Known in birding lingo as "RCWs," red-cockaded woodpeckers were once characteristic of mature, open pine forests of the southeastern United States. They are dependent on extensive stands of old pines for foraging, 75- to 95-year-old pines for nesting cavities, a relatively dense RCW population to accommodate their complex social structure, and fire to control understory growth. Commercial logging has taken its toll, because timber companies prefer to harvest their stands in less time than it takes for the pines to mature naturally. In addition, the RCW's favorite tree, the longleaf pine, is not easily cultivated and is usually substituted with slash pines when stands are replanted. RCWs were added to the federal endangered species list in 1970 and the state list in 1974. The state downgraded it to a species of special concern in 2003 because of a slight increase in population.

RCWs depend on the presence of the red heart fungus (*Phellinus pini*), which is a heart rot naturally found in older trees that makes the heartwood softer. These woodpeckers are unique because they excavate living trees for nesting cavities, as opposed to using dead trees as other woodpeckers do. It may take years to excavate enough for a nest, but the nest may be used for more than 50 years by succeeding generations.

Both sexes have white cheek patches and barred patterns on their backs. Males have a small red spot (cockade) on each side of head, displayed only during courtship and threatening behaviors. RCWs still persist in the slash pines of Big Cypress National Preserve and Corbett Wildlife Management Area.

Florida Scrub-Jays

Many of the wildlife species that inhabit the scrub of Florida are also found in the desert areas of the western United States, but not in the states in between. The scrub-jay is one of them. Climatic changes long ago caused the split that isolated the Florida jays, a separate species from the scrub-jays in the southwestern United States. Although the two populations of jays look nearly identical (the Florida ones have a lighter forehead), the behaviors differ markedly. The federally threatened, endemic Florida birds have evolved a complex social structure with nest helpers, possibly because the amount of scrub habitat is so limited (even without development). With most other animal species that have territories, the young must leave their parents' territory and seek their own. These scrub-jays, however, would die if they had to leave, because there is nowhere for them to go that isn't already taken by another jay. Thus, they stay with their parents and siblings, helping to raise more young by bringing them food and watching for predators. When death causes a territory to become available, one of the sons (evidence suggests the eldest) takes over. This results in a higher survival rate for the whole family.

Florida scrub-jays prefer oak habitats along ridges (such as the Atlantic Coastal Ridge) where Chapman oak, sand live oak, and myrtle oak provide their staple food, the acorn. The jays line their nests exclusively with the threadlike fibers from the leaf blades of the scrub palmetto. Territories cover about 20 acres each. Scrub-jays may be found along the Atlantic Coastal Ridge in Palm Beach County.

IV THE UNWANTED PESTS

South Florida has one of the highest concentrations of invasive plants and animals of any region in the country. These are nonnative species that become established in the wild and disrupt the natural ecological balance. Most invasive species come from other continents. Some are brought intentionally for agriculture, horticulture, and aquaculture, and many are brought for the pet industry. Others arrive accidentally as unintentional hitchhikers on ships, planes, or other vehicles. Some of these plants and animals live nearly innocuous lives, never spreading or causing harm, but many grow out of control. A few are extreme pests that must be controlled or we may face ecological disaster. These species grow or reproduce so fast or in such numbers as to outcompete native species for food and other resources. Some invasive animals are voracious predators that can devastate native species. If left unchecked, the natural habitats will gradually cease to function properly. For example, we may lose the productivity of our bountiful seafood-bearing Florida Bay.

The U.S. Fish and Wildlife Service, National Park Service, U.S. Department of Agriculture, and state and county agencies have programs to remove or control invasive species; millions of dollars are spent annually. It's a never-ending battle to eliminate organisms that spread faster than they can be removed.

Control of invasive species is extremely difficult and expensive (if possible at all), and conservationists stress that we can all do more to prevent their spread. The two most important tips are: 1) never release any plant or animal from captivity into the wild; and 2) clean all fishing equipment, boots, boats, and trailers completely upon leaving the water—make sure no tiny snails, eggs, pieces of plant, or other aquatic organisms are clinging to equipment, because these may survive out of water and start a new population in the next waterway they are dunked in.

Invasive Animals

One reason for the high concentration of nonnative animals in Florida is that the mild climate allows many people to keep exotic pets in outdoor pens year-round. Occasionally these escape or are released illegally when the owners tire of caring for them. Another reason is that Miami and Ft. Lauderdale are major ports of entry. Animals intended for the pet trade occasionally escape while the cargo crates are docked, or the animals are released by the shippers if the animals were smuggled and the authorities are closing in. Many of these animals can survive and even reproduce around the suburbs and natural areas.

Florida has the highest number of nonnative fish species in the lower 48 states, partly because the numerous wetlands contain warm water all year and the canal network, combined with seasonally flooding marshes, makes a convenient vehicle for widespread dispersal. Fishes from the aquarium trade, such as walking catfish, lionfish, and African jewelfish, have spread this way. Adding to the problem is that,

---

occasionally, even the state wildlife agency has intentionally introduced fish to promote sport fishing.

Parrots, snakes, and lizards are three types of animals that seem to adapt to the Florida suburbs with ease. Great flocks of monk parakeets (which destroy fruit crops) can be found in the skies and trees of southern Florida.

Also established are muscovy ducks and spot-breasted orioles. Muscovy ducks have become a nuisance around ponds near development. Their black or white (or both) plumages and red, warty faces are familiar around artificial ponds, which are abundant in south Florida. In this flat, low-lying terrain, builders must first dredge an area to provide the fill they need to build upon. This creates a depression that soon fills with water. As the new homeowners gaze across the barren pond, they yearn for something living to entertain them. They obtain one of the few animals that can survive above the water's surface in this artificial habitat—domesticated ducks. The domesticated muscovies and mallards do just fine, reproducing exponentially until the pond and all the surrounding lawns are filled with their droppings. Then neighbor confronts neighbor, tempers flare, and soon there are lawsuits over getting rid of the ducks.

Small lizards that have established populations include Cuban brown anoles, Mediterranean geckos, and Indopacific geckos. Large lizards include green iguanas and Nile monitors, both introduced through the pet trade. Green iguanas (averaging 6.5 feet) from Central and South America can munch away ornamental vegetation in a yard and like to defecate in swimming pools. When threatened, they jump into water to escape. This makes it hard to capture them. Nile monitors (native to Africa) can grow to 7 feet long (commonly to 5 feet), swim under water for up to an hour, climb trees and houses, are carnivorous with sharp teeth, and have no local predators. Estimates range in the thousands for Nile monitor populations in south Florida.

Invasive snakes that have become established in south Florida include boa constrictors and Burmese pythons. Since the first edition of this book, the problem of large constrictor snakes has gone from barely noticeable to increasingly severe. Boa constrictors, which grow to 13 feet, are established in the Deering Estate in South Miami. Burmese pythons are established in Everglades National Park and elsewhere. The pythons can grow to 20 feet, weigh 200 pounds, and eat animals the size of pigs and larger. While the threat to humans is minimal, pythons and boas can devastate populations of native birds, mammals, snakes, and fish, many of which are already rare. The longest snake native to Florida (the indigo snake) is only 8 feet long, so these large constrictors are far larger than the largest native predator snakes. Floridians must have a permit to own a Nile monitor lizard or any of seven species of large constrictor snakes (Burmese python, reticulated python, amethystine python, scrub python, Northern and Southern African pythons, and green anaconda) because of their potential to escape captivity or be released by disillusioned owners.

Two of the many introduced mammals that have become pests are the armadillo and feral hog. In 1943, a man brought a female nine-banded armadillo and six young from his native state of Texas to Wakulla, Florida. These reproduced, and probably others were introduced as well. Eventually, all the drier parts of Florida (except the Keys) became home to this prehistoric-looking species. Their primary food

Feral hogs in Everglades National Park

is insects and other invertebrates, but they will consume fruits and berries, seeds, mushrooms, and eggs. The eggs may be those of game birds, freshwater turtles, sea turtles, lizards, snakes, salamanders, or other ground-nesting animals. Their method of foraging by rooting around in the leaf litter destroys the integrity of that forest stratum. Armadillos have few enemies, since their armored skin protects them.

Feral hogs (also known as wild hogs and feral pigs) have been established in the southeastern United States for 400 years—so long that many people assume they are native. As descendants of the barnyard pigs that the Spanish explorers brought, they have thrived on eating fruits, nuts, ground-dwelling animals, and whatever other foods they can dig up. It is never difficult to tell when pigs have been around—the ground looks like a rototiller played hop-scotch in the woods. These telltale "rootings" may be all you see of these nocturnal animals. Feral hogs will eat almost anything edible they encounter: eggs, lizards, and snakes, including indigo snakes and other rare species. Some state parks have policies to eradicate the hogs from their lands. They cannot be released elsewhere without similar consequences. The carcasses are donated to state institutions for food. However, the hogs reproduce too fast for eradication efforts to keep pace. They will remain a pest for a long time to come. The only benefit that can be argued in their favor is that they are good prey for panthers. You can find feral hogs by walking at night wherever you see signs of recent rooting (such as Dupuis Reserve State Forest and Corbett Wildlife Management Area). Listen for gruntings and look with a flashlight, but keep your distance because they are wild.

Countless introduced animal species have become major pests in south Florida. Invasive amphibians include the Cuban treefrog and giant (cane) toad; fish include walking catfish, lionfish, and Asian swamp eel; birds include purple swamphen and sacred ibis; and invertebrates include island applesnail and Asian green mussel. Invasive insects include Asian tiger mosquito, lovebug, fire ant, and many fruit flies.

Invasive Plants

Some of the invasive, nonnative plants in south Florida have created great turmoil. More than a few biologists feel that they could be the ultimate destroyer of valuable habitat. Some of the plants were introduced from tropical and subtropical areas around the world and are cultivated in south Florida gardens. A number of plants were introduced for functions that were desirable at the time, such as coastal windbreaks and dewatering wetlands (because the plants drink more than their share of water). We have learned the hard way that their virtues did not outweigh their vices.

Some invasive plants are more destructive than others. An invasive plant can spread on its own, either reproductively (through seeds or spores) or vegetatively (by runners or budding). The main reason the invasive plants spread so rapidly is that they have no natural enemies in their new land as they do in their places of origin.

Some nonnative plants that initially did not spread have gradually adapted to local conditions over several decades and become invasive. Thus, the only truly safe plants for your garden are the native ones.

Invasive Trees

Three nonnative trees have made the local conservationists' "most unwanted to kill" list for decades. They are melaleuca, Brazilian pepper, and Australian-pine. Others are gaining momentum.

Melaleuca (also called punk tree or cajeput) was introduced to Miami in 1906 during the early swamp-draining era. Seeds of this tree were broadcast-spread by aircraft over the Everglades in the 1930s to facilitate draining the marsh. An eye-catching tree with papery white bark, melaleuca uses several times more water than our native vegetation does. A large stand of melaleucas steals water from and crowds out native plants, thereby outcompeting them. The phenomenal growth and reproductive rates, coupled with the variety of habitats melaleuca can grow in and the difficulty in killing it, make melaleuca one of the formidable environmental enemies south Florida faces. Melaleuca was added to the Federal Noxious Weed List in 1992, the first "weed" to be added in more than 12 years. Now, transportation of the plant into the U.S. and between states requires a permit from the U.S. Department of Agriculture. Other restrictions were enacted to prevent its spread. Stands of melaleuca can be seen along the Turnpike in Broward County, along Krome Avenue between Homestead and the Tamiami Trail, and along the Tamiami Trail west of Krome.

Brazilian pepper is a fast-growing, quick-spreading small tree that arrived from Brazil around 1941. Its clusters of bright red berries ripen around Christmas, and some people collect the branches (and encourage their growth) for Christmas wreaths. However, since Brazilian pepper is related to poison ivy (same family), touching it causes dermatitis for some people. The berries provide food for raccoons, robins, and other animals, but this benefit does not outweigh the detrimental properties. Brazilian pepper grows as an extraordinarily dense understory tree, impenetrable by all but the smallest animals. Brazilian pepper is now one of the most common plants along the roads of south Florida, where it is also known as Florida holly. Once Brazilian pepper becomes established, it is virtually impossible to eradicate, because

1. The colorful lubber grasshoppers are native to Florida.

2. Painted buntings are a treat to watch at Castellow Hammock Preserve and elsewhere in south Florida.

3. An Everglade snail kite hunts for its primary food—apple snails.

4. Water hyacinth, an introduced, invasive plant that chokes waterways, was imported for its attractive purple flowers.

5. Colorful fruits of beauty berry at Florida Panther National Wildlife Refuge

6. Observation platform at A.R.M. Loxahatchee National Wildlife Refuge

7. Rainbows are frequent in summer over A.R.M. Loxahatchee National Wildlife Refuge and the rest of the Everglades because of the frequent thunderstorms.

8. The Anhinga Trail boardwalk at Royal Palm in Everglades National Park is a superb place to see wildlife.

9. A male anhinga dries its wings after fishing underwater.

10. Bromeliads, also known as airplants and epiphytes, commonly grow on cypress trunks, such as these in Everglades National Park.

11. The purple gallinule, a chicken-like bird, can use its large feet to walk on aquatic vegetation.

12. A male green anole, a native lizard, showing its pink throat fan. Green anoles are only 8 inches long, including tail.

13. Dawn over the dwarf cypress trees in Everglades National Park

14. Fort Jefferson on Garden Key in Dry Tortugas National Park, with Bush Key on right

15. Boardwalk trail through hardwood hammock at John Pennekamp Coral Reef State Park in Key Largo

16. The Gumbo Limbo Trail at Royal Palm is named after the gumbo-limbo tree, such as the one with the reddish trunk on the left.

17. West Indian manatees live in clear, shallow water and graze on underwater vegetation.

18. Paurotis palms are native to Florida and grow to 25 feet tall in clumps.

19. Mangrove shoreline of Biscayne National Park

20. Palm Beach County marshland west of West Palm Beach (on horizon)

21. The hawksbill sea turtle, an endangered species, may be seen along the Florida coast.

22. The Florida softshell turtle is found in southern Georgia and across Florida.

23. Tarpon can grow to 8 feet and weigh more than 200 pounds; they are found around Florida Bay and the reefs.

24. French angelfish are common on the coral reefs.

25. Bahia Honda State Park

26. Sandhill cranes doing a courtship dance in the Everglades

27. Key deer are petite island-dwelling versions of the mainland's white-tailed deer.

28. Burrowing owls are commonly seen standing on the ground around suburban areas of Fort Myers, Marathon, Boca Raton, and Ft. Lauderdale.

29. Roseate spoonbills nest in south Florida where they feed on small animals in muddy water.

30. Storm clouds over Turner River Road in Big Cypress National Preserve

31. The Cuban treefrog, which grows to about 5.5 inches and climbs walls, is an invasive species in Florida.

32. An alligator tries to kill a Burmese python, one of thousands of the invasive species that is an increasing pest in the Everglades.

33. The zebra longwing butterfly is found only in Florida and Texas in the U.S.

34. Florida panthers are secretive and very rare.

35. Sunset at the Chekika section of Everglades National Park

36. Black-bellied whistling-ducks are a Florida rarity, unless you know where to look.

37. Brown pelican populations, once endangered from now-banned pesticides, have recovered.

38. Kayaking through the mangroves of the Florida Keys

39. The vegetation on the shore of Indian Key is scrubby, but small trees grow in the interior.

40. Limpkins are special Florida marsh birds, where they feed mostly on freshwater snails and mussels.

41. A green iguana, a nonnative pest, on a palm frond. Green iguanas can grow to 5 feet and weigh 20 pounds.

42. Some tricolored herons are year-round residents and some are migrants. They forage for small fish and amphibians in marshes and estuaries.

43. Two spotted eagle rays swim by red mangroves. These rays are common near shore in southeast Florida.

44. Fruits of the sea-grape tree resemble their namesake. Sea-grapes are common in the Keys.

45. Reddish egrets forage in shallow, coastal waters and actively chase fish.

Melaleuca tree trunks in Everglades, showing the papery bark and dense growth

it is resistant to fires, floods, and droughts. Approximately one million acres of Florida are infested with it.

Australian-pine, also known as Casuarina, is from Australia but is not a true pine. In fact, it's not even a conifer. Its wispy needles and small conelike fruits are reminiscent of pine trees. Australian-pines were introduced as soil retainers and windbreaks along the coast and canals. They outcompete native trees, but their weak branches make nesting risky for large birds, such as swallow-tailed kites, which prefer the native pines. The roots of Australian-pines growing along the beaches interfere with sea turtle and crocodile nesting. As windbreaks, they turned out to be worse than worthless when it really mattered. When Hurricane Andrew struck, the same Australian-pines that were planted along canals as windbreaks snapped in pieces and piled in the canals in a tangled mass. Hundreds of miles of canals were clogged. The resulting intensive and expensive debris removal prompted the South Florida Water Management District to cut the standing trees along the canals outside Andrew's path to prevent wind damage in the future. The Florida Department of Transportation spent $7 million removing Australian-pines from roadsides. Some local town ordinances now require homeowners to fell their Australian-pines.

Invasive Aquatic Plants

Alien (nonnative) aquatic plants have plagued Florida for decades by clogging waterways, interfering with fish reproduction, and reducing the dissolved oxygen. The latter effect has caused numerous fish kills. Three such plants are water hyacinth (from Venezuela), hydrilla (introduced from Sri Lanka for the aquarium trade), and water lettuce. All spread uncontrollably when dumped into canals. Water hyacinth was spread from one plant by a woman who brought it back from an exposition in New Orleans. She thought it would look pretty in her backyard fish pond by the St. Johns River. Some waterways have been rendered useless to wildlife and humans by these plants forming a solid mat on the surface, which blocks access to the water and prevents sunlight from penetrating to the native submersed plants. Hydrilla, which spreads vegetatively in Florida, covers more than 65,000 acres, or about half of the state's public waterways. Boaters inadvertently spread these plants when the plants hitch rides on their boats or trailers, which then travel to uninfested waters and start to grow.

Invasive Climbing Vines

Another group of invasive plants—the climbing vines—is also a scourge in Florida. Most were introduced as house or garden plants, and they thrive in the warm, humid climate. Two of the many compounding effects of hurricanes are to waft seeds and plant parts into pristine hammocks where they can grow into plants, and to open the canopy in the already affected areas to create a favorable environment for invasive vines. Some climbing vines have indeterminate growth, which means that they can keep growing as long as they have nutrients and proper weather. In comparison, determinate growers never grow more than a certain genetically determined height. Thus, a climbing vine can grow up a tree trunk to the upper branches, blanketing trees to death with shade. Examples of such vines are the air potato and Old World climbing fern. Air potato and other climbing vines may grow a foot a day. Air potato is rampant in Broward and Miami-Dade county parks. Climbing fern is visible at Hungryland Slough and has invaded Everglades National Park, A.R.M. Loxahatchee National Wildlife Refuge, and many other areas.

Old World climbing fern covering the trunks of cypresses at Hungryland Slough

V NATURAL AREAS OF SOUTHEASTERN FLORIDA

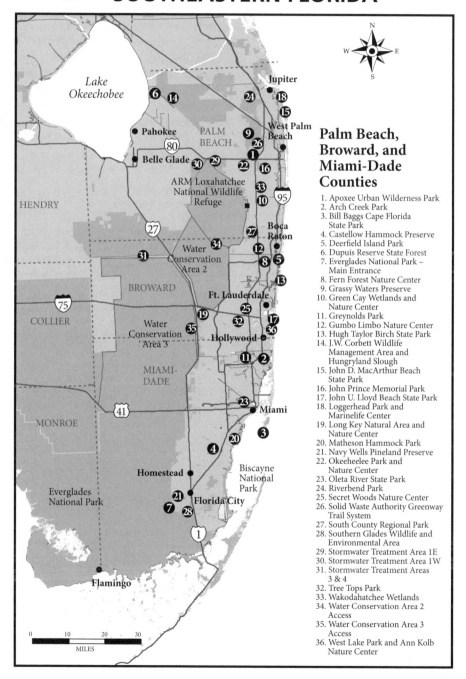

Palm Beach, Broward, and Miami-Dade Counties

1. Apoxee Urban Wilderness Park
2. Arch Creek Park
3. Bill Baggs Cape Florida State Park
4. Castellow Hammock Preserve
5. Deerfield Island Park
6. Dupuis Reserve State Forest
7. Everglades National Park – Main Entrance
8. Fern Forest Nature Center
9. Grassy Waters Preserve
10. Green Cay Wetlands and Nature Center
11. Greynolds Park
12. Gumbo Limbo Nature Center
13. Hugh Taylor Birch State Park
14. J.W. Corbett Wildlife Management Area and Hungryland Slough
15. John D. MacArthur Beach State Park
16. John Prince Memorial Park
17. John U. Lloyd Beach State Park
18. Loggerhead Park and Marinelife Center
19. Long Key Natural Area and Nature Center
20. Matheson Hammock Park
21. Navy Wells Pineland Preserve
22. Okeeheelee Park and Nature Center
23. Oleta River State Park
24. Riverbend Park
25. Secret Woods Nature Center
26. Solid Waste Authority Greenway Trail System
27. South County Regional Park
28. Southern Glades Wildlife and Environmental Area
29. Stormwater Treatment Area 1E
30. Stormwater Treatment Area 1W
31. Stormwater Treatment Areas 3 & 4
32. Tree Tops Park
33. Wakodahatchee Wetlands
34. Water Conservation Area 2 Access
35. Water Conservation Area 3 Access
36. West Lake Park and Ann Kolb Nature Center

1   Apoxee Urban Wilderness Park

Facilities: Hiking and bicycling trails, chemical toilets

Activities: Hiking, bicycling

Admission: Free

Hours: Daily 7 am–6 pm

Pets: Not allowed

Best Time of Year: November to April

This new park (pronounced "Ah-po'-ee") is managed by the City of West Palm Beach for water conservation and visitor use. It provides access to a short paved hiking trail with a 2.5-mile unpaved extension through wetlands, hammocks, and pine flatwoods. The park is approximately midway along the 16.5-mile Owahee Trail (northern terminus is at **Grassy Waters Preserve**). Hikers and bicyclists can go north for about 8 open and level miles to the Northlake Blvd. access of the Owahee Trail, or south, then west, and then north for 8 miles to the Preserve boundary, where there is no public access (must return to Apoxee). The habitat is wetlands. Bring drinking water.

DIRECTIONS
Take Florida's Turnpike to Exit 98 (Jog Road). Go north to parking lot on left, one mile past Okeechobee Boulevard.

CONTACT
Apoxee Urban Wilderness Park
3125 North Jog Road
West Palm Beach 33411
561-804-4985
www.cityofwpb.com/park/park.php?id=47#tabs

Arthur R. Marshall Loxahatchee National Wildlife Refuge

Facilities: Headquarters: Visitor center, observation tower, self-guided nature trails, canoe and kayak rentals, boat ramps (Loxahatchee Canoeing, Inc.; 561-733-0192; www.canoethe everglades.com) Hillsboro: chemical toilets, boat ramp

Activities: Wildlife viewing, paddling, boating (except airboats), hiking, bicycling

Admission: U.S fee area

Hours: Refuge open daily, sunrise to sunset; Hillsboro entrance open 6 am–8 pm; Visitor center hours vary seasonally (core hours 9 am–4 pm)—closed Mondays and Tuesdays May–mid-October, closed Thanksgiving and Christmas; paddling trail at main entrance usually closed in summer

Pets: Not allowed

South Florida Birding Trail: 81

Best Time of Year: November–April for observing birds and other wildlife, paddling, and hiking. Canoe Trail may be closed in summer; perimeter canal open all year. Mosquitoes rarely noticeable except in summer twilight.

Originally, the Everglades covered almost 4,000 square miles. It now covers less than half of that. Part of what remains is contained in A.R.M. Loxahatchee National Wildlife Refuge (221 square miles or 143,874 acres). The refuge contains the largest remaining undisturbed northern Everglades habitat. In fact, it was established in 1951 to protect this unique habitat, which is surprisingly different from the southern Everglades. The southern Everglades is fairly open, with relatively few scattered large tree islands and shallow peat. The refuge contains thousands of small tree islands and deep peat—up to 12 feet thick. While the tree islands in the south are formed on the limestone bedrock that breaks the water's surface, tree islands in the refuge are formed from floating peat mats that eventually become rooted to the bottom.

The refuge, which includes **Water Conservation Area 1**, is located downstream of one of the country's most valuable agricultural areas. The agricultural runoff has caused water pollution, leading to a severe habitat imbalance in the part of the refuge that receives these excessive nutrients. As a result, the U.S. Department of the Interior has undertaken a massive multi-faceted program to clean the water before it enters the refuge (**Stormwater Treatment Areas 1 East and 1 West**) and the rest of the Everglades.

Much of the refuge is off-limits to the general public. This prevents disturbance to the wildlife and the habitat. The primary visitor facilities (visitor center and trails) are at the main entrance. A 30,000-acre public use area at the refuge's southern entrance (Hillsboro Recreation Area) is also available for day use. This part of the shallow marsh can only be accessed by boat. This southern area is used primarily by anglers year-round and waterfowl hunters from Thanksgiving to mid-January.

Canal and boat launch at Headquarters entrance

Loxahatchee is undeniably a wetland, but the levees and the boardwalk through the cypress swamp provide hikers a way to see some of the refuge while keeping their feet dry. Alligators, turtles, limpkins, anhingas, and purple gallinules are common residents. River otters and gray foxes are occasionally seen. Bobcats and deer roam the levees, especially at dusk. As many as 257 species of birds have been seen here. Wood storks and many other wading birds forage in the marsh all year. Black-necked stilts are easily seen in the summer when they nest in the impoundments. Thousands of ducks winter at the refuge, including fulvous whistling-ducks, mottled ducks, ring-necked ducks, and blue-winged teal. The refuge is designated as critical habitat for the endangered Everglade snail kites that nest on the refuge in some years. Snail kites are most likely to be seen between March and May.

Trails

The profusion of bromeliads along the Cypress Swamp Boardwalk near the Headquarters (0.4-mile loop, handi-capped-accessible) was impressive until Hurricane Wilma blew them off in 2005. Every cypress was festooned with plants—cardinal air plants, giant wildpines, needle-leaved wildpines, reflexed wildpines, and reddish wildpines to name some. They are slowly growing back. A red lichen known as baton rouge (French for "red stick", after the lichen-covered trunks) brightens the shady cypress swamp. Otters and alligators may be seen.

The grassy Marsh Trail (0.8-mile loop, handicapped-accessible) circum-navigates a 31-acre impoundment. Wading birds, waterfowl, turtles, and alligators are frequently seen. An observation tower is located about halfway around. Other impoundments are easily accessible, allowing for several miles of hiking. In spring, nesting anhingas and great blue herons are occasionally seen from the levee. Allow at least an hour.

Part of the levee that surrounds Water Conservation Area 1 is accessible to pedestrians and bicyclists. The 12-mile section from the Headquarters south to the Hillsboro area provides views of the marsh to hikers and bicyclists. Also from Headquarters, hikers can walk the levee north to Acme 1 pump station (about 12 miles) and must return the same way; no bicycles.

The expanded visitor center opened in 2009 with a variety of videos, a simulated airboat ride, and exceptional exhibits of wildlife of the Everglades. The book store has a large selection concentrating on local natural history.

Paddling

A good way to see the refuge is on the Everglades Canoe Trail at the Head-quarters Area. This 5.5-mile loop passes through wet prairies and deeper sloughs of northern Everglades habitat. In April and May, tricolored and little blue herons occasionally nest in the willows along the trail. Snail kites may infrequently be seen. Listen for the "click, click, click" of cricket frogs any time of day. Look for the clumps of pearl-like eggs of the apple snail on blades of sawgrass or pickerel-weed. Along the trail is a picnic platform and chemical toilet. Allow about one hour per mile, since submerged vegetation often slows paddling. Call ahead to see if the trail is open; it is often closed in summer when floating and submerged plants become too dense. No motors allowed.

Visitors may also paddle along the perimeter canal at the edge of the refuge. Long, straight distances can be paddled—it is 52 miles around! However, since camping is not permitted, only boats with motors can circumnavigate the entire distance in a day. Canal paddlers must share the water with the occasional motorboat. Invasive, nonnative water lettuce and water hyacinth sometimes hinder paddling.

Canoes and kayaks may also be launched at the boat ramp at the Hillsboro entrance where there is a large open marsh.

Bicycling

A 12-mile trail tops the unpaved L-40 Levee between Headquarters and Hills-boro. Mountain or hybrid bikes are recommended. Bicyclists should wear helmets and carry drinking water. There is no shade or shelter.

DIRECTIONS

Main entrance (Headquarters Area): From I-95 (Exit 57) or Florida's Turnpike (Exit 86), take CR 804 (Boynton Beach Boulevard) west to US 441 (SR 7). Turn left, go south 2 miles, and turn right at refuge sign (Lee Road).

20-Mile Bend entrance and boat ramp: From I-95 Exit 68 or Florida's Turnpike Exit 97, go west on SR 80 (Southern Blvd.) for about 11 miles. Turn left on SR 880, cross small steel bridge and take immediate left onto 20-Mile Bend Boat Ramp Road to automatic gate on right, then drive 0.7 miles, cross one-lane bridge, to trailer parking lot.

Hillsboro Recreation Area entrance: From US 441 (SR 7; 12 miles south of main refuge entrance), go west on Loxahatchee Road for 6 miles to end.

CONTACT

A.R.M. Loxahatchee
National Wildlife Refuge
10216 Lee Road
Boynton Beach 33473
561-734-8303 Visitor Center
561-732-3684 Office
www.fws.gov/loxahatchee

3 Bill Baggs Cape Florida State Park

Facilities: Nature trails, historic lighthouse, snack bar, bicycle and kayak rentals

Activities: Swimming, birding, picnicking, fishing, bicycling, kayaking

Admission: State Park fee

Hours: 8 am to sunset

Pets: Allowed on leash in picnic areas, along the sea wall, bike trails, and hiking trails; may not be left unattended; not allowed on the beach, wetlands, in lighthouse, or other buildings

South Florida Birding Trail: 99

Best Time of Year: Late March–May and September–November for migrating birds; year-round for all other activities, such as swimming and fishing

In 1966, the state bought 406 acres at the south end of Cape Florida and named the new park after a Miami newspaper editor who was instrumental in getting the area protected. Because of the Cape's proximity to the dangerous shoals and reefs of the Atlantic Ocean and Biscayne Bay, a lighthouse was built in 1825. Through the bitter Seminole Wars, the lighthouse was alternately lit and darkened. It survived Hurricane Andrew, underwent major renovations in 1996 restoring it to its 1825 appearance, and then was relit after a long darkness.

Cape Florida is part of a large barrier island that protects the mainland. Beaches and dunes are a natural part of the Cape. In 1992, the island was put to the test when Hurricane Andrew blew ashore about 15 miles south. The southern tip of Cape Florida was at the outer edge of the northern eye wall. Virtually every tree in the park was blown down. These were primarily the unwanted Australian-pines, which are clearly not hurricane adapted. The park staff took this opportunity to initiate major habitat restoration. They cleared all the downed nonnative trees, removed the surviving invasive species, and replanted native species (such as sea-grape, Geiger-tree, and cabbage palm). The result is a spectacular improvement of this park as a natural area.

The waters around Biscayne Bay have attracted a rather unusual group of squatters. If you go to the seawall at the southwest corner of the park and look out into Biscayne Bay, you'll see the famed neighborhood known as "Stiltsville." Through the years, people have built houses on stilts in the bay, obviously accessible only by boat. The seven buildings that remained after Hurricane Andrew now belong to the National Park Service.

Cape Florida is primarily a recreational area, with Miamians flocking to the beaches in the summer and the picnic areas on holidays. For a few months in the fall, Cape Florida shines as a birding hotspot. Because migrating birds, particularly warblers and raptors, follow the coastline from the north, they often congregate on the south end before venturing across the water. You may see as many as 20 species of warblers in one day when unfavorable winds or weather frontal systems concentrate migrating birds at coastal sites. Shorebirds frequent the long stretches of beaches.

A self-guided nature trail cuts through a hammock for about 0.5 miles one way on the park's western side. Interpretive signs describe the native vegetation and habitat. A bicycle path circumnavigates most of the park, but joins with the road for a short stretch. Look for magnificent frigate-birds and gray kingbirds in spring and summer, and songbirds in the winter. The 1.25-mile-long swimming beach on the Atlantic Ocean side is often ranked as one of the best beaches in the country. The seawall along Biscayne Bay is a popular fishing place. Anglers can catch snappers, groupers, jacks, snooks, and other game fish.

The 95-foot lighthouse is an interesting historic site. Tours inside are given periodically during the day (fee charged). The lighthouse area is a good place to watch for migrating birds in spring and fall.

DIRECTIONS
Park is located at the southern end of Key Biscayne (southeast Miami). From the southern end of I-95, take the Rickenbacker Causeway south to the park entrance.

CONTACT
Bill Baggs Cape Florida
State Park
1200 S. Crandon Boulevard
Key Biscayne 33149
305-361-5811
www.floridastateparks.org/capeflorida

Aerial view of Cape Florida, showing the lighthouse (center) and the sandy beach

Biscayne National Park

Facilities: Visitor center, canoe launch and rentals, hiking trails, glassbottom boat tours, interpretive programs

Activities: Snorkeling, scuba diving (including lessons), swimming, picnicking, paddling, hiking, camping

Admission: No entrance fee; fees for concession tours and rentals

Hours: Convoy Point open 7 am to 5:30 pm; visitor center open 9 am to 5 pm; Adams Key is day-use; the water portion of the Park is always open

Pets: Allowed at Convoy Point and the developed areas of Elliott Key on a leash; prohibited in other areas of the park except for service animals

South Florida Birding Trail: 103

Best Time of Year: January to April has the fewest insects and the driest weather. Ocean water temperature and clarity are best from April to October (for swimming, snorkeling, and diving) but they are generally good year-round. Glassbottom boat trips are worthwhile any month, since the reef is more protected from heavy seas here than off Key Largo. Nevertheless, high winds and winter cold fronts may cause boat tours to be canceled.

Other: No lodging and limited food (snacks) in park (see nearby Homestead for lodging and meals)

This is truly one of the underappreciated gems of the national park system. In 1968, President Lyndon Johnson turned the barrier islands into a national monument to protect them from inevitable development. After an enlargement in 1974 and another in 1980, it became a national park. Ironically, the coral reef, the northernmost in North America, was not the original concern. Now it is the main attraction. Farther down the Keys, the barrier islands (such as Key Largo, Plantation Key, and Upper Matecumbe) are developed and cause pollution problems for the adjacent reefs. At Biscayne, since the barrier islands are relatively pristine, the coral is healthier and the water crystal clear.

Besides the 44 barrier islands and the reef, the park protects 14 continuous miles of mangrove shoreline, the longest uninterrupted stretch of mangroves along the eastern coast. But of the 173,000 acres the park encompasses, 95 percent is water. Newcomers to the park arrive at Convoy Point, the mainland "jumping off" point, take one look at the parking lot, the visitor center, the boat dock, and the gift shop, and say "Is this it?" The answer is most emphatically "No!" But you have to find your way onto or into the water to see the best part. Fortunately, the National Park Service and the concession company make that easy. See this gorgeous reef by snorkeling or by taking a glassbottom boat trip, and try a paddling trip along the mangrove shoreline. You may see manatees or dolphins or the colorful reef fish. Biscayne Bay is a sanctuary for spiny lobsters where they are thoroughly protected.

The park hosts 10 species of federally threatened and endangered animals: American crocodile, hawksbill sea turtle, green sea turtle, leatherback sea turtle, loggerhead sea turtle, eastern indigo snake, piping plover, wood stork, West Indian manatee, and Schaus' swallowtail butterfly

(*Papilio aristodemus ponceanus*). Biscayne National Park is one of the few remaining places left to see the Schaus' swallowtail butterfly, listed as endangered in 1984. The chief contributor to the species' demise is the long-term destruction of native hardwoods, like torchwood and wild-lime, on which it feeds. Since 1972, aerial spraying outside of the park with pesticides targeted at mosquitoes has been contributing to the mortality. This beautiful butterfly, about 3.5 inches across, is black with yellow diagonal bands and black tails edged with yellow. The adults normally live only three or four days but may survive several weeks. Look for them from late April through mid-July. The islands in Biscayne National Park are one of the few places left to see this rare butterfly.

During the autumn and spring migrations of raptors, passerines, and shorebirds, Elliott and Adams Keys are resting and foraging places, thus also great for birding. Birding is good all winter. LaSagra's flycatchers have been seen on Elliott during several winters.

Mexican red-bellied squirrels (introduced) were occasionally seen foraging in the treetops of Elliott Key by hikers before Hurricane Andrew. These nonnative squirrels are black with a rusty-colored belly. They somehow survived Hurricane Andrew.

Hurricane Andrew made landfall at Convoy Point in 1992. The entire park was directly in the path of the worst winds and storm surges. Damage to this park was extensive. All buildings (except the old stone ones on the islands) were damaged or destroyed. Most of the park's mangroves were damaged. There was damage on all reefs, but most was minor.

CONVOY POINT

Dante Fascell Visitor Center

The large visitor center at Convoy Point has innovative techniques for bringing the reef and the hammocks close up and inside for easier visitor viewing. Natural history books, including marine and seashore field guides, are for sale. Videos and slide programs on the area's cultural and natural history are available on request.

Jetty

A boardwalk leading to the breakwater jetty goes from Convoy Point into Biscayne Bay. Winter shore-birding can be great. White mangrove, sea-grape, sea purslane, and sea ox-eye daisy grab a tenuous roothold along the rocky jetty.

Paddling

You can bring your own watercraft (free launch at Convoy Point) or rent a canoe or sit-on-top kayak from the concession. You can paddle along the shore, around the mangroves and lagoons, and to nearby islands. You may see small sharks, spiny lobsters, and crabs. Canoeists should not go far from shore. However, experienced sea kayakers can tackle the 7 miles to Elliott Key and camp overnight. If you plan to park a vehicle overnight at the visitor center, let the rangers know. Be careful of the tides, since the currents can be very strong. Check with a ranger for the tide schedule and plan your trip so you paddle with the current. Also watch for strong winds and choppy waters that are frequent in the winter. Park rangers periodically provide guided paddling trips, so call the visitor center or check the park's website for the schedule.

Boating

Visitors with their own motor boats will find much to see and do. Hiking and picnicking on the islands are popular, and it's easy to find snorkeling hot spots on your own. Mooring buoys are provided at several places around the reef to protect the coral, since it is illegal to anchor on coral. If no mooring buoys are available, you must anchor on sand. Because of the shallowness of Biscayne Bay and the reef, you should carry a NOAA nautical chart (#11451, "Miami to Marathon and Florida Bay," available at Convoy Point) with you. The adjacent Homestead Bayfront Park (a county park) has a boat launch and gas dock. Biscayne National Park has no such facilities. The national park concession also provides shuttle boat service to take you to one of the islands for the day by prior arrangement.

The harbor by the Ranger Station on Elliott Key has slips for the public, as does Boca Chita Key. They are free and available on a first-come basis for day use; fee for overnight. No-fee docks are available at Adams Key for day-use.

Swimming and Snorkeling

There are many places to swim, although the area you can access without a boat (only at Convoy Point) is small. The coral reef must be reached by boat. Protected and shallow swimming areas are found at Elliott Key on the bayside. Seagrasses shelter the barracudas, grunts, and snappers that are commonly seen.

ELLIOTT KEY

Elliott Key (7 miles long, accessible only by boat) has a boat dock, a campground (first-come basis), drinking water, restrooms, showers, and picnic tables with grills. The Ranger Station has restrooms, picnic areas, and a few wall displays. In the winter (usually Christmas to Easter), it is staffed by an interpretive volunteer intermittently on weekends.

Hiking Trails

A loop trail, about 1.5 miles round-trip, with a section of boardwalk on the ocean side, begins on the bayside near the Ranger Station. Interpretive signs tell the natural and human history of Elliott Key. The trail meanders through a West Indian hardwood hammock and mangroves. The mangrove land crabs (*Ucides cordatus*) scurry around by the dozens under the mangroves, above the tide line. The vivid purple and orange shells of these land crabs are a spectacular sight.

A much longer straight trail (an old road) runs almost the entire length of the island. From the Ranger Station, the trail goes 2.5 miles north and 4.5 miles south. The habitat is tropical hammock, and many native hardwoods can be found.

ADAMS KEY

This small island has a boat dock, picnic area, and restrooms. The 0.5-mile-loop hiking trail penetrates a hardwood hammock with seven-year apple, white stopper, pigeon-plum, and poisonwood; in the openings are buttonwood, bay-cedar, and sea ox-eye daisy. Adams Key is partially composed of fill pumped up from the ocean floor. That's why you'll see piles of clamshells on the island, re-

Walking trail on Elliott Key in Biscayne National Park

sembling Indian middens. Camping on Adams is reserved for school groups.

BOCA CHITA KEY

This small Key has a 0.5-mile loop hiking trail, as well as a lighthouse, picnic area with grills, and campground. There are saltwater toilets but no fresh water. The 65-foot-tall, nonfunctioning lighthouse is open whenever staff or volunteers are available, and the view of the bay from the observation deck is stunning.

Camping

Tent camping is allowed on Elliott and Boca Chita Keys; both have cooking grills and bathrooms. They are accessible only by boat. There is a fee for camping. The concession will bring groups by boat to the camping areas on Elliott or Boca Chita Keys for overnight camping from autumn through spring. The fee for the boat depends upon the group size. Make arrangements at least a few weeks in advance. You may also paddle to the islands on your own.

Concession Tours and Rentals

The concession offers ways for almost everyone to enjoy the coral reef. At the store at Convoy Point, you can reserve space on the glassbottom boat or the snorkel and dive trips. While tours are regularly scheduled, you can also arrange special group tours in advance. Make reservations and check schedules in advance for all trips, either in person or by phone: 305-230-1100. All trips leave from Convoy Point and may be cancelled due to weather.

The concession maintains scuba certification facilities. Divers will see some of the thousands of patch reefs that have formed on the ocean side near Elliott Key. A patch reef is a small, circular coral reef (usually only a few hundred yards in diameter) surrounded by a ring of sand. When snorkeling or diving, do not touch the corals, because simply touching can kill them. Enjoy watching the colorful angelfish, parrotfish, blue tangs, and butterflyfish. You may even see a complacent nurse shark.

The concession has a glassbottom boat that was custom-built for the reef, with recessed propellers to prevent turbulence to and siltation of the reef. The 28-inch draft is small for a boat that size allowing it to venture into shallow water without scraping the coral. An interpretive ranger will be on board each trip to narrate about the reef. The 3-hour trip leaves twice daily and is wheelchair-accessible.

DIRECTIONS

From US 1 in Homestead, go east on SW 328th St. (N. Canal Drive) 8 miles to end (Convoy Point).

CONTACT

Biscayne National Park
9700 SW 328th Street
Homestead 33033-5634
305-230-PARK (230-7275)
www.nps.gov/bisc

CONCESSION:

Biscayne National Underwater Park, Inc.
305-230-1100
www.biscayneunderwater.com

Broward County Parks

For more information on the 24 Broward County regional parks contact Parks and Recreation Division, 950 NW 38th Street, Oakland Park 33309-5982; 954-357-8100; www.broward.org/parks. Fifteen parks are described below; the remainder are community parks and other nonnatural areas.

5   **Broward County Parks**

Deerfield Island Park

Facilities: Nature trails, guided walks, marina with 6 boat slips, picnic tables and grills, primitive camping for youth groups by reservation (954-360-1315)

Activities: Hiking, boating, picnicking

Admission: Free entrance and boat shuttle

Hours: Boat shuttle on weekends only, from 10 am–3 pm on the hour

Pets: Not allowed

Best Time of Year: No preference

This 53-acre island was created by dredging the Intracoastal Waterway. It is maintained as habitat for gopher tortoises. Native trees include red mangrove, sea-grape, and cabbage palm, while the introduced Australian-pine dominates. The park is accessible only by boat (private boats are permitted). No vehicles are permitted, so it is a great urban escape. The county provides free weekend boat transportation.

Trails

The Coquina Trail (0.5 miles) goes through a coastal hardwood hammock to an observation platform on the Intracoastal Waterway. The Mangrove Trail is 0.75 miles and includes a boardwalk through mangroves. Obtain the free trail guide at the park office.

DIRECTIONS

Park is located on an island in the Intracoastal Waterway. To get to the park's boat ramp for free boat shuttle, take I-95 to Exit 42A and go east on Hillsboro Boulevard 2 miles to Riverview Road. Follow signs to dock at Sullivan Park.

CONTACT

Deerfield Island Park
1720 Deerfield Island Park
Deerfield Beach 33441
954-357-5100

Broward County Parks

Fern Forest Nature Center

Facilities: Nature center, nature trails, interpretive programs, picnic tables

Activities: Hiking, picnicking

Admission: Free

Hours: 8 am–5 pm; closed Tuesday and Wednesday, some holidays and some Fridays

Pets: Not allowed

South Florida Birding Trail: 88

Best Time of Year: Fall and spring for migrating passerines; winter and spring for walking on trails (wet in summer)

Fern Forest is part of a cypress slough that once drained the area from Coral Springs to the ocean at Pompano Beach. It was also part of the cypress strand that stretched from Lake Okeechobee to Fort Lauderdale. The cypresses were logged by the Seminoles. The 254-acre park contains 10 habitat types: oak–pine–cabbage palm; mixed temperate–tropical hardwood hammock; maple; ficus–tropical hardwood hammock; cypress–maple; oak–cypress–cabbage palm; prairie; oak–ficus–cabbage palm; tropical hardwood hammock; and invasives (Brazilian pepper–guava). Look for such ferns as resurrection, marsh, leather, swamp, strap, shoestring, golden polypody, and maiden; such trees as gumbo-limbo, cypress (bald and pond), satinleaf, paradise, and wild-lime; such shrubs and other plants as marlberry, wild coffee, firebush, beauty berry, and coontie.

Boardwalk trail at Fern Forest

The modest Nature center contains exhibits and live reptiles; a few field guides and local natural history books are sold.

Trails
Three short trails bring the visitor close to the various habitats of Fern Forest. The Cypress Creek Trail is a 0.5-mile, handicapped-accessible boardwalk through one of the last cypress strands in Broward County. The Maple Walk is a 0.3-mile non-wheelchair-accessible trail through a red maple swamp lush with ferns; it can be wet in summer. The 1-mile Prairie Overlook Trail leads to an observation platform over a former cattle pasture now used by gopher tortoises.

DIRECTIONS
From I-95, take Exit 36 and go west on Atlantic Blvd. 3 miles to Lyons Rd. Go south on Lyons a short distance.

CONTACT
Fern Forest Nature Center
201 Lyons Road South
Coconut Creek 33063
954-970-0150

Broward County Parks

Long Key Natural Area and Nature Center

Facilities: Nature center, hiking and equestrian trails, guided nature walks and programs

Activities: Hiking, horseback riding

Admission: Free entrance to trails (small fee for nature center)

Hours: Open 9 am–5 pm, closed Tuesday and Wednesday

Pets: Not allowed

Best Time of Year: No preference

This 164-acre site opened in March 2008. Before the region was drained for development, Long Key was a hammock, one of several local islands of the Everglades. These islands were the home of Seminoles until the 1800s and the Tequesta before that. The site contains well-preserved archaeological resources that are considered the best preserved archaeological record of Seminole life in Broward County.

Nature Center

This 18,000-square-foot center (Exhibit Hall) has live-animal educational displays, an interactive replica of an archaeological dig, exhibits, and classrooms.

Trails

On the 0.5-mile hiking trail through the oak hammock, you may see such hardwood trees as live oak, red bay, paradise-tree, satinleaf, strangler fig, hackberry, cabbage palm, and gumbo-limbo. A remnant orange grove is evidence of a bygone local livelihood. Constructed wetland marshes attract a variety of wetland birds, including great egrets and little blue herons that nest there. Guided walks are available by reservation (954-357-8797) and last about an hour. The 1.5-mile equestrian trails traverse less sensitive areas and connect to the Davie Multipurpose Trail.

DIRECTIONS

From I-595: Exit 1B (Flamingo Road) and go south to SW 36th Court. Turn west across from Flamingo Gardens and follow 36th Court until it curves to the right (north) to become SW 130th Avenue. Entrance to natural area on left (west).

From I-95: Exit 23 (Griffin Road) and go west to Flamingo Road. Turn right (north) on Flamingo and go to SW 36th Court. Turn left and follow directions above.

CONTACT

Long Key Natural Area
and Nature Center
3501 SW 130th Avenue
Davie 33330
954-357-8797

Broward County Parks

Secret Woods Nature Center

Facilities: Nature center, nature trails, butterfly garden, interpretive programs

Activities: Hiking, nature viewing

Admission: Free

Hours: 9 am–5 pm, closed Tuesday and Wednesday and some holidays

Pets: Not allowed

Best Time of Year: Spring and fall for migrating warblers; year-round for walking on trails

Nestled between superhighways and a river thoroughfare is a cool green patch of untamed woodland. Three plant communities are found within this 57-acre urban wilderness area: cypress–maple wetland, pond-apple–mangrove wetland, and laurel oak upland. The New River runs along the edge of the woods. The 2,000 square-foot Nature Center houses an aquarium; live reptiles; quality exhibits of the local plant communities, wildlife, and Native American culture; and offers free interpretive programs. The Butterfly Island is a 3,800-square-foot butterfly garden. You might see giant swallowtails and atala hairstreaks.

Trails

The New River Trail is a 0.6-mile wheelchair-accessible boardwalk that passes through oak uplands to the river. Near the river are cypress and maples in the freshwater swamp and salt-tolerant mangroves along the river. Due to the diversion of fresh water upstream, saltwater is creeping farther inland. Look for the resulting dying cypress trees. Watch for wading birds year-round in the wetlands. Yellow-crowned night-herons are commonly seen. Some native plants to look for: firebush, beauty berry, rouge plant, dahoon holly, red and white mangroves, royal palm, and pond-apple. Pick up a trail guide at the office.The 0.2-mile mulched Laurel Oak Trail visits the oak hammock (laurel oak, live oak, sabal palm, coco-plum, white stopper, and white mangrove). Look for the inch-long fiddler crabs that scurry into the small holes in the ground around the boardwalk sections. The larger holes are from land crabs, which are a type of hermit crab.

DIRECTIONS

From I-95, take Exit 25 onto SR 84. Go west on 84 for 0.5 miles to nature center.

CONTACT

Secret Woods Nature Center
2701 W. State Rd. 84
Dania Beach 33312
954-791-1030
www.broward.org/Parks/Secret
WoodsNatureCenter/Pages/Default.aspx

Broward County Parks

Tree Tops Park

Facilities: Nature trails, observation tower, butterfly garden, equestrian trails and guided horse rides, primitive campsites for nonprofit groups, canoe and boat rentals, picnic tables and grills

Activities: Hiking, fishing, horseback riding, camping, canoeing, picnicking

Admission: Entrance fee on weekends, holidays

Hours: 8 am–6 pm in Standard Time, 8 am–7:30 pm in Daylight Savings Time, closed Tuesday and Wednesday

Pets: Allowed on a leash in designated areas

South Florida Birding Trail: 93

Best Time of Year: No preference

The live oak hammock, marsh, and pine ridge are the main natural features of this 243-acre park. The oaks are carpeted with bromeliads and epiphytic ferns. The 23-acre marsh has been restored and is edged by a 1,000-foot-long boardwalk. The Pine Island Ridge rises 29 feet above the surrounding land—not much to brag about, but still the highest natural elevation in Broward County (the landfills are higher). A pond provides boating and fishing recreation.

Some of the native plants you can find in the park are beauty berry, rouge plant, coontie, bromeliads, and swamp fern. Several of the trails, such as the Live Oak Trail near the boardwalk, are particularly infested with nonnative plants, such as oyster-plant, Brazilian pepper, and (perhaps the worst of all) air potato. The air potato is a vine with large heart-shaped leaves that will climb the trunk of a tree and shade the tree to death. Eerie ghostly images rise from the floor of the woods where the air potato reigns. Park staff, assisted by volunteers, constantly battle the invasive plants.

Trails

There are about two miles of nature trails, some paved and some wood-chipped, and more than 3.5 miles of trails for horseback-riding. A self-guiding trail booklet is available from the office and marina for the 1,000-foot-long Sensory Awareness Trail. One trail goes to the slash pine ridge (the Pine Island Ridge Natural Area). The trail to the marsh boardwalk is wheelchair-accessible. Look for mottled ducks, least bitterns, and purple gallinules. The 28-foot-high observation tower brings you to "tree-tops" level.

DIRECTIONS

From Florida's Turnpike, take Exit 53, go west on Griffin Rd. for 1.7 miles past University Drive. Then right onto SW 100th Ave. for 0.5 miles to entrance.

CONTACT

Tree Tops Park
3900 SW 100th Avenue
Davie 33328
954-370-5130

West Lake Park and Ann Kolb Nature Center

Facilities: Nature center, nature trails, environmental education programs, boat tours (school and summer camp groups only); canoe, kayak and bicycle rentals; observation tower, gift shop, summer camp

Activities: Hiking, paddling, bicycling, picnicking

Admission: Entrance fee for nature center, rentals, boat tours; no fee for nature trails, personal boat use, observation tower; entrance fee for West Lake Park (recreation section, south side of Sheridan Street) on weekends and holidays

Hours: Park gates open at 8 am and close at 6 pm Standard Time (Daylight Savings Time to 7:30 pm); closed Tuesday and Wednesday; nature center open 9 am–5 pm, closed Tuesday and Wednesday

Pets: Allowed on leash in designated areas in south section

South Florida Birding Trail: 92

Best Time of Year: No preference

One of the largest urban parks in Florida, West Lake Park is a relative youngster. The recreational section (south side of Sheridan St.) opened in 1978, but the outstanding nature center complex opened in 1996. Located by the 1,500+-acre West Lake, this 88-acre complex offers a variety of nature-oriented activities. West Lake was created by dredging in the 1920s and is connected to the Intracoastal Waterway; thus it is salt water. Miles of undeveloped mangrove shores beckon paddlers. Ecological restoration activities are ongoing. West Lake is home to many types of fish, crabs, shrimp, and wading birds. If you live in or visit Broward County, this is the place to come to learn and to appreciate it.

Ann Kolb Nature Center

The theme of the exhibits is the mangrove ecosystem. The 3,500-gallon saltwater aquarium features mangrove plants and animals. The introductory video explains the interactions of the mangrove creatures. The gift shop offers limited nature-related articles and packaged snacks. The 68-foot-high Observation Tower was built with the acrophobic person in mind—it is solidly built and has an elevator. A wide variety of educational programs are scheduled. Ask for their species inventory, which includes plants, vertebrates, and invertebrates.

Nature Trails and Boardwalks

Obtain a trail guide first. Two walking trails are on the north side: Lake Observation (1,374-foot boardwalk) and Mud Flat (1,552-foot boardwalk). On the south side is South Trail (2.3 miles). All boardwalks through the mangroves are constructed of recycled plastic. Among the red and black mangrove roots, you may see crabs and white ibises feeding.

Canoe Trail

Obtain the canoe trail guide first; it will serve as your map and interpretive guide. The trail goes through West Lake's mangrove perimeter where you may see roseate spoonbills, least terns, black-necked stilts, and yellow-crowned night-herons. Rentals are available at the marina.

DIRECTIONS

From north or south, take I-95 to Exit 21,
go 2.7 miles east to nature center.

CONTACT

Ann Kolb Nature Center
751 Sheridan Street
Hollywood 33019
954-926-2480

Yellow-crowned night-herons are common around water. This one perches on a red mangrove root.

Broward County Natural Areas

The following are unstaffed natural areas that are suitable for a short visit, especially if you are in the vicinity; open to the public during normal seasonal park hours.

Name, Size, Habitat Type	Location, Phone Number
Crystal Lake Sand Pine Scrub 24.3 acres; sand pine scrub	3299 NE Third Ave., Pompano Beach; 954-357-8700
Helene Klein Pineland Preserve 13 acres; mesic flatwood	4701 West Hillsboro Blvd., Coconut Creek; 954-357-8700
Highlands Scrub 34.3 acres; sand pine scrub	4050 N Dixie Hwy., Pompano Beach; 954-357-8700
Hillsboro Pineland 44 acres; pine flatwoods, cypress, open prairie	5591 NW 74th Pl., Coconut Creek; 954-357-8700
Pine Island Ridge 101 acres; live oak ridge, slash pine; SFBT #93	3900 SW 100 Ave., Davie; 954-357-8727
Snake Warrior's Island 53.3 acres; upland hammocks, created wetlands; SFBT #95	3600 SW 62nd Ave., Miramar; 954-926-2480
Tall Cypress Natural Area 66.4 acres; pine flatlands, cypress swamp	3700 Turtle Run Blvd., Coral Springs; 954-357-8700
Woodmont Natural Area 21.6 acres; mixed slash pine and cypress	7250 NW 80th Ave., Tamarac; 954-357-8700

6 Dupuis Reserve State Forest (Dupuis Management Area)

Facilities: Visitor center; hiking, bicycling, and equestrian trails

Activities: Hiking, wildlife viewing, mountain bicycling, primitive backpack camping, horseback riding

Admission: Small entrance fee; fee for camping

Hours: Gate open dawn to dusk; may be closed on weekends during hunting season in the autumn and winter (call FWC for hunt schedule); visitor center open Tuesday–Friday 8 am–4 pm, Saturday 9 am–noon

Pets: Not allowed

South Florida Birding Trail: 54

Best Time of Year: December–April for the driest trail conditions

The 21,875 acres of Dupuis Reserve State Forest contain a variety of habitats: pine flatwoods, wet prairies, cypress domes, and marshes. Bald eagles, wood storks, limpkins, bobcats, deer, armadillos, and many other kinds of wildlife may be seen.

The reserve, located two miles east of the eastern shore of Lake Okeechobee, straddles Martin and Palm Beach counties. It was purchased in 1986 by funds from "Save Our Rivers," a program maintained by South Florida Water Management District to protect water resources. This former ranchland is managed as a limited multi-use area, allowing hiking, hunting, and horseback riding. The Florida Trail Association created and maintains the hiking trails. The DuPuis Horsemen's Association developed and maintains the equestrian trails.

Cattle and sheep ranching operations by former owner John H. DuPuis (pronounced doo-pwee') are evident by the park-like understory and the drainage ditches and

Main gate to auto road and campground at Dupuis Reserve State Forest

fences still crossing the land. The South Florida Water Management District is gradually filling ditches to restore the natural hydrology of the land.

Hiking (Gate 2)

You can easily plan an all-day hike. Four stacked loop trails give hikers a choice of four distances: 4.3, 6.8, 11.5, or 15.5 miles. These trails are for hiking only; the horse trails are separate. The Ocean to Lake Trail, which goes from Jonathan Dickinson State Park to Lake Okeechobee and is maintained by the Florida Trail Association, passes through Dupuis. From the last hiking loop, hikers can go another 7 miles to **J.W. Corbett Wildlife Management Area**.

The trails are flat, grassy, occasionally wet (especially in the summer and autumn), and can be bumpy because of feral hog rootings. The canopy is open slash pines and live oaks (little shade) with frequent cabbage palms. The understory is open, grassy parkland and saw palmetto clumps. Some plants you may encounter are round-leaved sundew, bog bachelor-button, gallberry, white sabatia, celestial lily (endangered), glades lobelia, and spider orchid. Wildlife abounds for the observant. Deer, gray foxes, bobcats, bobwhites, wild turkeys, and raptors are common. Bald eagles, sandhill cranes, alligators, and indigo snakes may also be seen. Waterfowl and wading birds feed in the marshes.

Bicycling (Gates 1 and 2)

Bicycling is allowed on the named and numbered roads. From Gate 1, bicyclists can go on Jim Lake and Dupuis Lake roads for 7 miles to the fishing pier and on the Auto Tour road (7.5 miles).

Camping (Gate 5)

The distance from the trailhead to the West Route primitive campsite is 5.7 miles and from the trailhead to the East Route primitive campsite is 9.7 miles. Campers pay a small fee at the gate. There is no potable water. There are also four backpack sites, an equestrian site, and a family campsite.

Equestrian Trails (Gate 3)

At Gate 3 are four loop trails, with the shortest at 7.2 miles long and the longest at 17.5 miles long. Overall, there are 40 miles of trails. These trails are located in the same general area as the hiking trails (which they occasionally cross), so the habitats are similar. However, the horse trails are placed on the higher land within the area. Camping and use of the barn and paddock are allowed at the equestrian center by the parking lot (extra fee).

Auto Tour (Gate 1)

The 7.5-mile graded marl road goes through slash pines that were injured by bark beetles in the late 1990s. An area of pines is being restored for the endangered red-cockaded woodpecker. Areas are being cleared of invasive plants, such as Brazilian pepper and Old World climbing fern. Other habitats include a marsh and oak–cabbage palm hammock. Return the same way (15 miles roundtrip). Bicycles allowed.

DIRECTIONS

The State Forest is on SR 76 (Kanner Hwy.), about 6 miles west of the Beeline Highway (SR 710) on left or 3 miles east of SR 441 on right. The gates are spaced along SR 76. Gate 1 is the Auto Tour and main entrance; Gate 2 is the hikers' trailhead parking lot; Gate 3 is the equestrian trailhead; Gate 5 is the visitor center, campground, and other end of auto tour.

CONTACT

Dupuis Reserve State Forest
23500 SW Kanner Highway
Canal Point 33438
www.sfwmd.gov/recreation

Hiking information, camping and horseback riding permits:
South Florida Water Management District
561-924-5310

Hunting dates:
Florida Fish and Wildlife Conservation Commission (FWC)
561-924-5310
www.myfwc.com/media/185604/
10-11_Dupuis.pdf

Everglades National Park

Facilities: Nature, hiking, and paddling trails; boat and tram tours; boat, houseboat, and canoe rentals; bicycle rentals, interpretive activities, wildlife observation areas, visitor centers (main park entrance, Royal Palm, Flamingo, Shark Valley, and Everglades City), marina, gift shops

Activities: Camping, hiking, wildlife observation, paddling, bicycling, freshwater and saltwater fishing, boating

Admission: U.S. fee area (entrance fee good for all park entrances for 7 days); Everglades City is free

Hours: The park is always open, except during major emergencies, such as fires and hurricane warnings; see park entrances below for their specific hours

Pets: Must be on a six-foot leash, must not be left unattended; not allowed on trails, in buildings, in amphitheaters, or on boat and tram tours

Best Time of Year: Overall, November–April (the dry season). At this time, wildlife is concentrated around remaining fresh water, biting insects are minimal, weather is cooler and drier, and park facilities are fully open. In summer, visitor facilities (campsites, visitor center hours, concession operations, and ranger programs) are reduced, and biting insects, humidity, and daily thunderstorms can be annoying. However, paddling on freshwater may be difficult during the dry season.

Other: No airboat tours or private airboating in the park. Literature is available in many foreign languages at the main and Shark Valley visitor centers. Visitors should stop at the visitor center serving the area they are about to explore to gather tour schedules, trail maps, and other helpful materials. Most of the park's facilities are accessible to the handicapped and assistance is available. Operations (such as tours and naturalist programs) are reduced during the summer, so call ahead to confirm schedules.

The name "Everglades" conjures up images in tourists' minds of vast tangled jungles with vines and snakes dripping from the trees. Park rangers frequently hear visitors comment, "This isn't like I pictured." Indeed, the Everglades does have vine-covered jungles, but they are not vast, and the snakes don't drip from trees. The "jungles" are mostly in the form of isolated tree islands and mangrove stands. The major habitat types are the open freshwater marshes, coastal mangroves, and island-studded bay.

The Everglades is a unique ecosystem—there is no other like it anywhere in the world. That is why so many people (starting with Ernest Coe in 1928) led the fight to protect it, culminating with the dedication of this national park in 1947.

Many other honors have been bestowed upon it: The park was designated an International Biosphere Reserve in 1976; UNESCO, the United Nations Educational, Scientific, and Cultural Organization, named it a World Heritage Site in 1979; and in 1987 it was named a Wilderness of International Importance. Two canoe trails were designated as National Trails in 1981. There is no doubt the Everglades has played and will continue to play a major role in Florida's mental and environmental health.

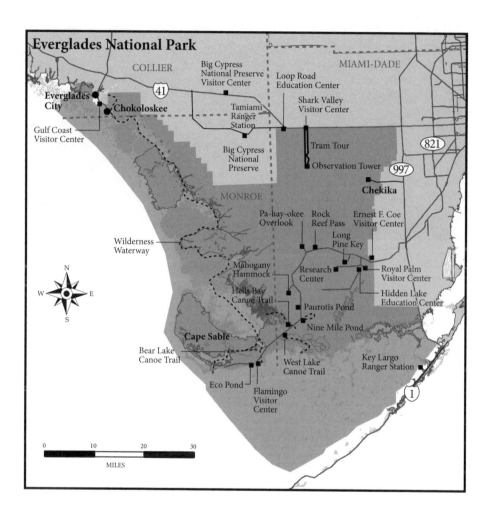

Everglades National Park is the largest subtropical national park in the United States. Visitors can find extensive backcountry paddling, camping, and hiking with some of the best wildlife sights east of the Mississippi River.

Typical marsh habitat in Everglades National Park

Everglades National Park plays another unique role. It was the first national park to be established at the mouth of a waterway, rather than at the source. Most parks are at the headwaters of rivers (such as Glacier, Yellowstone, Grand Teton, and Yosemite), where the water is pure and the main administrative problem is the overabundance of visitors. Everglades National Park is at the end of a water system that has environmental insults thrown at it every step of the way, causing major ecological problems.

Less than 20 percent of the original Everglades region is contained within the park boundaries. The boundary encompasses 1,509,000 acres. About a third of that is Florida Bay and the Gulf of Mexico.

Sixteen species of animals found in the park are federally endangered or threatened. They are the American alligator; American crocodile; eastern indigo snake; loggerhead, green, Atlantic Ridley, Atlantic hawksbill, and leatherback sea turtles; piping plover, roseate tern, Cape Sable seaside sparrow, Everglade snail kite, wood stork, Florida panther, West Indian manatee, and Schaus' swallowtail butterfly. Red-cockaded woodpeckers are no longer found in the park. However, there is still a rich variety of native plants and animals that includes approximately 370 native species of birds, 40 mammals, 17 amphibians, 50 reptiles, 300 fish, 120 trees, and 1,000 flowering plants. More than 25 types of orchids grow in the park.

The 137-mile coastline attracts many people for the saltwater fishing. Others come for the excitement of seeing alligators, flocks of wood storks, and other fascinating wildlife. Still others come to camp in the solitude of the Ten

Thousand Islands. Park visitation has steadily increased from 7,482 people in 1948 to around a million each year.

The duration of your stay depends on how much time you have, since you can easily fill a two-week stay. If you have only a day in the winter, you should at least see the Anhinga and Gumbo Limbo Trails at Royal Palm. If you have only a day in the summer, you may be better off paddling away from land and the mosquitoes at Flamingo or taking a boat tour of the Ten Thousand Islands at Everglades City. A two-day trip could include a camping stay at the quiet outpost of Flamingo, with a canoe trip or boat tour. Hopefully, you will have at least a week, with time to see Royal Palm, Flamingo, Shark Valley, and Everglades City. Take advantage of the ranger-led trips and programs to learn about the Everglades. Wildlife observing, canoeing, hiking, and photographing opportunities are excellent.

Camping

Two campgrounds (Long Pine Key and Flamingo) provide basic camping facilities for tents and can accommodate RVs. Stays are limited to 14 days. Golden Age and Golden Access cardholders pay half price for sites. Although the campgrounds are open year-round, the summer heat, insects, and thunderstorms can be intense. Summer camping (approximately June to August) is free, but sites are reduced in number (never a problem) and ranger assistance is reduced. December through April are the best camping months.

Long Pine Key
The Long Pine Key campground turnoff is about 7 miles from the main park en-

trance. The 108 sites have minimal facilities (no showers). Camping is pleasant under the shady slash pine trees. You're more likely to be kept awake by a barred owl than by your neighboring campers. The lake next to the loop road usually has alligators. Miles of hiking trails through the pinelands originate from the campground. Campground information: 305-242-7873.

Flamingo
The other campground is at the far end of the Main Park Road (38 miles). The 234 drive-in sites are more open and sunny than Long Pine Key. It has water and bathrooms plus a sewage dumping station, but no hook-ups. This is the only camping area with showers. But be prepared—they are cold water only and they are open topped, so take your shower before a cold front hits.

The 40 walk-in sites are great for tent camping. Picture a large grassy field sprinkled with palm trees perched next to Florida Bay. The parking lot where you leave your car is at most a few hundred yards away. You can pick a spot near your car or near the bay. From your tentsite, you can see reddish egrets lurching drunkenly for prey in the shallow water, a bald eagle stealing food from an osprey overhead, a corn snake sliding down from an arboreal hiding place, and dolphins spouting plumes of vapor as they surface. Red-bellied woodpeckers love the coconut palms and can easily be identified by their trilling calls. Each site has a grill and table, and bathrooms are nearby; showers at the drive-in sites are walking distance away. The walk-in sites are closed in summer. For reservations, call 877-444-6777.

Backcountry Sites

There are 47 designated primitive back-country sites from Everglades City to Flamingo and in Florida Bay that are accessible only by canoe or motor boat. These are chickees, ground sites, and beach sites. Two more sites along the Old Ingraham Highway (trail) can be reached on foot. All sites require backcountry permits.

The chickees (named after the Miccosukee word for house) are 10-foot by 12-foot wooden platforms on stilts over water in areas where no high ground is available. They are suitable for self-supporting tents or open-air sleeping. The chickees have roofs and chemical toilets. The maximum group size is six people. Some are double chickees, with enough room for two groups. One chickee at Pearl Bay (a four-mile canoe trip from the Main Park Road) is adapted for wheelchairs: it has an accessible toilet, railings, ramp, and a boat slip for canoe stability.

The ground sites are on relatively high ground away from the water. Some (like Willy Willy) are located on old Indian middens, which explains the higher ground. They have docks, chemical toilets, and picnic tables. Beach sites are on beautiful shell beaches, with open views and cooling breezes, but none has tables and most have no toilets. Remember to pitch your tent well above the high tide line.

The backcountry sites are within easy canoeing distance from each other (some are as little as a mile apart). However, conditions can be difficult (high winds, strong currents, heavy rains, getting lost), so you must get a backcountry permit from a ranger at the Flamingo or Everglades City Ranger Stations.

Camping is permitted in Florida Bay on North Nest, Johnson, and Little Rabbit Keys. These are beach sites and the permits may be obtained from Flamingo or Key Largo Ranger Stations. Length-of-stay limits vary for each site from one to seven nights during the peak visitor season (December 1 to April 30). During the summer, mosquitoes and no-see-ums can make camping unbearable, so visitation drops off; however, you still need a permit. Call the Key Largo Ranger Station (305-852-0304) to ask about permits.

Campfires are permitted only at some beach sites below the storm surge line. Driftwood on the ground may be used for fires. At all other sites, fires are permitted only in camping stoves; no grills are provided at the sites. Particularly at the ground and beach sites, raccoons spell trouble for your food—they are relentless in their pursuit of it. You should have a hard-sided cooler (raccoons can break styrofoam) or a way to keep food out of reach of the raccoons. Raccoons will also chew through soft-sided water containers, particularly in the dry season.

Lodging

As of this printing, no lodging facilities exist within the park. In 2005, Hurricanes Katrina and Wilma destroyed the Flamingo Lodge and cabins beyond repair. Plans are underway to build a more environmentally friendly and hurricane-proof lodge. Except for Flamingo, the other main visitor areas are near enough to towns to be easily accessible to commercial lodging.

Fishing

About one third of Everglades National Park is water, and fishing has always been popular. Noncommercial fishing is permitted and regulated in the park. A freshwater license is needed to fish in Nine-Mile Pond and all waters north of the Main Park Road or to possess freshwater fish caught in brackish waters. You will need a saltwater license for Florida Bay, the Gulf of Mexico, Long Sound, Little Blackwater Sound, and Blackwater Sound. These licenses are not sold at Flamingo (purchase before entering the park). Live or dead fish, amphibians, and nonpreserved fish eggs or roe are prohibited as bait.

Because of mercury found in largemouth bass, the park has issued the following warning: "Do not eat bass caught north of the Main Park Road. Do not eat bass caught south of the Main Park Road more than once a week. Children and pregnant women should not eat any bass." Less restrictive warnings apply to some saltwater fish. Some of the main freshwater ponds are posted with warning signs. Too bad the otters and alligators can't read.

Areas closed to fishing for wildlife protection include the ponds by the main visitor center and Royal Palm Visitor Center area and trails, the first three miles of the Main Park Road, Taylor Slough, Mrazek Pond, Eco Pond, Coot Bay Pond, along the Shark Valley tram road, and Chekika Lake.

Saltwater anglers may encounter any of the following fish: snook, spotted seatrout, redfish, mangrove snapper, sheepshead, and black drum. Tarpon, ladyfish, and shark are also good possibilities, as well as dozens of other species. Guides are available for hire by calling the Flamingo Marina.

Boating

The boat ramps are located at Flamingo (Florida Bay side and Buttonwood Ca-nal side), West Lake, Little Blackwater Sound, and Everglades City. Southern Florida Bay is accessible from the Keys via boat ramps at marinas or at public ramps and may have a fee. A fee is charged for all vehicles entering the park with boats (minimal for nonmotorized boats); this covers launching for a week.

Some areas are off-limits to boats (including kayaks and canoes). Boats are prohibited from landing on all the mangrove islands in Florida Bay, with the exceptions of Little Rabbit, North Nest, Johnson, and Bradley Keys (Bradley Key during daylight hours). This is to protect the nesting birds and other wildlife. A crocodile refuge exists in northeast Florida Bay; therefore, seasonal restrictions exist for when boats are allowed in the waters of Little Madeira and Joe bays or in the waters of the back bays from Little Madeira Bay east to US 1. Boats are allowed to land on any of the keys in the Ten Thousand Islands, except the southern part of Pavilion Key.

Motors are prohibited from some parts of the park, including all freshwater lakes. Prohibited brackish areas include (but not limited to) the canoe trails of Bear Lake, Noble Hammock, Coot Bay Pond, and Mud Lake, Raulerson's Marsh, the southern part of Hell's Bay canoe trail, and the creek at the southeastern end of West Lake through to Garfield Bight. On West Lake, only motors of less than 6 horsepower are permitted. "No Wake" zones exist around Everglades City, Flamingo, and Key Largo. Waterskiing and jet-skiing are prohibited throughout the park. Coast Guard regulations require that all watercraft carry a personal flotation device, quickly accessible, for each person on board.

The Marina at Flamingo (239-695-3101), operated by a concession, has gas pumps and slips with water and electric hookups for at least 50 boats. Skiffs, kayaks, canoes, and bicycles may be rented at the marina.

Birding

The vastness of the park, the warm climate, and the rich variety of habitats and plants contribute to the exceptional birding enjoyed by visitors to Everglades National Park. As of 2009, the park's bird list included 368 species. Birds from temperate North America and the tropical Caribbean thrive in South Florida. Tropical storms blow accidentals from far out at sea.

An interesting bird may show up at any time. The following are the most reliable, easily accessible places to start: Anhinga Trail, Mahogany Hammock, West Lake, Snake Bight Trail, the mud flats in front of the Flamingo Visitor Center, and the Shark Valley Tram Road.

The use of audiotape recordings to attract birds is prohibited within the park. Such tapes interfere with the birds'

natural activities. Binoculars may be rented at the Flamingo Marina and the Shark Valley tram office.

DIRECTIONS

There are four land entrances: Main (in Florida City), Shark Valley, Everglades City, and Chekika. Key Largo has a ranger station and science center (MM 98.6 Overseas Highway Bayside; 305-852-0304). The main park entrance is west of Florida City on SR 9336 about 10 miles southwest of the intersection of SW 344th St. (Palm Drive) and US 1. Chekika, Everglades City, Flamingo, Royal Palm, and Shark Valley are regions of the park that are covered separately below.

CONTACT

Everglades National Park
40001 SR 9336
Homestead 33034-6733
305-242-7700
www.nps.gov/ever

| 7 | **MAIN PARK ENTRANCE** |

The main park entrance station is open 24 hours. Ernest Coe Visitor Center (the main park visitor center) is located before the fee station and is open 9 am to 5 pm daily. Information for any part of the park can be obtained here. A large selection of books about the Everglades (natural and human history) is for sale.

ROYAL PALM

Royal Palm has a visitor center, birding and other wildlife viewing, nature trails, photographic opportunities, and ranger programs. Turn left off the Main Park Road about 2 miles past the fee station.

Royal Palm was the nucleus of the new national park in 1947. It was the site

of the first state park in Florida, formed in 1916 by the Florida Federation of Women's Clubs to preserve the fabulous hammock at Paradise Key with its stately native royal palms. The state gave it to the National Park Service in 1947.

Visitor Center

Displays illustrate the intricate web of life in Taylor Slough. The small gift shop sells Everglades books, field guides, and insect repellent. Restrooms are available. Vending machines dispense snacks and drinks. Open 8 am–4:15 pm. The best time of year is December to April; anhingas nest from late January to April.

Anhinga Trail

The most famous trail in the park, the Anhinga Trail, is also one of the most famous trails in the National Park system. One of the reasons is how accessible it is from a major metropolitan area. Another is the ease of walking it. Most thrilling of all is the reward of fantastic views of wildlife found few other places in the country.

What makes this trail so attractive to wildlife? If you look on the official Everglades National Park map, you'll see that Taylor Slough flows through the Royal Palm area. The slough is a region of slightly deeper water than the surrounding area. During the dry season, much of the water in the Everglades disappears through evaporation, transpiration through plants, and run-off to the coasts, but water always remains in the Taylor and Shark River sloughs. Wildlife is forced to concentrate around these watering holes. The Anhinga Trail boardwalk passes right over Taylor Slough. Over the years the animals have become habituated to the presence of humans on the trail. They seem to know that the wingless, two-legged creatures stay within a certain territory and won't bother them. In fact, the anhinga (the bird the trail was named for) even nests within plain view of the trail. Visitors have observed courtship displays, eggs, fluffy pink chicks, and awkward fledglings,

without disturbing the birds. Caution is advised whenever wild animals dwell so close to visitors. Stay at least 15 feet away from any animal.

The wildlife concentrations begin around November or December, depending on the local water levels. From January to April, visitors may be treated to excellent views of alligators, frogs, snakes, turtles, gar (a fish), ospreys, anhingas, herons, bitterns, raccoons, deer, marsh rabbits, and much more. The anhingas generally nest beginning in January or February. Look for these birds swimming gracefully under water, then watch them climb onto a branch and spread their wings to dry and warm themselves. During the winter, the pond at the start of the trail is a sure place to find alligators.

The trail (mostly boardwalk) is only 0.5 miles long, but you won't want to hurry around it. The only part on dry land is where the Old Ingraham Highway (the original route from Homestead to Flamingo) passed. You can watch anhingas spear bass under water, purple gallinules step lightly on water lily pads and rummage for insects, and soft-shelled turtles glide silently by. Look for black racers, rough green snakes, and water snakes. Short-tailed hawks have been seen soaring overhead from October to March.

Since the trail is mostly open, mosquitoes are less pesky here than on most other trails in the park. The trade-off is that it is often scorching in the sun. So, just as mamma says not to salt your food before you taste it, refrain from applying insect repellent until you get to the trail and are sure you'll need it.

The trail is in the open because it courses through the sawgrass marsh. This is an excellent place to see sawgrass close up and even touch it. Beware of its telltale name—the blade's edge can cut your skin like a knife. Other common plants are willow, coco-plum, and pond-apple.

Photographing opportunities are wonderful, and you don't even need a supertelephoto lens (unless you want a photo of an alligator's eye).

Check the announcement board by the visitor center for the schedule of ranger activities. Rangers give talks in the shade by the visitor center and lead groups around the trail every day. This trail is easily accessible to the handicapped.

Gumbo Limbo Trail

A few yards to the right of the start of the Anhinga Trail is the beginning of the Gumbo Limbo Trail. The opposite of the Anhinga Trail, the Gumbo Limbo is cool, shady, and buggy. This narrow, paved footpath, also 0.5 miles long, wanders through the Paradise Key hammock. The hammock is densely vegetated by West Indian hardwood hammock trees, orchids, bromeliads, ferns, and climbing vines, lending a jungle feel to the trail. Look for tree snails, anole lizards, and golden orb-weaver spiders. Some common plants are strangler fig, lance-wood, poisonwood, wild-tamarind, and pigeon-plum.

The unusual name of this trail comes from the like-named tree. Plenty of gumbo-limbos inhabit the hammock, displaying their satiny bronze bark to the visitors. Although the hammock is lush with epiphytic plants, you won't find them attached to gumbo-limbos. This is because the bark is smooth and flakes off easily, like birch bark, so the plants can't get a good grip. Epiphytes like to grow on fissured and firmly attached bark.

Because the vegetation grows densely, the mosquitoes find a haven from intense sun and debilitating breezes in the summer. Photographers will have a more difficult task in capturing the plants and animals on this trail. Most of the animals are the small types (that is, songbirds and tree snails rather than great blue herons and alligators). The filtered sunlight will make metering tricky, and the closeness of the subjects will make focusing harder. Handicapped-accessible with caution.

LONG PINE KEY

Long Pine Key offers hiking, bicycling, a campground, and a picnic area. Turn left at the sign for Long Pine Key past the fee station on the Main Park Road.

The main draw for people to Long Pine Key is the campground (see "Campgrounds" above). But there are other reasons to go, even if you're not camping. Forty-three miles of trails offer hiking and some allow bicycling. Get the trail map from the main visitor center. Botanizing is exceptional, with about 30 species of plants found here and nowhere else. Located in a large stand of slash pines, the habitat is maintained by periodic burns conducted by the National Park Service.

Long Pine Key Trail

Just before the fee station at the campground entrance is the beginning of this trail (look for Gate 4 on the side of the road). The gate is locked and the only vehicles allowed past it are Park Service; human feet, bicycles, and horses are the permitted alternatives. The trail is an unpaved fire road that the rangers occasionally use, so it is wide, hardpacked, and passable by bicycle. In the summer, large puddles from rain and large clouds from mosquitoes may form. Winter is beautiful hiking weather and the trail will most likely be dry. From Gate 4 to the end of the trail at the Main Park Road (Gate 8), the trail is 7 miles long. You can return the same way, walk along the Main Park Road (5 miles to campground turnoff), or find another (but longer) footpath back.

The trail heads west from Gate 4. It passes alternately through tall pine stands and open marshes. Despite a few turns and occasional side trails, the main trail is obvious. Besides the slash pine, you should see the small satinleaf trees, one of the most beautiful tree species in the park. The leaves are dark green above

A solution hole in the limestone at Long Pine Key

and shiny bronze underneath. When the wind blows, the satiny undersides shine in the sun. Other common species are beauty berry, rough velvetseed, tetrazygia, and willow bustic. The trail ends at the small Pine Glades Lake, near Gate 8 on the Main Park Road.

Pinelands Trail

This trail is located 2.1 miles west of the entrance to Long Pine Key Campground on the Main Park Road. Look for the sign "Pine Land" with a parking lot on the right. The trail is a half-mile paved loop through typical slash pine habitat. Although the trail is gentle enough to walk on, the ground beside the trail is treacherous. The soil is shallow, and the limestone substrate rock pokes through numerous places. The limestone is pockmarked from dissolving by rainwater mixed with acidic plant matter. Most solution holes are small and hardly noticeable. Some are a foot or more across and several feet deep. Picture the early explorers trying to hike across this unforgiving land. The larger solution holes serve as refuges during the dry season for small fish and other aquatic organisms. The holes may be the only places left in the dry season with drinking water for deer, panthers, northern bobwhite quail, and other terrestrial creatures.

The predominant shrub-like palm forming the understory is saw palmetto. Look also for tetrazygia, wild-tamarind, satinleaf, Florida trema, and beauty berry. The trail is punctuated with interpretive signs about the plants and animals and the role of fire in the ecosystem.

Unnamed Trails

Several other trails originate at the Long Pine Key Campground. One starts at Gate 3, directly opposite the gate for the Long Pine Key Trail above (Gate 4). This trail runs east, with two right turns along the way. The first right turn takes you on a 3-mile round-trip hike. The second right is a 5-mile round-trip. Both require walking a short distance on a paved road (Research Road).

Research Road

This 4-mile stretch of paved road (accessible from Royal Palm Road) leads to the Research Center for Everglades National Park. The Research Center is the working office for the many biologists and hydrologists who are seeking ways to understand and protect the Everglades.

The road is a popular wildlife crossing. You may see a white-tailed deer, bobwhite, short-tailed hawk, gray fox, pygmy rattlesnake, Everglades racer, barn owl, or glass lizard. Panthers and black bears have been seen on this road.

Hidden Lake

Named for its seclusion, this lake is not on the main tourist list. You can find it by turning off the Main Park Road onto the Royal Palm Road, then turning right toward the Research Road, and going straight past the turnoff for the Research Center (see sign for Hidden Lake). The road becomes unpaved. Look for Gate 13 off the left side of the road 0.3 miles past the turnoff to Research Road. Park your car and walk the short distance in to the pond. The pond is good for quiet wildlife observations. There are no facilities, no interpretive signs, and no provisions for handicapped people. Programs at the nearby interpretive center are for school groups by reservation only.

Old Ingraham Highway

The original highway to Flamingo, built in 1922, was the first land link. Before that, Flamingo residents traveled by boat, usually to Key West, for supplies. When the Park Service rerouted part of the road, they closed this section to vehicular traffic. It is now a good hiking and bicycling road.

To find the start of the road, turn off the Main Park Road at Royal Palm, make the first right (as if you're going to the Research Center), but keep going straight past Research Road. Pass the gate for Hidden Lake on the unpaved road. At 1 mile past the turnoff for Research Road, Gate 15 crosses the road and blocks vehicular traffic. The road continues for 11 miles.

This road through the marsh was built with material that was dredged from what is now the parallel canal. Look through the trees on the north side of the road and you will see the canal. The canal is the reason you may see semi-aquatic animals cross your path, such as otters, alligators, water snakes, anhingas, and turtles. It's a good hike to take in the dry season, when wildlife is concentrated around watering holes. The road may be flooded in the wet season.

Two backcountry campsites are along this road: Ernest Coe (at about 4 miles) and Old Ingraham (at about 10 miles). Neither has any facilities and no ground fires are permitted; backcountry permits are available at the main visitor center.

MAIN PARK ROAD FROM ROCK REEF PASS TO FLAMINGO

Many people see Everglades National Park only from a road, usually this one. Established stops along the road at all the main habitat types provide people with convenient places to view the land. Some of the stops have only overlook platforms with interpretive signs, but some have in-terpretive trails. Allow extra time on your drive to Flamingo (38 miles from park entrance) to stop at these trails.

Rock Reef Pass
(11 miles from park entrance)
This is marked by a sign on the road bragging that the elevation is three feet. Although Coloradans may snicker, this is not an insignificant landmark. In this flat land, just barely above sea level, every inch counts. On both sides of the road, the trees grow on this narrow strip of higher land. From the air, this narrow band of trees resembles an anaconda snaking through the marsh. The slight extra elevation above the adjacent marsh keeps the trees' roots dry enough to grow here and not in the adjacent marsh. Changes in the Everglades are indeed subtle!

Pa-hay-okee Overlook
(13 miles from park entrance)
A short boardwalk (0.25 miles; wheelchair-accessible, no bicycles) leads to a two-level observation platform that overlooks the sawgrass prairie. In fact, the name Pa-hay-okee means "Grassy Waters" in the Seminole language. The panoramic view includes tree islands (hammocks), wading birds, and hawks. It is an excellent spot for using your binoculars, spotting scope, and camera. At certain times of the year, brush fires and thunderstorms can be seen in the distance.

Along the boardwalk leading to the platform, look over the railing into the sawgrass for the shells of the apple snails (*Pomacea paludosa*), about 1.5 inches in diameter. These are the famed snails that the endangered Everglade snail kites feed on almost exclusively. Also look for their pearl-like egg clusters clinging to a

Dwarf cypress tree in winter—cypress trees lose their needles in winter and hence are called "bald."

plant stem near the water's surface.

Along the Main Park Road near Pa-hay-okee Overlook, you will start to see stunted cypress trees. These are dwarf pond-cypress that may be more than 100 years old but only 15 feet tall. Their growth is limited by the depth of water and soil under them; generally, taller cypresses grow in deeper water and soil. Most visitors see these trees in the winter when they lack their foliage. The needles are dropped in the autumn at the start of the dry season, theoretically to conserve moisture.

Mahogany Hammock
(20 miles from park entrance)
To many people, Mahogany Hammock is what the Everglades is supposed to look like—dense and jungly, with vines strangling every tree. This is one of the most interesting places in the park that is easily accessible by wheelchairs (no bicycles). The 0.5-mile boardwalk winds through the interior of one of the largest tropical hardwood hammocks in the park. The hammock's name is derived from the huge West Indian mahogany tree along the boardwalk that is the U.S. champion (that is, the largest mahogany in the United States). Many smaller mahoganies exist in the hammock.

At the "doorway" into the hammock, notice the clump of skinny palms with fan-shaped leaves. These are the state-threatened paurotis palms, native to southern Florida and restricted to the transitional (brackish) marshes between the fresh water and the estuary.

Notice the bromeliads, orchids, and ferns growing in the upper branches of the mahoganies and live oaks. This microhabitat of plants creates places for treefrogs, anoles, insects, and snakes to find food, water, and hiding places without ever descending to the ground. Most of the ferns in the upper branches are resurrection ferns. In the dry season, these ferns dehydrate and wither into brown leaves that look dead. But a soaking rainfall will saturate these plants and allow them to "resurrect" into vibrant, green, growing plants.

As you stroll through the hammock, keep an eye peeled for anoles, warblers, and tree snails. The snails may be on a tree trunk or on the boardwalk. Don't even touch a tree snail, for touching it may cause it to break its moisture seal, which in the dry season will kill it. In winter, white-crowned pigeons are occasionally found feeding here; they are common in the summer. The hammock is also a reliable place to see and hear barred owls. Be patient, and look and listen quietly for them.

If you visit in the dry season, the vines, ferns, bromeliads, and orchids will make the hammock look luxuriant. However, the summer rains really spur the growth in the hammock, and the lush vegetation in July, August, and September is phenomenal (but be prepared for mosquitoes).

The pines across the Main Park Road from Mahogany Hammock are a traditional roost for bald eagles. At dawn, they depart the pines, heading south to the lakes and bays. At dusk, they return from the south, and you should see the eagles as they approach. December and January are the best months and evening is the best time for viewing the eagles.

In the summer, a few sandhill cranes return to the marsh around Mahogany Hammock. Look for them along the Main Park Road near the Mahogany Hammock turnoff.

Paurotis Pond
(24 miles from park entrance)

This small artificial pond was named for the paurotis palms on the island. The pond has a ramp for small paddle craft and picnic tables at the pond's edge. This pond sometimes offers views of wood storks, which have nested on the spoil islands, and a variety of other wading birds (such as roseate spoonbills, black-crowned night herons, white ibises). The area will likely be closed past the parking lot from January to late May to protect nesting waterbirds, but you can see the birds from the parking lot.

West Lake
(30 miles from park entrance)

A nature trail (wheelchair-accessible, no bicycles) and a canoe trail originate here. The nature trail is a boardwalk (less than 0.5 miles) that bisects a mangrove stand. The four tree species collectively known as mangroves can be seen from the boardwalk. During the wet season, this section can be buggy. The boardwalk ventures out onto the open water and refreshing breeze of West Lake. In late winter, hundreds of ducks of at least half a dozen species can be seen. Alligators, coots, and wading birds are commonly seen. In fact, West Lake is a great place to sit and watch the water—a lot goes on because of the abundant life beneath the water's surface. Redfish, snook, mullet, and other fish need this brackish lake for feeding.

Interpretive signs along the trail explain the mangrove ecosystem. The only restroom facilities between Long Pine Key and Flamingo are located here.

Snake Bight Trail
(33 miles from park entrance)

The old road to Snake Bight formerly served a fishing camp on Florida Bay. The road is 1.6 miles long and terminates at a boardwalk on the edge of Florida Bay. The boardwalk is an exceptional place for birding most of the year. It is tidally influenced, rather than seasonally influenced, meaning you must catch the right tides for good birding. An outgoing tide is best; a high tide is worst, except for flamingos. Shorebirds and wading birds (including roseate spoonbills) use this shallow, rich, protected edge of the bay as a feeding ground. It is here that the rare views of flamingos are seen from land. However, flamingos are more easily seen by paddling to Snake Bight from Flamingo.

Along the trail are excellent opportunities to view wildlife. Alligators find this trail a convenient place to rest. If you see one, keep your distance, since it can fool you with its sluggish appearance. Snakes are common, and treefrogs can be found in the bromeliads. Warblers and mangrove cuckoos are active here. Bobcats prowl frequently. Perhaps the best known inhabitant of the Snake Bight Trail is the mosquito. If mosquitoes are anywhere around, they'll show up here first. Vegetation can get tall on the trail, so chiggers may be plentiful. Bicycling is permitted. Not wheelchair-accessible.

Mrazek Pond
(34 miles from park entrance)

Park Ranger Vincent Mrazek must have had a glorious view of wading birds as he gazed out over this pond in the 1950s and 1960s. Judging by the activity 50 years later, it must have been quite a sight. Mrazek Pond is one of those spe-

Snake Bight on Florida Bay, which is in the distance

cial birding spots that almost every local birder and every birder who has been to the park knows about. Finding it and getting to it couldn't be easier. The pond is viewable from the Main Park Road.

The birds seem to habituate to people watching quietly from the grassy shore, so it's easy to observe them feeding and resting. Some of them get too close to focus a telephoto lens. In fact, Mrazek Pond is known even more as a photographic hotspot than for birding. Probably more photos of wading birds have been published from here than from Anhinga Trail, which is saying a lot.

The bad news is that the avian activity doesn't last all year. The peak months are December to March, when water levels in the park are dropping. Sometimes the activity is reduced to a hectic few weeks during those months, when it seems like every wading bird from Cape Sable to Taylor Slough is visiting. You're likely to see great egrets, snowy egrets, great white herons, great blue herons, little blue herons, tricolored herons, roseate spoonbills, wood storks, white ibises, green herons, white pelicans, black skimmers, common moorhens, rails, blue-winged teal, and other ducks. The birds disappear when their feeding frenzies have depleted the fish populations. In drought years, the pond may dry completely in late winter. You also may see alligators, turtles, and maybe even a bobcat.

Coot Bay Pond
(34 miles from park entrance)
Just past Mrazek Pond is the small channel known as Coot Bay Pond, leading from the Main Park Road to Coot Bay. In late winter and spring, it is a good place to watch ducks and wading birds. There are picnic tables and a canoe launch.

Rowdy Bend Trail
(35 miles from park entrance)
This unpaved road winds through stands of buttonwood trees and coastal prairie for 2.6 miles and ends at the Snake Bight Trail. Buttonwoods were used by the early South Florida settlers for making charcoal for cooking. Cactus and yucca grow here because of the lack of fresh water. Wet and buggy in summer. Bicycles are allowed but not recommended.

Christian Point Trail
(37 miles from park entrance)
Remnants of a buttonwood forest are evident along the trail, where the weathered trunks that once surrendered to a hurricane lie prone on the coastal prairie. The trail is 1.8 miles one way and ends at the western part of Snake Bight. Ospreys are usually seen along this trail. Keep your eyes open for a rare indigo snake, the longest native snake in Florida.

FLAMINGO

Flamingo offers a campground, hiking trails, paddle trails and rentals, boat tours, tram tours, bicycling and rentals, naturalist programs, motorboat and houseboat rentals, boating, boat ramps, birding and other wildlife viewing, a visitor center, and a marina. During the winter season, the rangers lead walks, slogs, canoe trips, and lectures. At the amphitheater next to the walk-in campsites, expert scientists and naturalists present slide shows every evening. Schedules can be found at the ranger station information desk. The campground was discussed above under "Camping."

Flamingo was a quiet fishing village in the late 1800s. No roads led to it; it was accessible only by boat. Families built houses on stilts and farmed small patches of land for bananas, tomatoes, sugar cane, and squash. They made charcoal from buttonwood trees for shipment to Key West. Smudge pots inside the houses were a way of life to prevent mosquitoes. Every few years a hurricane would level most of the houses and destroy the crops, so the village never grew large. In fact, after the road from Florida City was completed in 1922 and villagers discovered a way out, more people left than arrived.

Some Flamingo residents made a living by plume hunting. Many of the colonies of birds the plume hunters sought were near Flamingo. Around the turn of the century, the killing of egrets, herons, and spoonbills for their feathers was lucrative. The long breeding plumes of the great egret brought $32.00 an ounce (more than gold). In 1905, National Audubon Society warden Guy

---

Bradley, who lived in Flamingo, was shot to death by plume hunters while protecting a colony of birds. His death stirred a major crusade, sparked several years earlier by women outraged that the birds were killed for so worthless a purpose. In 1910, the governor of New York signed a landmark bill making the sale of plumes illegal in that state. The political attack against the center of the plume market in New York City effectively curtailed much of the slaughter.

The town was named in 1893, when residents had to identify the post office they had requested. Knowing their town was unique and rather hellish, they wanted to name it something exotic and distinctive. A flock of a thousand flamingos, probably from the Bahamas, had been seen on Cape Sable a few years previously and lent their name to the town. Since then, only a handful of flamingos are seen occasionally in Florida Bay.

Since 1947, when the Park Service became caretakers, the village has included only Park Service and concession employees, their families, and tourists. Hurricanes Katrina and Wilma caused extreme damage to the village, destroying the lodge and cabins beyond repair in 2005. The only overnight facility is the campground.

Marina and Store

The marina (239-695-3101) is open daily year-round, offering automobile and boat fuel pumps; boat ramps to the Florida Bay side and to the Buttonwood Canal side; rental skiffs, canoes, kayaks, houseboats, binoculars, and bicycles; boat tours; and the marina store, which is more like a general store, with groceries, basic boating and camping equipment, fishing bait and tackle, books,

snacks, and souvenirs. Campers often use the pay hot showers. Boaters can pay for overnight docking here (limited water and electric hook-ups).

Reservations are accepted for canoes. Skiffs may be used only on the Whitewater Bay side (not in Florida Bay). For a total water experience, you can rent a houseboat that sleeps 6 to 8 people for up to a week. Houseboat renters can rent a canoe for a discount and bring it on the houseboat for exploring shallow places.

Boat tours operated by the concession (fees charged) are available by reservation. They operate in Florida Bay and Whitewater Bay.

Visitor Center

The visitor center (239-695-2945) near the marina includes a ranger station, museum, and observation deck; open from 9 am–4:30 pm. Go to the ranger station if you need to plan a backcountry trip or get a permit (24-hour self-service permit applications set-up if the ranger station is closed). Information on ranger-led activities is also posted. Next to the ranger station is the small museum with exhibits of local Everglades ecology.

The observation deck is a great place to be at low tide. Wading birds and shore birds are abundant and easily observed. Pelicans, ospreys, terns, skimmers, cormorants, and gulls round out the complement of birds. Peregrine falcons hunt for shorebirds and ducks over the mud flats in the winter. Bottlenose dolphins are frequently seen in the bay by Flamingo.

Walking Trails
Eco Pond
Located between the marina and the campground on the main road, this

eight-acre freshwater pond is a good place for observing wildlife. The treated effluent from the lodge at Flamingo was discharged into this shallow evaporation pond for years, but now that the lodge is gone and the observation platform was destroyed by hurricanes in 2005, the old trail and pond are not maintained. The pond is reverting to natural Everglades habitat. You may see herons hunting for fish, gators hunting for herons, and raccoons hunting for just about anything. Eco Pond is a popular roost for white ibises and roseate spoonbills at sunset or sunrise. Look for rails, smooth-billed anis, painted buntings, shorebirds, baby gators, frogs, and bobcat tracks around the pond.

Guy Bradley Trail

If you're looking for a shortcut by foot or bicycle from the campground to the marina, take this one-mile trail located at the eastern end of the campground by the amphitheater. It meanders partly along the shore and gives a good view of the mud flats at low tide where you may see a reddish egret. Marsh rabbits often feed along the trail.

Coastal Prairie Trail

This 7.5-mile trail, which follows an old roadbed beginning at the western end of campground Loop C, goes through buttonwood forests and coastal prairie. There is little shade and the breeze never seems to reach here. It is often hot, humid, buggy, and wet. On a cool winter day, none of these are a problem, and the trail is delightful. Salt-tolerant plants (like saltwort, glasswort, prickly-pear cactus, sea purslane, yucca, and coral bean) dominate. A hardy backpacker can hike to Clubhouse Beach at the trail's end to camp. The white sand beach is beauti-

ful, and with the prairie behind and the mangroves on either side, you can feel isolated. Bring plenty of drinking water for this 15-mile roundtrip; there are no comfort facilities. Bicycles not permitted.

Bayshore Loop

This trail begins at the western end of the drive-in campground Loop C, where the Coastal Prairie Trail starts. It's a 2-mile unmarked loop that goes from the Coastal Prairie Trail to the shore of Florida Bay. To find it, turn left at the sign "Coastal Prairie Trail" that's part way down the Coastal Prairie Trail. Florida box turtles are frequently seen. In summer, it is muddy and overgrown. It's a convenient walk from the campground (no bicycles).

Paddling Trails

Check with a ranger for current conditions before embarking.

Nine Mile Pond

This is a nice trip for the summer months, when the water level is high, since mosquitoes are less prevalent here. Late February through May may be too dry. The trail is a 5.2-mile loop and takes about four hours to complete. A shortcut shaves 1.5 miles off. Ask at the visitor center for the printed trail guide that is coordinated with numbered signposts. Motors are prohibited.

Noble Hammock

The trail originally was used during Prohibition by bootleggers going to their stills in the hammocks. The 2-mile loop is marked with numbered floats and takes about three hours. Low water may present a problem during the dry season. Narrow passages and tight corners make this trail tricky for novices. Motors are prohibited.

Hell's Bay

You'll understand the origin of this trail's name when you paddle your way through the dense mangroves, cutting through spider webs, clouds of mosquitoes, and branches masking the trail. The trail is marked with floats. The distance is 3 miles to Lard Can, the first campsite (about two hours). About 0.5 miles farther is the Pearl Bay Chickee, and about 2 miles past Pearl Bay is the Hell's Bay Chickee. Not for novices.

West Lake

A 7.7-mile trail starts from the launch by the West Lake Interpretive Shelter. The trail first crosses a long stretch of open lake, making for windy, strenuous paddling much of the time. The marked trail progresses through a series of smaller lakes connected by creeks and terminates at Garfield Bight on Florida Bay. The Alligator Creek campsite (primitive) is located at Garfield Bight. Allow about seven hours travel time one way.

Coot Bay

Three places are available to launch a boat headed for Coot Bay: in the Buttonwood Canal at the Flamingo Marina (3.6 miles to Coot Bay); at the north end of Bear Lake Road (1.6 miles); and at Coot Bay Pond (short paddle). Coot Bay Pond is the shortest route, and the Bear Lake Road may be closed by poor conditions. The Buttonwood Canal is straight and easy paddling, a good choice for novice paddlers or windy days. The freshwater Coot Bay can be windy. Paddlers can continue to Mud Lake then circle back via the Bear Lake Canoe Trail to Bear Lake Road. That loop is 4.8 miles long.

The bay is named for a past era when coots, aquatic chicken-like birds, were abundant here. They fed on the aquatic vegetation until it was wiped out by saltwater intrusion from construction of a canal that connected Coot Bay to Florida Bay. The salinity has been reduced since 1982, when the "plug" (a concrete dike) was installed at the Florida Bay end of the canal to prevent further intrusion.

Bear Lake

As with the Coot Bay Trail, there are the same three launch sites: the Flamingo Marina; the north end of Bear Lake Road; and Coot Bay Pond. The Bear Lake Road requires a 200-yard portage, but the road may be closed. From the Bear Lake Road portage, it's 1.6 miles to Bear Lake along a narrow mangrove-lined canal. The canal was dug in 1922 to drain Cape Sable and provide access to the Cape. Motors are not permitted on Bear Lake Canal.

Cape Sable

The Bear Lake Trail Canoe Trail past Bear Lake was impassable after the hurricanes of 2005, but the Park Service is clearing it and it should be open as of this printing; check with the ranger station. Experienced canoeists who desire a two- to three-day camping trip can continue past Bear Lake to Cape Sable. The total distance from Bear Lake Road to Cape Sable is 12 miles and includes a second portage on East Cape Canal. Parts of the western stretch can be impassable during the dry season. The destination is a campsite on East Cape, which means a paddle of about one mile on open Gulf of Mexico waters; tides and winds make the Gulf section not recommended for novices. Camping on Cape Sable is remote and peaceful. Aside from an old dock, no reminders of civilization remain. The sand on the beach is made of broken shells, not quartz like most other beaches.

Florida Bay

Canoeing on Florida Bay can be wonderful or miserable, depending on the weather and tides. Check with a ranger or concession employee about those two factors before setting out into Florida Bay. Winds and tides can be strong, and thunderstorms can make it hazardous to paddle out in the open. Low tides can strand boats for hours. The marina will not rent canoes for Florida Bay on windy days.

On calm days, canoeing on shallow Florida Bay presents an unbeatable way to see flocks of wading birds and shorebirds. Dolphins are frequently seen around Flamingo. Manatees and sea turtles are possibilities. Small sharks (such as blacktip, bonnethead, and lemon) are common; their dorsal fins break the water's surface, revealing their presence. They pose no threat to people in canoes, but it is not advisable to wade in the shallow water.

Much of Florida Bay, including the Flamingo area, is carpeted with three common kinds of seagrass: turtle grass, manatee grass, and shoal grass. Turtle grass, with flat blades up to a half inch wide, is grazed by green sea turtles. Manatee grass, which (along with other seagrasses) is grazed by manatees, has leaves that are round in cross-section. Shoal grass, with narrow, flat leaves, is important as an early colonizer of disturbed underwater sites.

During daylight hours, boaters are permitted to land on Bradley Key. This is a worthwhile and easy destination. The island was named for Guy Bradley, the Audubon warden who was killed nearby while protecting a colony of wading birds from plume hunters. Boaters may also land on Carl Ross Key. Another destination is Snake Bight, the cove to the east of Flamingo. At low tide, hundreds of wading and shore birds gather to feed on the mud flats laden with invertebrates.

Boating

Flamingo is a popular launch site for small, shallow-draft motor boats. There are two ramps: the Florida Bay ramp, and the Whitewater Bay ramp on the Buttonwood Canal.

Although Florida Bay was once artificially connected to Whitewater Bay by the Buttonwood Canal, passage is now blocked by the dike that keeps salt water from intruding into the mostly fresh canal. A boater who wishes to pass through Flamingo from one bay to the other and who doesn't have a boat trailer at Flamingo must have the boat mechanically hoisted over the dike at the marina (fee charged).

Florida Bay is shallow and laced with mud banks. At low tide, much of the bay is exposed, and the sight of thousands of wading birds and shorebirds feeding on the invertebrates and trapped fish is spectacular. The shallow water attracts small sharks, rays, dolphins, sea turtles, and occasionally a manatee. Local boaters learn to "read" the water. That is, they can tell by the size of the waves and the water's color if they are about to hit a shoal. A newcomer to Florida Bay boating should get a nautical chart at the marina and stick close to Flamingo. Running aground is not just an inconvenience for the boater—it's destructive to the seagrass beds.

Fishing

All year long the lure of saltwater fishing draws people to Flamingo. Locals make frequent weekend trips for sport or to stock their freezers. For those who prefer shallow calm water and light tackle to deep sea fishing, Florida Bay is the perfect place. If you prefer, you may hire a fishing guide through the Flamingo Marina.

The most sought-after food fish are snook, redfish, spotted seatrout, black drum, mangrove snapper, tripletail, and sheepshead. Other popular targets are tarpon and ladyfish. The warm shallow waters of Florida Bay are a rich nursery for invertebrates (such as shrimp, crabs, lobsters, and mollusks) and larval fish. This gives the larger gamefish plenty to feed on.

In recent years, a combination of habitat destruction and sport fishing pressure has severely stressed the Florida Bay fisheries. Some guides claim the problem is with the commercial fishermen outside the park. However, on any one weekend day or holiday, several hundred recreational boats may be in the bay fishing. These boats are taking the fish that may be ready to spawn in the estuary. The toll on the seagrass beds scarred by propellers and on the thousands of fish that were caught and kept (plus the released fish that may not spawn that year or even survive from handling stress) every weekend of the year cannot be ignored.

DIRECTIONS

From the north: Take Florida's Turnpike Extension south to the end in Florida City. Turn right onto SW 344th St. (Palm Drive) and follow the signs on SR 9336 to Everglades National Park.

From the Keys: Take US 1 to first traffic light in Florida City at SW 344th St., turn left and follow the signs on SR 9336.

CHEKIKA

Chekika offers a short trail, a boardwalk, and a picnic area. It is open dawn to dusk but closed May to November because of seasonal flooding.

This is the most recent addition to Everglades National Park. The 640 acres that formerly comprised Chekika State Recreation Area were turned over to the National Park Service in 1991. From this eastern access, visitors will see a tropical hardwood hammock surrounded by sawgrass marsh. Visitors traveling between the main park entrance and Shark Valley or Everglades City will find a convenient place to hike or have a picnic lunch.

The area was named for a famous Seminole, Chief Chekika. Chekika was hanged in 1840 in a nearby hammock by Lt. Col. William Harney in revenge for several earlier attacks by the Seminoles.

As late as 1903, local Indian families camped in the high ground of the hammock. In 1943, oil prospectors drilled 1,250 feet into the underlying aquifer and struck water instead of oil. The resulting artesian well released 2.5 million gallons of sulphurous water a day. The deep well was later capped to prevent the ground water, having one type of chemical composition, from mixing with surface water, which has a different composition. Now the water is recirculated by a pump, so it looks like a spring.

The Hammock Trail is a short footpath through a hardwood hammock, labeled with interpretive signs (not handicapped-accessible). A boardwalk crossing the sawgrass is also labeled with interpretive signs. The pond was created by directing the artesian well into a natural depression.

DIRECTIONS
From Florida City, go north on SR 997 (Krome Ave.) about 9 miles to SW 168th St. (Richmond Dr.). Turn left, go 6 miles to SW 237th Ave., then right for 0.6 miles.

SHARK VALLEY

Shark Valley has a visitor center, bicycling and rentals, nature trails, birding and other wildlife viewing, interpretive programs, a tram ride, and an observation tower. Entrance station hours are 8:30 am to 6:00 pm. Visitor center hours are 9:15 am to 5:15 pm in summer and 8:45 am to 5:15 pm in winter. December to April (the dry season) is the best time of year because wildlife will be concentrated in the water along the road and the weather is cooler. However, in summer, high water levels may drive snakes, frogs, and mammals onto the roads and trails where they are more visible.

Shark Valley is at the northern boundary of Everglades National Park, easily reachable from Miami and Naples. It provides access for visitors to the Shark River Slough, a wide but shallow and slowly moving body of water that supports much wildlife. A trip on the Tram Road to the Observation Tower, whether by tram or bicycle, is a good way to see alligators and wading birds.

Visitor Center
This small center contains educational displays and items for sale, including local human and natural history books and videos. You can obtain the schedule for the many ranger-led programs offered. These include a 3.5-hour bicycle tour to the observation tower, a 3-hour get-your-feet-wet "Slough Slog" to a gator hole or hammock, a 45-minute walk on an elevated boardwalk, or a 20-minute sit-down talk next to the visitor center.

Vending machines for chips, snacks, and soft drinks provide the only food on the premises. Across the Tamiami Trail from the entrance station is a restaurant operated by the Miccosukee Indians, serving Miccosukee and American food. The marsh behind the restaurant is a good place to check for snail kites.

Tram Road

The main "trail" is the 15-mile paved, loop road that leads to the Observation Tower. The road was built by Humbel Oil (now Exxon) in 1946 for oil drilling. The distance between the visitor center and the Observation Tower is seven miles on the western side of the loop and eight miles on the eastern side. Plenty of alligators, including babies, can be seen at close range, such as in the culverts on the side of the road (but keep at least 15 feet away). Wood storks, deer, otters, water snakes, snail kites, and many other animals can be seen. The road intercepts Shark Slough and is the only way most people will get to see the slough. A slough is a slow-moving channel in the marsh that has slightly deeper water than the rest of the marsh. It holds water longer (has a longer hydroperiod), looks greener from the air, and serves as a refuge for wildlife when other areas dry up. Shark Slough is the largest slough in the park.

The only motorized vehicles allowed are the tour trams and official vehicles. Visitors can travel the road one of three ways: taking the tram, riding a bicycle, or walking. Because of the openness and heat, not many people choose to walk the entire length, although many people walk shorter segments.

The two-hour tram tours are run by the concession seven days a week all year (weather permitting). The tram makes a half-hour stop at the Observation Tower (see below) and riders are encouraged to disembark and ascend the ramp to the tower. Occasional stops are made elsewhere if the guide sees something interesting, but riders must stay on the tram. Reservations are suggested from December to March. Tickets are available at the Tram Tour Office (fee charged). Call first for departure times, since they vary seasonally. In the busy season, the schedule includes moonlight and early morning tram tours.

An excellent way to see and feel the Everglades more closely is to bicycle the 15-mile road. Visitors may bring their own bicycles or rent them from the concession. Specify if you want a bicycle with a basket for carrying your field guides and lunch. Bicycling is easy on the flat terrain, but it can get very hot. Bring plenty of drinking water and sun protection. Don't attempt to bicycle in thunderstorms. You will not be safe from lightning on a bicycle as you would be in a car, and there is little protective cover along the road. Allow at least two to three hours to pedal the route.

Bobcat Trail

A short walk from the parking lot is a 0.5-mile, handicapped-accessible boardwalk that connects the two legs of the Tram Road. The boardwalk trail leads to the bayhead habitat and is punctuated by interpretive trail signs. A small gazebo midway along the trail provides a place to rest and enjoy the quiet. Look for rails, particularly the king rail, along the boardwalk.

Otter Cave Trail

A 0.5-mile walk along the western leg of the Tram Road (from the parking lot) will bring you to the start of the Otter Trail, which is about 0.25 miles long. It is a narrow footpath through a hammock, also with interpretive signs, and emerges on the same side of the Tram Road.

Observation Tower Trail

Originally built as a fire tower, the current observation tower was remodeled in the 1960s for park visitors. A long spiral ramp (handicapped-accessible) now leads to the top of the 65-foot tower, which yields a glorious panoramic view

Shark Valley Observation Tower provides a panoramic view of Shark Slough.

of the Shark Slough. This is one of the more popular photography spots in the park. During the spring months, the drying of the glades forces alligators, turtles, fish, and other wildlife to concentrate in the water at the base of the tower. Several dozen alligators may be seen at once. The trees surrounding the tower also serve as a diurnal roost for yellow-crowned night herons. At the base of the tower are restrooms and drinking water.

The Tower Trail, a small side trail near the base of the Observation Tower, is 0.25 miles long. It is good for observing butterflies and great blue herons and for photography.

DIRECTIONS
Drive on U.S. 41, 18 miles west of the intersection with Krome Ave. (SR 997).

CONTACT
National Park Service
36000 SW 8th Street
Miami 33194
305-221-8776

Concession:
Tram tours, bicycle rentals
305-221-8455
www.sharkvalleytramtours.com/

EVERGLADES CITY

This entrance offers canoe and kayak launches, canoe rentals, boat ramp, boat tours, a visitor center, and gift shop. Access is always open and there is no entrance fee at this location. The visitor center is open 9 am–4:30 pm mid-April to mid-November, 8:30 am–4:30 pm mid-November to mid-April. Generally, the best time of year is November to April. Winter has fewer mosquitoes, cooler temperatures, less rain, and more wading birds. In the summer, though, waters are calmer for boating. Some Park Service programs may not be offered during the summer.

Tucked up in the northwest corner of Everglades National Park is a region called the Ten Thousand Islands. Named for the myriad of small, irregularly shaped mangrove islands, this area is popular with paddlers and anglers. This vast wilderness abounds with wildlife. Manatees, dolphins, alligators, rays, sharks, sea turtles, spoonbills, and white ibises are visible at certain times of the year. This is a water-oriented area; there are mangrove islands but no trails. You'll just have to find a boat if you want to see this area.

Visitor Center

The visitor center is also the ranger station where boaters and paddlers get back-country permits and maps. The visitor center is located on the second floor of the building and is not accessible to the handicapped. Handicapped people should ask on the first floor for park information. Hours vary seasonally, but generally 9 pm–4:30 pm.

A concession operates the gift shop, boat tours, and rentals on the first floor and sells souvenirs, Seminole crafts, and a small assortment of books. Vending machines dispense sandwiches, snacks, and drinks. More substantial meals are available in restaurants across the street.

Boat Tours

Two boat tours (fee charged) make it easy for visitors to see the Everglades coast by water. The Ten Thousand Island Tour is a 1.5-hour trip through the coastal mangrove islands and estuaries. The Mangrove Wilderness Tour is on a smaller boat that is able to navigate up the Turner River. The concession will assist with wheelchairs.

Paddling

Canoeing and kayaking are excellent ways to see the Ten Thousand Islands. Trips of several hours to several days can be planned. Everglades City is the northern terminus of the Wilderness Waterway, a 99-mile canoe trail to Flamingo (see "Wilderness Waterway" below).

All paddling trips should be carefully planned in advance. Proper safety equipment includes a Coast Guard-approved personal flotation device for each person. The Coast Guard recommends all boaters bring a current NOAA nautical chart covering their route and vicinity. The chart for the Everglades City area day trips is #11430 ("Lostmans River to Wiggins Pass"). For the Wilderness Waterway trip, you would also need #11432 ("Lostmans River to Shark River") and #11433 ("Whitewater Bay"). The National Park Service recommends each person bring at least one gallon of water per day planned, plus enough for one extra day. Since strong tides can greatly impede your progress, check with a ranger for the local tide schedule.

Day trips don't require a backcountry permit, but it is best to check with a ranger for the latest information on tides, winds, and storms before departing. Tides can be strong, and, combined with a head wind, it can be impossible for a strong canoeist to make headway. There aren't many places to pull over and rest either. The mangroves can be confusing to navigate if you deviate from a marked trail or encounter decreasing visibility. However, with careful planning, you can ensure the tides are with you and enjoy a most delightful canoe trip.

The National Park Service distributes printed guides with maps for day paddling trips. The trips will be briefly described in the next two paragraphs for advanced planning, but you should ask the Park Service for these guides when you arrive or send for them earlier (request the canoe guides for Everglades City; www.nps.gov/ever/planyourvisit/loader.cfm?csModule=security/getfile&PageID=297367).

You can bring your own boat or rent one at the concession at the Ranger Station. You can launch at the Ranger Station or at the privately operated Outdoor Resorts on Chokoloskee Island (Outdoor Resorts also rents canoes).

The Sandfly Island trip will take about 2.5 hours paddling time (round-trip). Sandfly Island is about 2 miles from the Ranger Station across open water. There is a dock at the near end, and a walking trail on the island, so get out and stretch your legs.

If you prefer an "inland" canoe trip, you can choose several routes through narrow mangrove and sawgrass channels. You can leave either from an access road on US 41 (about 11 miles east of SR 29), from the Gulf Coast Ranger Station, or from Chokoloskee. The Turner River trip takes about five hours from US 41 (embark 0.6 miles east of SR 29) to Chokoloskee and is not a loop (so an upriver return or alternate transportation back to your car must be planned). From Everglades City or Chokoloskee, you can take a shorter loop through Halfway Creek and Left Hand Turner River. This will take about three hours, depending on wind and tides. Because of the intense mosquito population, the inland trips are best avoided in summer.

You can plan other nice routes for day trips using a nautical chart. The rangers at Gulf Coast Ranger Station will be glad to help you plan a route.

Overnight Paddling Trips

Numerous combinations of routes can be used to plan overnight trips—too many to describe here. The backcountry chickees and campsites are strategically placed by the Park Service for overnight convenience (see "Backcountry sites" under "Camping" above). As mentioned above, you need a permit from a ranger to stay at a backcountry site. During the busy winter season, you will have a better chance of getting the backcountry camping site of your choice if you avoid holidays and begin on a weekday. Also see "Paddling" under **Big Cypress National Preserve**.

Wilderness Waterway

The super-adventurous, super-experienced paddlers with 7–10 days available can tackle the Wilderness Waterway, a 99-mile marked canoe trail between Everglades City and Flamingo. The trail can be traveled just as easily in either direction.

While paddling along the waterway, you'll pass seemingly endless miles of mangroves. Concealed in the tangle of living trunks and prop roots are the skeletal ghosts of giant mangroves destroyed in hurricanes. Occasionally, a shell mound will create enough elevation for a change of vegetation. The shell mounds are remnants of the Calusa Indians, who lived along the southwest coast possibly as early as 1450 BC. These indigenous people depended on shellfish, primarily oysters, clams, and conchs. They left the empty shells in huge piles that became mounds. Other mounds were burial sites and some were structured for habitation. Some reached extraordinary proportions. The town of Chokoloskee, at the northern end of the Wilderness Waterway, is built on a 150-acre shell mound that is 20 feet high. Sandfly Island, west of Chokoloskee, is a 75-acre shell mound. While clams have since been depleted by canneries early in the 20th century, the oysters are still abundant. This will be gratingly obvious every time your boat scrapes over an oyster bar.

The waterway bisects some of the wildest country left in the eastern United States. That is why people who are looking for solitude and wilderness head for this unique trail. It is also why anyone who undertakes this journey must be experienced, well-prepared, and willing to take a risk. Risks are mostly in the form of strong tides, high winds, choppy water, lightning, sun exposure, hypothermia, lack of drinking water, and getting lost. The last one is not a problem if you keep the markers in sight. If you explore off the trail or encounter poor visibility, you can easily get confused in the tangle of mangrove islands. Other than rainfall, no source of drinking water is found between Everglades City and Flamingo. All boaters must carry their own in heavy duty (preferably hard-sided) containers that won't puncture and will be secure from raccoons. During the dry season, the lack of fresh water can drive raccoons and other animals to seek it from humans. Raccoons can chew through soft-sided containers.

The campsites (chickees and ground sites) are spaced at irregular intervals along the trail. Some are as little as a mile apart and some have almost 10-mile gaps. Since most campsites are slightly off the marked trail, they can be difficult to find. They are marked on the NOAA nautical charts #11430, 11432, and 11433. Be sure to get the Park Service brochure "Backcountry Trip Planner" that explains where the campsites are.

A long-distance trip like this must be planned well in advance. Because the trail is not a loop, you will need to arrange transportation from your destination back to your car, unless you plan to paddle the 99 miles back! The drive around by land between Flamingo and Everglades City is about 3.5 hours.

Plan your Wilderness Waterway trip carefully. The Park Service brochure "Introduction to Canoeing the Everglades" includes an excellent checklist of items to carry. You'll

need a permit for the campsites (see "Backcountry Sites" under "Camping").

Motorboating

Boats can be launched at the Barron Marina on SR 29 in Everglades City (239-695-3591) or at Outdoor Resorts in Chokoloskee (239-695-3788).

If you bring your own boat, you had better be good at reading the local nautical charts. The water is so full of shoals, it's almost impossible to drive in a straight line. During extremely low tides, boating to or from Chokoloskee may be impossible for several hours.

DIRECTIONS

The Gulf Coast Ranger Station is at 815 Oyster Bar Lane, Everglades City 34139. It's on SR 29, 4.8 miles south of the intersection with Tamiami Trail.

CONTACT

239-695-3311 or 305-242-7700

Concession
Boat tours, canoe rentals
239-695-2591 or 800-445-7724

9

Grassy Waters Preserve

Facilities: Nature center, boardwalk, hiking and bicycling trails, guided canoe trips and walks

Activities: Hiking, bicycling, paddling

Admission: Free

Hours: North side open daily 7 am to 5:30 pm; south side open Monday–Saturday 8 am–4:30 pm, Sunday 8:30 am–5 pm; nature center closed Monday and federal holidays

Pets: Not allowed

Best Time of Year: No preference

Once upon a time the Everglades overflowed into the Loxahatchee Slough then out to the ocean during the wet season. During the dry season, however, water from the coastal ridge sometimes flowed the other way from the Slough into the Everglades! Grassy Waters Preserve (formerly Loxahatchee Preserve) is contained within the now-fragmented Loxahatchee Slough. The Slough was once connected at the south end to the area that is now **A.R.M. Loxahatchee National Wildlife Refuge** and at the north end to the Loxahatchee River. The Preserve is part of the 20-square-mile Water Catchment Area that is owned by the City of West Palm Beach.

The City operates a nature center and trails within the Preserve. Good vistas of sawgrass marshes, cypress strands and domes, and some pinelands are visible. Everglade snail kites nest on an adjacent site and are occasionally seen. Bald eagles, limpkins, and otters may also be seen.

The nature center is accessed from the south entrance and contains classrooms, meeting halls, and educational exhibits. The 0.65-mile Cypress Boardwalk, additional trails, and the wide-vista observation platform are at the nature center. Call ahead to arrange guided canoe trips.

Trails
To find the unpaved Owahee Trail (hiking and bicycling), bicycle or walk east from nature center along Northlake Boulevard for 0.5 miles; trail is on right (no parking). This trail follows levees and berms south to **Apoxee Urban Wilderness Park** about 8 miles to the south, then west along the southern end of the preserve, then north along the western side of the preserve, totaling 16.5 miles. Trail open dawn to dusk. The trailhead has no parking, so if you park at the nature center or northside lots, watch out for their earlier closing times.

On the north side, Hog Hammock Trail is 2.8 miles and Eagle Trail is 0.5 miles for hiking and bicycling through an oak-palmetto hammock.

DIRECTIONS

Preserve is 1 mile west of Beeline Highway (SR 710) on Northlake Boulevard, south entrance on left, north entrance on right.

CONTACT

Grassy Waters Preserve
8264 Northlake Boulevard
West Palm Beach 33412
561-804-4985
www.wpb.org/park/center.php?id=3

River otters may be seen at Grassy Waters Preserve.

12

Gumbo Limbo Nature Center and Red Reef Park

Facilities: Nature center, boardwalk, nature trail, observation tower, butterfly garden, educational programs, gift shop

Activities: swimming, snorkeling, nature viewing

Admission: Free

Hours: Monday–Saturday 9 am–4 pm, Sunday 12–4 pm; closed July 4, Thanksgiving, December 25, January 1; Red Reef Park open 8 am–10 pm daily

Pets: Not allowed

South Florida Birding Trail: 87

Best Time of Year: No preference

The nature center is part of the Gumbo Limbo Environmental Complex at Red Reef Park, which is operated by the City of Boca Raton. The 20-acre complex also includes classrooms, biology laboratory, amphitheater, marine observation tanks, and marine research facility. Its location between the Intracoastal Waterway and the Atlantic Ocean affords the opportunity for studies of tropical hammocks, coastal dunes, mangroves, sea turtles, and manatees. Florida Atlantic University runs the marine research, which includes the large seawater tanks. The 67-acre Red Reef Park (separate entrance) includes dune and hammock habitats and oceanside swimming and snorkeling activities. Loggerhead sea turtles nest on the 0.75-mile-long beach in summer.

Nature Center
The forte of this educational center is the marine aquaria containing local fish and invertebrates. Other live exhibits include gopher tortoises, snakes, and lizards. Displays of sea turtles, local birds, reptiles, fish, and a comparison of the wood from native trees round out the exhibits. Outside are a butterfly garden and live sea turtle tanks. Sea turtle nesting programs are conducted from May to July (call for reservations).

The nature center's name was borrowed from a tropical tree called the gumbo-limbo, which grows commonly here. The wood is easily carved and was used in bygone years to make carousel horses. A remarkable feature of the wood is that a branch stuck in the ground will sprout roots and leaves and become a whole tree.

Boardwalk, Observation Tower, and Trail
The 0.3-mile-long boardwalk rambles through high and low hammocks and mangroves along the Intracoastal Waterway. It also leads to the 40-foot observation tower

that affords a view above the tree tops. A small oyster-shell midden is along the way.

Native trees include paradise-tree, pigeon-plum, tallowwood, mastic, guiana-plum, white indigo-berry, lancewood, Spanish stopper, and Jamaica caper. The North Trail, shorter than the boardwalk, passes by the Intracoastal Waterway and is lined by white mangroves.

DIRECTIONS
From northern Boca area, take NW 40th Street east to SR A1A (Ocean Blvd.), turn south and go about 1.5 miles to nature center. From southern Boca area, take Palmetto Park Road east to SR A1A, turn north and go 1.1 miles to nature center.

CONTACT
Gumbo Limbo Nature Center
1801 N. Ocean Boulevard
Boca Raton 33432
561-338-1473
www.gumbolimbo.org

Red Reef Park
1400 N. Ocean Boulevard
Boca Raton 33432
561-393-7974
www.ci.boca-raton.fl.us/rec/
parks/redreef.shtm

Hugh Taylor Birch State Park

Facilities: Nature trails, canoe rentals, visitor center, swimming beach, primitive youth-group campground

Activities: Hiking, paddling, swimming, camping

Admission: State Park fee

Hours: 8 am to sunset; see page xx for details

Pets: Not allowed overnight in campground

South Florida Birding Trail: 90

Best Time of Year: No preference

When attorney Hugh Taylor Birch came to Florida from Chicago in 1893, he settled in the small village of Ft. Lauderdale. By the time he died, urbanization surrounded his 180-acre seaside estate. Birch donated his barrier island property to the people of the state as a recreation spot for all to enjoy. The park preserves some of the last coastal hammock habitat in Broward County. Two self-guided nature trails, a small freshwater lagoon for canoeing, and access to a swimming beach on the ocean are the attractions to this urban park.

The visitor center, which now contains natural and cultural history exhibits, was formerly Birch's house. Canoes are available for rent for use on the 0.6-mile-long lagoon.

Trails

A leisurely 20-minute walk will take you through the coastal hammock on the Beach Hammock Trail. Here you'll see pond-apple, sea-grape, Spanish stopper, marlberry, mastic, coontie, and torchwood plants labeled. The coontie is a reminder that this was one of the last strongholds of the atala butterfly larvae, which feed on the plant. The short Exotic Plant Trail has a brochure indicating native and nonnative plants. The nonnatives include kalanchoe, oysterplant, banyans, and Australian-pine.

DIRECTIONS

From I-95, take Exit 29 to Sunrise Boulevard (SR 838), east 3.8 miles to entrance.

CONTACT

Hugh Taylor Birch State Park
3109 E. Sunrise Boulevard
Ft. Lauderdale 33304
954-564-4521
www.floridastateparks.org/hughtaylorbirch

John D. MacArthur Beach State Park

Facilities: Nature center, nature trails, butterfly garden, kayak rentals, guided programs, gift shop

Activities: swimming, snorkeling, hiking, paddling, picnicking

Admission: State Park fee

Hours: Nature center open daily from 9 am to 5 pm

Pets: Not allowed on beach

South Florida Birding Trail: 67

Best Time of Year: Summer for snorkeling and swimming, fall–spring for birds (roseate spoonbills April–October)

While the Palm Beaches continue to squeeze out the surrounding green spaces, MacArthur Beach remains a precious remnant of the subtropical coastal habitat. The 325 acres include coastal hammock, dunes, and mangroves, as well as underwater habitats. The beach and the reef are on the Atlantic Ocean, while the mangroves are on Lake Worth and Lake Worth Cove. Several nature trails and a pristine beach are the main attractions of this park.

The 0.25-mile pedestrian boardwalk bridges the gap over Lake Worth Cove to the beach. From the boardwalk may be seen red, white, and black mangrove species. The mud flats along the boardwalk are a good place to find wading and shore birds. Free trams run periodically from 10 am to 4 pm to transport people who don't want to

A just-hatched leatherback sea turtle crawls to the relative safety of the ocean.

walk to the beach. The boardwalk is a good place to look for wading birds and shorebirds on the mud flats. Lucky visitors may see a manatee in Lake Worth.

The 4,000-square-foot Kirby Nature Center contains exhibits of Jaega tribe artifacts found at Riviera Beach, live snakes, and live mangrove and reef tanks. Guided nature walks are offered year-round and snorkeling trips are offered in summer. From the self-guided trail through a butterfly garden, you can see a variety of native shrubs that butterflies depend on, such as indigo-berry, wild-lime, and fiddlewood. Some butterflies found here are Gulf fritillary, Julia heliconian, zebra longwing, mangrove skipper, and statira sulphur. The new 5,000-square-foot Pew Family Natural Science Education Center (with classrooms, a gift shop, and more) opened in 2011.

Paddlers may launch their canoes or kayaks from the public canoe and kayak launch (ask directions at entrance gate) and paddle around the estuary. You may also join a 2-hour ranger-led tour of the estuary, Lake Worth Cove, and Munyon Island (first-come basis, kayaks included with tour fee).

Two nature trails provide access to the upland habitats. At the north end of the parking lot is the Satinleaf Trail, a leisurely 20-minute walk. The emphasis is on the mixture of temperate and tropical plant species. Satinleaf is tropical, as are paradise-tree, mastic, and strangler fig. Temperate species include redbay, live oak, and red mulberry. Other species include pigeon-plum, wild coffee, Spanish stopper, and coral bean. The Dune Hammock Trail next to the beach contains torchwood, Jamaica caper, blolly, paradise-tree, gumbo-limbo, mastic, and others.

The pristine beach, nearly two miles long, is a prime nesting area for loggerhead, green, and leatherback sea turtles. About 1,000–1,500 sea turtles nest on the beach from May through August. Loggerheads are the most prevalent of the three. The lack of artificial lighting on the beach makes this one of the best turtle nesting areas in Palm Beach County. Night programs are offered in June and July to observe the turtles laying their eggs (call the nature center for information).

Snorkelers can wade from shore to the rock reef at high tide to see such fish as blueheaded wrasse, sergeant major, puffers, jacks, gray angelfish, and stingrays. On the reef are loggerhead turtles, tarpon, snook, and barracuda. Snorkelers must have their own "diver down" flag.

DIRECTIONS

Park is located on Ocean Blvd. (SR A1A) on N. Palm Beach's barrier island; take I-95 to Exit 79AB, go east on PGA Blvd. (CR 786) which turns into Ocean Blvd. (A1A) at US 1. Follow south on Ocean Blvd. about 2 miles.

CONTACT

John D. MacArthur Beach State Park
10900 Jack Nicklaus Drive
N. Palm Beach 33408
561-624-6950
www.floridastateparks.org/
macarthurbeach

Nature Center:
561-624-6952

17

John U. Lloyd Beach State Park

Facilities: Nature trail, boat rentals, boat ramp

Activities: Beach swimming, snorkeling, paddling, picnicking

Admission: State Park fee

Hours: 8 am to sunset

Pets: Allowed only in picnic area

South Florida Birding Trail: 91

Best Time of Year: Winter for fewer crowds and greater chance of manatees and birdlife

In the summer, a constant stream of beach-going traffic is the norm. Human activity slows down a little in the winter, although Sundays are always crowded. The narrow beach must be maintained by beach renourishment projects that pump sand from offshore back onto the beach. This affects the sea turtles that nest here in the summer. The 310-acre park on the barrier island (between the Atlantic and Intracoastal) also contains a less crowded, mangrove-lined waterway for canoeing and a short nature trail. Mostly local residents use this park.

Manatees occasionally use the narrow waterway that divides the park. Canoes and kayaks can be rented from the concession for use on this waterway. The Barrier Island Trail is a 45-minute self-guided walk through a subtropical coastal hammock.

DIRECTIONS
From I-95, take Exit 22 to Stirling Road (CR 848), east to US 1, then left (north) to US A1A (Dania Blvd.), right to E. Dania Beach Blvd., then left 1.5 miles to park entrance.

CONTACT
John U. Lloyd Beach State Park
6503 N. Ocean Drive
Dania 33004
954-923-2833
www.floridastateparks.org/lloydbeach

J.W. Corbett Wildlife Management Area and Hungryland Slough

Facilities: Boardwalk, trails, primitive campsite

Activities: Hiking, bicycling (allowed on all trails except Hungryland and Florida Trail), horseback riding, camping

Admission: Free entrance for Hungryland; State Wildlife Management Area Stamp needed for rest of Corbett

Hours: Hungryland Slough open sunrise to sunset

Pets: Pets restricted depending on location and season; permitted on leash at Hungryland

South Florida Birding Trail: Corbett is 52 and Hungryland is 53

Best Time of Year: Do not go hiking on trails (except Hungryland) during hunting season (peak is October–December); Hungryland Slough is open year-round and is away from the hunt area

Formerly timber company land, the 60,348 acres of Corbett encompass slash pine flatwoods, hardwood hammocks, freshwater marshes, and dense cypress domes—a transition between the uplands of central Florida and the Everglades. Hungryland Slough, which has standing water at least 9 or 10 months of the year, flows slowly through the center; part flows east into Loxahatchee Slough and part flows west into Allapattah Slough. The lower portions of these sloughs once flowed into the Everglades. Now, however, canals surround Corbett, but the Florida Fish and Wildlife Conservation Commission (FWC) is trying to restore the hydroperiods. The FWC has been managing the area for hunting since 1948. The Florida Trail passes through Corbett and a boardwalk built for nature observing at Hungryland Slough invites non-hunters.

Native people constructed mounds around 500 BC, and the Calusa lived in the area until around AD 1500. Between the 1500s and 1800s, the Seminoles roamed in small bands locally. They were chased into the slough by nonnatives until they were starving and had to surrender. The area became known to local cattlemen as "the hungryland."

Corbett provides habitat for many types of wildlife besides the deer, turkeys, small game, and feral hogs that draw the human hunters. The endangered Bachman's sparrows and red-cockaded woodpeckers reside there. A 3,000-acre sawgrass area provides habitat for Everglade snail kites. This is one of Palm Beach County's better easy-access getaways.

Hungryland Slough Boardwalk and Trail

The upland segment of this 1.2-mile trail passes through slash pine flatwoods with coco-plums, dahoons, and wire grasses. Along the boardwalk are cypresses accompanied by pond-apples, red maples, bromeliads (needle-leaved wildpine, cardinal air plant, giant wildpine, twisted air plant, ballmoss, Spanish moss), and 13 species of ferns (including strap, swamp, giant leather, chain, royal, bracken, resurrection). The open wetlands are dominated by sawgrass. In the hardwood hammock, where typical fires can't penetrate, are oaks, paradise-trees, wild coffees, redbays, and stoppers. Turkeys roost in the cypress at night, nest in the pine flatwoods, and feed in the hammocks. White-tailed deer, otters, limpkins, wood storks, sandhill cranes, and barred owls may be seen, as well as alligators, corn snakes, indigo snakes, cottonmouths, pygmy rattlesnakes, and green treefrogs. The state is in a constant battle to control invasive plants, such as Old World climbing fern.

Florida Trail

This trail goes west 17 miles from the Hungryland parking lot to **Dupuis Reserve**. Along the way are two primitive campsites (at 6 and 12 miles). These are available for hikers during the non-hunting season (fee included with WMA Stamp, register at trailhead). The trail goes through seasonally wet pine flatwoods.

Corbett Wildlife Management Area Trails

The wildlife management area is composed of former tomato fields that the state is converting into wildlife food plots. With luck, the southeasternmost population of endangered red-cockaded woodpeckers may be seen in the pines around trails 8, 14, and 15.

DIRECTIONS

North entrance (Corbett): From West Palm Beach, take Exit 77 from I-95 west on Northlake Blvd. Turn right at Beeline Hwy (SR 710) and go about 15 miles to Wildlife Management Area on left, at intersection with CR706.

South entrance (Hungryland Slough): From West Palm Beach, take I-95 north to Exit 77, go west on Northlake Blvd (CR 850), which turns into CR 809A after passing the Beeline Hwy. (SR 710). Go 8.7 miles past Beeline to Seminole Pratt Whitney Road, then right for 2.9 miles to left turn, then 0.7 miles to grassy parking area (past "Everglades Youth Camp").

CONTACT

Florida Fish and Wildlife Conservation Commission
West Palm Beach
561-640-6100
myfwc.com/viewing/adventures/where-to-go/by-region/southeast/jw-corbett/
www.myfwc.com/media/185580/10-11_Corbett.pdf

Miami-Dade County Parks

For more information on the Miami-Dade county parks, contact Miami-Dade Park and Recreation Department, 275 NW 2nd Street, Miami 33128; 305-755-7800; www.miamidade.gov/parks.

2 **Miami-Dade County Parks**

Arch Creek Park

Facilities: Nature trail, historic museum, butterfly garden

Activities: Nature viewing, picnicking

Admission: Free

Hours: 9 am–5 pm, closed Monday and Tuesday

Pets: Not allowed

Best Time of Year: No preference

The 40-foot oolitic limestone arch that once spanned a small creek and served as a thoroughfare for the Tequesta Indians collapsed mysteriously two hours after the surrounding land was purchased for use as a park in 1973. No evidence could be found linking the collapse to threats by opponents to bomb it if the purchase went through. The area is, nevertheless, a welcome green haven in an urban environment.

The Tequestas dwelled here from 500 BC to AD 1300. The land was higher and drier than the surrounding land, and it was close to Biscayne Bay and the Everglades. The natural arch formed a bridge that facilitated travel. A midden is visible from the trail. Arch Creek is one of the only preserved archeological sites in Miami-Dade County.

Owing to its reputation as one of the greatest natural wonders in south Florida, later residents often used the area for picnics, meetings, and stagecoach rest stops. In 1858, new settlers built a coontie mill to grind the roots of the plant into starch, using water from Arch Creek to turn the water wheel.

The small museum was designed as an old Florida pioneer home, with high ceilings, many windows, and a shady porch. The building contains historical artifacts found around the bridge and natural history displays. A short trail goes through a mature live oak hammock. Among the native plants you'll see are rouge plant, paradise-tree, wild coffee, gumbo-limbo, pigeon-plum, white stopper, and bromeliads. Coontie plantings have encouraged the rare atala butterflies to lay their eggs at Arch Creek. Special walks and programs offered (especially Saturdays)—call for information and reservations.

DIRECTIONS
From I-95, take Exit 14 east on NE 135th Street (SR 916) for 2.8 miles; entrance is less than 1 block west of US 1.

CONTACT
Arch Creek Park
1855 NE 135 Street
North Miami 33181
305-944-6111
www.miamidade.gov/parks/parks/arch_creek.asp

Miami-Dade County Parks

Castellow Hammock Preserve and Nature Center

Facilities: Nature center, trail, butterfly and hummingbird garden, nature programs

Activities: Birding, hiking, nature viewing

Admission: Free

Hours: Nature center open 9 am–5 pm, closed Monday and Tuesday; grounds open daily dawn to dusk

Pets: Not allowed

South Florida Birding Trail: 102

Best Time of Year: In summer, the graceful swallow-tailed kites roost in the hammock, and in the winter the hammock is a roost for black and turkey vultures. Many warblers feed in the hammock during migration. Buntings and hummingbirds are frequent in winter, and butterflies are common throughout the year. The bird feeders are frequented by painted and indigo buntings from October through April and white-winged doves year-round.

The 112-acre Castellow Hammock was established as an environmental education center in 1974 and boasts of a tropical hammock with more than 250 species of plants. Castellow Hammock is probably best known for its wintering painted buntings. People come from all over the country in the winter to watch and photograph these brilliantly colored birds. Hurricane Andrew appears to have improved the habitat for the buntings, which prefer more open areas than dense hammocks. Hummingbirds regularly visit from September to April. The park's bird list includes 126 species of resident and migratory birds, such as mangrove cuckoos, smooth-billed anis, scissor-tailed flycatchers, and purple martins. Wintering hummingbirds frequent the butterfly garden.

Butterfly-watchers will also find much to see in this densely vegetated hammock. More than 70 species of butterflies and skippers have been identified at and around Castellow. Many species (such as fulvous, gray, red-banded, and amethyst hairstreaks) are tropical and are found nowhere else in the United States.

Castellow was in the center of the worst winds of Hurricane Andrew. Damage to the hammock and visitor facilities was extreme. The County rebuilt the nature center after leveling the remnants. It took four years of intensive trail work and invasive-plant removal to reopen the trail.

Nature Center

The center includes environmental exhibits, classrooms, and a display of 61 species of native butterflies. Call for nature program schedule; naturalists also lead tours outside of Castellow Hammock Preserve.

Nature Trail

The self-guided trail through the hammock is 0.5 miles one way; rocky and narrow (not handicapped-accessible). Some trees likely to be seen along the trail are wild-tamarind, mastic, gumbo-limbo, pigeon-plum, paradise-tree, lancewood, and West Indian cherry. Look for limestone solution holes along the way.

DIRECTIONS
Preserve is south of Miami in Goulds, half-mile south of SW 216th Street.

CONTACT
Castellow Hammock Preserve
and Nature Center
22301 SW 162nd Avenue
Miami 33170
305-242-7688
www.miamidade.gov/parks/parks
/castello_hammock.asp

Ruddy daggerwing butterflies (orange with black markings) are found only in central and south Florida. They can be seen at Castellow Hammock.

Miami-Dade County Parks

Greynolds Park

Facilities: Nature trails, bird roost, guided birding, nature walks, field trips (305-948-2891 for reservations), nature center, bicycling paths, picnic tables, snack bar, children's playground, canoe, kayak and paddleboat rentals (weekends, holidays)

Activities: Birding, hiking, bicycling, paddling, picnicking

Admission: Entrance fee on weekends and holidays only

Hours: Open sunrise to sunset; office hours Monday–Friday 8:30 am–4:30 pm. Nature center open weekends and holidays. Call for schedule of guided walks.

Pets: Not allowed

South Florida Birding Trail: 96

Best Time of Year: March to April and October to November for warblers

A former rock quarry on the Oleta River within the urban confines of Miami, Greynolds Park has a special claim to fame. The 249-acre park was renowned for the water birds that nest on the mangrove islands in close proximity to the trails. Such species as great egret, great blue heron, tricolored heron, little blue heron, snowy egret, cattle egret, anhinga, and cormorant commonly nested here. Sometime in the 1980s, the rookery (nesting colony) collapsed for unknown reasons. It is still a good place to see wading birds.

Of further interest is the history of the scarlet ibis's introduction into the park. In the 1950s, a neighbor living next to the rookery imported scarlet ibis eggs from Trinidad and Surinam to place into the nests of the white ibises already nesting there. He hoped that the scarlet ibises would reside at Greynolds when they grew up and would be visible from his yard. The first batch of eggs failed, and a second batch was imported in the early 1960s. Some chicks survived and later mated with the white ibises. The resulting pink or orange offspring have been seen occasionally around south Florida since then.

The Lakeside Nature Trail circum-navigates the mangrove pond and islands where the wading birds roost. It is narrow and rocky, not handicapped-accessible; other trails, however, are accessible.

A bird checklist, containing more than 130 species, is available from the office. This is a good place to see the many introduced parrots and parakeets that have become established in the Miami area. Warblers pass through the park in large numbers during the spring and fall. Short-tailed, broad-winged, and other hawks are seen here. Spot-breasted orioles are found from March to October. Herons come to roost in the mangroves at dusk. At sunrise, they'll be off again to their favorite feeding sites in nearby marshes. Yellow-crowned night herons and great blue herons nest in the spring.

DIRECTIONS
From Exit 14 of I-95, go east on NE Miami Gardens Drive about 2.5 miles. Turn right onto West Dixie Hwy for 0.7 miles. Another entrance is on NE 22nd Ave., just south of Miami Gardens Drive.

CONTACT
Greynolds Park
17530 West Dixie Highway
North Miami Beach 33160
305-945-3425
www.miamidade.gov/parks/parks/greynolds.asp

Matheson Hammock Park

Facilities: Nature trails, bicycle path, picnic tables with grills, boat ramp and canoe launch, canoe and kayak rentals, snack bar, wading and swimming beaches, large marina

Activities: Walking, birding, bicycling, picnicking, boating, paddling, swimming

Admission: Trails and picnic areas free, all others are fee areas

Hours: Open sunrise–sunset

Pets: Not allowed

South Florida Birding Trail: 100

Best Time of Year: March and April, September and October for migrating warblers and small land birds in the hammock

When William J. Matheson donated 84 acres to Dade County in 1930, he stipulated that the hammock be used as a botanical park for the public's benefit and that it be preserved in its natural state. The park now covers 629 acres of land, much of which is left natural.

This park along Biscayne Bay has two sections, a water recreation-based fee area (free for bicyclists) and a land-based non-fee natural area. The water recreation, which contains a full-facility marina, restaurant, and swimming areas, is frequently crowded. The land-based area has picnic areas, playing fields, and nature trails. If you happen to be in the area (to visit adjacent Fairchild Tropical Garden, for example) with a little extra time, the West Hammock Trail is worth a short side trip.

The water sports area has little to offer an exploring naturalist. Go instead to the non-fee picnic area for the few foot trails off the beaten path. The parking lot is a few hundred yards north of Fairchild Tropical Garden. Near the parking lot are the picnic tables around which spot-breasted orioles and hill mynas may be seen. Several small ponds surrounded by red mangroves occasionally harbor alligators and wading birds. The East Hammock Trail is a short, paved trail with interpretive signs.

The better trail is on the other side of Old Cutler Road in a remnant West Indian hardwood hammock. The West Hammock Trail passes through mostly native vegetation. The trail was rebuilt and improved after Hurricane Andrew. Much invasive plant removal has been accomplished and a trail guide identifies hammock plants. Look for white-crowned pigeons and Caribbean vagrants.

DIRECTIONS

From Exit 20 of Florida's Turnpike, go east on SR 94 (Kendall Dr.) for 7.8 miles. Turn right on Old Cutler Rd. and go 0.6 miles to park on left.

CONTACT

Matheson Hammock Park
9610 Old Cutler Road
Miami 33156
305-665-5475
www.miamidade.gov/Parks/Parks/
matheson_beach.asp

Miami-Dade County Parks

Navy Wells Pineland Preserve

Facilities: Hiking trails, no visitor facilities

Activities: Hiking, birding

Admission: Free

Hours: Sunrise–sunset

Pets: Not allowed

Best Time of Year: Winter and spring for weather and birding

Scattered throughout Miami-Dade County are remnant patches of pinelands. The largest patch outside of Everglades National Park survived because it happened to be perched atop an important water wellfield. In 1940, the U.S. Navy built an 18-inch diameter pipeline to supply the naval station on Boca Chica, near Key West. The source of the water was a well in Florida City on the mainland 130 miles away. The Florida Keys Aqueduct Authority bought water from the Navy to sell to civilian Keys residents. The 310-acre slash pine preserve surrounds the original wellfield compound. The aqueduct has since been purchased by the Aqueduct Authority and enlarged to meet the growing need for water in the Keys. The Miami-Dade County Park and Recreation Department now owns most of the land around the wellfield.

Walk through the gate to the left of the parking area and along the

Slash pines at Navy Wells Pineland Preserve

grassy firebreak roads throughout the preserve. The surficial limestone bedrock makes this a rough area to walk around, complete with frequent poisonwood trees.

Swallow-tailed kites may be seen from March to August. Look for coontie, the ancient cycad. The starchy root of the coontie was a staple food of the Seminoles and Miccosukees. The larvae of the Florida atala (*Eumaeus atala*), a threatened tropical butterfly, depends on the coontie for food as well. The adult butterflies feed on the nectar of palmettos and other flowers. The pineland croton is the host plant of the Florida leafwing (*Anaea floridalis*) larvae. This rare butterfly is endemic to the pinelands of southern Florida. Other butterflies include Bartram's scrub-hairstreak (*Strymon acis*), tropical buckeye (*Junonia genoveva*), and variegated fritillary (*Euptoieta claudia*).

Other plants of special interest include silver palm, tetrazygia, and pineland jacquemontia. Forty-six species of grasses sprout beneath the pines in this preserve, including the south Florida endemic gamagrass.

DIRECTIONS

From Krome Ave. or US 1 in Florida City, turn west onto SW 344th St. (Palm Drive). Turn left at 192nd Ave. (at "Robert Is Here" Fruit Stand) and drive 0.5 miles. Turn right at the sign "Water Treatment Facility."

CONTACT

Navy Wells Pineland Preserve
SW 354th Street
Florida City
305-755-7800
www.miamidade.gov/parks

Oleta River State Park

Facilities: Canoe, kayak, and bicycle rentals, primitive youth-campground, primitive rental cabins

Activities: Paddling, swimming, bicycling, picnicking

Admission: State Park fee

Hours: 8 am to sunset

Pets: Allowed except on beach

Best Time of Year: Winter for manatee sightings

The location right in Miami makes Oleta crowded year-round. This is the largest urban wilderness park in Florida (1,032 acres). Most folks come to picnic, some come to swim in the lagoon, and some come to bicycle on the trails. The persistent urban canoeist will find a surprisingly good maze of mangrove-lined waterways to explore. The park is at the northern end of Biscayne Bay and is named for the Oleta River, which intersects the bay. This is the only reason the park is included here. The upland sections of the park are dominated by Australian-pine and other invasives.

Canoeing

Canoes and kayaks may be rented at the park's concession. Ask for their canoeing map. Canoes can stick to the protected lagoon waters or venture into Biscayne Bay (which is also the Intracoastal Waterway here) and then into the Oleta River, which is less than 2 miles away and less than 2 miles long (full round trip is approximately 7 miles). Mullet, tarpon, and snapper are present, as are brown pelicans, white ibises, bald eagles, herons, and egrets. Manatees, dolphins, and crocodiles may be seen.

Bicycling

Mountain bikers have 10 miles of short trails, and paved trails are available for road bikes.

DIRECTIONS

From I-95, take Exit 12B east (N. Miami Beach Blvd. (SR 826)), going 1.1 miles past US 1 (where road becomes Sunny Isles Blvd.) to entrance.

CONTACT

Oleta River State Park
3400 NE 163rd Street
North Miami 33160
305-919-1846
www.floridastateparks.org/oletariver/

Concession:
305-957-3040
www.bluemoonmiami.com

Palm Beach County Parks

For more information on Palm Beach County Parks contact Palm Beach County Parks and Recreation, 2700 6th Ave., South Lake Worth 33461-4799; 561-966-6600; www.co.palm-beach.fl.us/parks/.

10 Palm Beach County Parks

Green Cay Wetlands and Nature Center

Facilities: Nature center, boardwalk, gift shop, educational programs

Activities: Wildlife viewing

Admission: Free

Hours: Wildlife observation trails open year-round, 7 am–sunset; nature center open Tuesday–Friday 10 am–4:30 pm, Saturday 8:15 am–4:30 pm, Sunday 9:30 am–3 pm; closed Monday.

Pets: Not allowed

South Florida Birding Trail: 82

Best Time of Year: Winter and spring for weather and wildlife viewing

Green Cay Nature Center (containing live animal exhibits, lecture rooms, and gift shop) opened its doors in 2005. It high-lights the 100-acre manmade wetlands, the newer cousin of its neighbor, **Wakodahatchee Wetlands**. You can observe the wetlands wildlife from a 1.5-mile interpretive boardwalk across cypress swamps and cabbage palm hammocks. Waterfowl, gulls and terns, shorebirds, and wading birds (such as black-bellied whistling duck) may be seen.

DIRECTIONS
Located in Delray Beach, 2.2 miles north of Atlantic Ave. (SR 806) on Hagen Ranch Road, entrance on east side.

CONTACT
Green Cay Wetlands and Nature Center
12800 Hagen Ranch Road
Boynton Beach 33437
561-966-7000
www.pbcgov.com/parks/nature/green_cay_nature_center

Boardwalk at Green Cay Wetlands

Palm Beach County Parks

John Prince
Memorial Park

Facilities: Nature trails, bicycle-jogging path, campground

Activities: Hiking, bicycling, birding, boating, picnicking, camping

Admission: Free

Hours: Sunrise–sunset

Pets: Allowed on leash

Best Time of Year: No preference

Lake Osborne (338 acres) is the focus of the activities in this 726-acre park. The long, narrow lake (about 3 miles long) is a mecca for water birds such as limpkins, anhingas, moorhens, herons, and egrets. The limpkins are residents and have become accustomed to humans, so it is almost guaranteed that you'll see one if you walk around the shore. A 5-mile paved bicycle path circumvents the lake.

Nature Trails
The several short trails at the south end of the park (S. Congress Ave. entrance) have been restored by replacing nonnative plants with native species. This was a massive effort because many mature Australian-pines were felled. The endeavor was greatly aided by volunteer help from the local Audubon Society. Native plants that you may see are coreopsis, wax myrtle, coco-plum, cypress, wild-tamarind, and paradise-tree. The Custard Apple Trail (0.5 miles) has a concentration of pond-apple (also known as custard apple) trees in the wetland area.

Campground
Situated on an isolated spit of land mostly surrounded by water and accessible only through the campground gate, this 48-acre camping area is relatively quiet, especially for suburbia. It contains 266 recreational vehicle and tent sites, all with water and electric hookups and nearby showers. Some are on the waterfront. Reservations are accepted.

DIRECTIONS
From I-95, take Exit 63 (6th Ave. S) and go west less than a mile. Entrances are also at 2520 Lake Worth Road and 4759 S. Congress Ave.

CONTACT
John Prince Memorial Park
2700 6th Avenue South
Lake Worth 33461
561-582-7992

Palm Beach County Parks

Loggerhead Park and Marinelife Center

Facilities: Short hiking trails, overlook tower, and picnic area in park; museum, gift shop, and turtle nesting and rehabilitation programs in Marinelife Center

Activities: Hiking and picnicking in park

Admission: Free

Hours: Park open sunrise–sunset; Marinelife Center open Monday–Saturday 10 am–5 pm, Sunday Noon–4 pm, closed major holidays

Pets: Not allowed in Marinelife Center or on beach; allowed in Loggerhead Park on leash

Best Time of Year: June and July when the sea turtles nest, if you can arrange to go on a night walk; otherwise, no preference

This is a good destination for anyone interested in marine life. Allow a few hours for the park trails and marinelife center.

Loggerhead Park (17 acres) is named for the loggerhead sea turtles that come ashore every summer to lay their eggs on Juno Beach. In 2009, 4,017 loggerhead nests were found, as well as 335 green turtle and 316 leatherback nests. This park has a 2-acre coastal scrub area preserved as relatively natural with a network of sandy trails. The overlook tower allows a 360-degree coastal view. Plants include coral bean, prickly-pear cactus, saw palmetto, and poisonwood. Look for land crab holes and gopher tortoise burrows. Look for shorebirds and sea turtle tracks on the beach.

On the park property is Marinelife Center, a nonprofit educational and conservation facility dedicated to protecting marine creatures, particularly sea turtles. The center maintains large outdoor rehabilitation tanks to care for injured turtles. Indoor museum exhibits highlight different types of marine and non-marine life. Many hands-on activities for children make this a great afternoon outing for youngsters. Special school group tours can be arranged.

Marinelife Center is small but packed with exhibits in every corner. The live tanks have small sharks and turtles, crabs, sea urchins, and other local marine creatures. Kids do much of the volunteer work of caring for the rehabilitating animals. From April to October each year, the volunteer staff conducts counts of sea turtle nests on the adjacent 8-mile stretch of beach. Turtle nesting watches for the public are held several nights a week during June and July; call for reservations. Lectures are held in winter for adults.

DIRECTIONS

From Exit 83 of I-95, go about 4.5 miles east on Donal Ross Rd. Turn left onto US 1. The park is 0.3 miles north of Donald Ross Road.

CONTACT

Loggerhead Park
14200 US 1
Juno Beach 33408
561-966-6600
www.pbcgov.com/parks/locations/loggerhead.htm

Marinelife Center
561-627-8280
www.marinelife.org

Palm Beach County Parks

Okeeheelee Park and Nature Center

Facilities: Nature center, nature trails, bicycle and jogging path

Activities: Birding, picnicking, bicycling, wildlife viewing

Admission: Free

Hours: Nature center open Tuesday–Friday 10 am–4:30 pm, Saturday 8:15 am–4:30 pm, Sunday 10 am–4:30 pm; closed Mondays and major holidays; trails open sunrise–sunset daily

Pets: Not allowed on trails or in nature center, allowed elsewhere in the park

Best Time of Year: Winter and spring for weather and wildlife viewing

DIRECTIONS
Take I-95 Exit 49 (Forest Hill Blvd.) west about 5 miles.

CONTACT
Okeeheelee Park and Nature Center
7715 Forest Hill Boulevard
West Palm Beach 34413

General:
561-966-6600

Nature Center:
561-233-1400

Most of the 1,700-acre park is reclaimed from a shellrock quarry. Most is developed as multi-use, but 100 acres were set aside as a natural area, managed with prescribed burns and invasive plant control. It has grown into a lovely setting of native pines and wetlands. Several miles of trails and a nature center attract visitors.

The nature center has natural history displays, live animal exhibits, and provides programs for all ages. The 2.5 miles of trails twist through pine flatwoods and wetland habitats. The Pine Trail and Cypress Trails (totaling one mile) are paved and the others are shellrock.

Palm Beach County Parks

Riverbend Park

Facilities: Bicycling, hiking, and equestrian trails; canoe, kayak, and bicycle rentals

Activities: Hiking, bicycling, horseback riding, paddling, picnicking

Admission: Free

Hours: Park open sunrise–sunset daily; rental concession open weekdays 9 am–5 pm (closed Tuesday–Wednesday), weekends 8 am–5 pm

Pets: Not allowed

Best Time of Year: Water level is higher in summer, which is better for paddling

The 680-acre park is situated on the Loxahatchee River and provides recreational access to it. The Loxahatchee River is a nationally designated Wild and Scenic River (the first so-designated river in Florida) that winds through subtropical cypress and mangrove swamps and empties into Jupiter Inlet. Pond-apple trees, orchids, and ferns also line the tannin-stained waters. The skeletal ghosts of the cypress trees and cabbage palms are evidence of the increase in the river's salinity. Red mangroves encroach farther upstream each year as the line of fresh water recedes and the salt water intrudes. This is caused by channelization and diversion of fresh water upstream for drainage.

About four miles between Riverbend Park and Jonathan Dickinson State Park in Martin County is the landmark destination of Trapper Nelson's cabin. Before he died in 1968, Trapper Nelson, known as the "Wild Man of Loxahatchee," lived off the land without electricity in his self-built cabin. The

Loxahatchee River at Riverbend Park

cabin is on the highest land along the river. He trapped otters and raccoons for pelts. He planted fruit trees and kept penned gopher tortoises for food. He earned money by housing and feeding river-going travelers. His homestead is now maintained by Jonathan Dickinson State Park and is a popular stop by canoeists. A ranger is often present to give short tours.

Canoe Outfitters of Florida provides complete canoeing service for the 8.5-mile trip downstream to Jonathan Dickinson State Park, including the return bus shuttle. Allow 5–6 hours for paddling one-way with a stop. Canoeists planning to return by bus should enter the water by 10 am. You can paddle upstream for the return if you prefer. Independent wanderers can paddle with their own canoes and kayaks and put in later in the day. The trip downstream is approximately 8 miles and of moderate difficulty. Two water control structures necessitate minor pull-throughs, depending on water levels.

Otters, raccoons, bobcats, ospreys, bald eagles, wading birds, and alligators live along the river. Turtles frequently bask on fallen logs in midstream, alluding to the source of the river's name "Loxahatchee," which means River of Turtles in the native tongue. Peninsula cooters, softshells, and Florida snapping turtles are common.

DIRECTIONS
Take SR 706 (W. Indiantown Road) for 1.5 miles west of the Turnpike (Exit 116 West) or I-95 (Exit 87b).

CONTACT
Riverbend Park
8900 W. Indiantown Road
Jupiter 33478
561-966-6617
www.pbcgov.com/parks/riverbend

Concession:
Canoe Outfitters of Florida
561-746-7053 or
toll-free 888-272-1257
www.canoeskayaksflorida.com

Palm Beach County Parks

South County Regional Park

Facilities: Nature center, short trails, boardwalk, observation tower, butterfly garden, guided walks, and programs; multi-use recreation

Activities: Nature viewing

Admission: Free

Hours: Trails open sunrise–sunset; nature center open 10 am–4:30 pm Tuesday–Sunday, closed Mondays

Pets: Allowed on leash

Best Time of Year: No preference

This 848-acre park opened in 1996 with numerous ball fields, a 2.8-mile bike path, and a nature center complex. The 3,000-square-foot nature center contains an exhibit area, classrooms, and amphitheater. A 0.6-mile boardwalk penetrates a 40-acre cypress forest. Special group programs are available. Later phases will include a recreational vehicle and tent campground, equestrian facilities, and an aquatic complex.

The Daggerwing Nature Center has exhibits, live native reptile displays, and an auditorium. The boardwalk winds through a hardwood hammock with red maples, strangler figs, pond-apples, and wild coffee. The ferns are prolific, including strap, resurrection, leather,

sword, and giant sword. The 40-foot observation tower overlooks part of the hammock and some playing fields. You may see bobcats, wood storks, anhingas, alligators, and other wetland animals.

The nature center's name comes from the ruddy daggerwing butterfly (*Marpesia petreus*) that is found in the hammock along the boardwalk. This orange butterfly with long dagger-like extensions on its wings is found in hardwood hammocks of southern Florida. The larvae feed on strangler fig leaves and the adults feed on sea-grape nectar. You may also see zebra longwings, atalas, and polydamas swallowtails.

DIRECTIONS
From Exit 75 of Florida's Turnpike, go west on Glades Road (SR 808) for 2.9 miles to Cain Blvd.; turn right, go 0.4 miles to Park Access Road, then left. Nature Center Complex entrance is 0.4 miles on left.

CONTACT
South County Regional Park
11200 Park Access Road
West Boca Raton 33498
561-629-8760
www.pbcparks.com/nature

Palm Beach County Parks

Wakodahatchee Wetlands

Facilities: Wildlife observation boardwalk

Activities: Wildlife viewing

Admission: Free

Hours: Sunrise to sunset daily

Pets: Not allowed; service animals may be asked for documentation

South Florida Birding Trail: 83

Best Time of Year: Winter and spring for birding

DIRECTIONS

From Florida's Turnpike: Exit at Atlantic Avenue (exit 81). Drive east 1.7 miles to Jog Road. Turn left and drive north 1.5 miles to entrance.

From I-95: Exit at Atlantic Avenue (SR 806, exit 52), go west 3.5 miles to Jog Road and north 1.5 miles to entrance.

CONTACT
Wakadahatchee Wetlands
13026 Jog Road
Delray Beach 33446
561-493-6000 (weekdays)
www.pbcgov.com/waterutilities/
wakodahatchee/location.htm

This 50-acre site is a manmade wetland, which is what "Wakodahatchee" means in Seminole. The Palm Beach County Water Utilities Department pumps highly treated water into the wetland, which then filters additional nutrients from the water. The 0.75-mile boardwalk gives a good vantage for viewing wetland wildlife. Different sections of the wetland were designed as different habitat types of varying water levels. Look for black-bellied whistling-ducks, least bitterns, purple gallinules, and limpkins. Spot-breasted orioles are occasionally in the area. During winter, look for wintering ducks, American bitterns, sora and Virginia rails, and Wilson's snipe. Also look for smooth-billed anis, wood storks, white and glossy ibises, herons, egrets, gulls, terns, and songbirds. More than 140 bird species have been recorded here. Alligators, frogs, turtles, and other wetland vertebrates can also be found.

Solid Waste Authority Greenway Trail System

Facilities: Hiking and bicycling trails

Activities: Hiking, wildlife viewing, bicycling

Admission: Free

Hours: Daily dawn to dusk; bird nesting area (rookery) closed from February–September

Pets: Not allowed

Best Time of Year: Winter and spring for weather and wildlife viewing

The Solid Waste Authority (SWA) set aside 300 acres for a conservation area. Before the plant was built, a roost of 372 snail kites was found in a drought year on the site intended for the plant. Modifications were made to the construction plans to keep the roost area intact. Thousands of wading birds nest in a small area (rookery) each spring and summer including snail kites and wood storks. Herons, egrets, spoonbills, ibises, and sandhill cranes are frequently seen, as well as otters, bobcats, and alligators.

Trails

Trails at the northern entrance include the Loop Trail (1.9 miles) and the Malachite Trail (0.4 miles); from the south entrance is Rookery Loop (2 miles, seasonal closure); and from either parking lot is the Dragonfly Trail (0.67 miles). The area is adjacent to **Grassy Waters Preserve**, and the Owahee Trail (16.5 miles) is accessible from both parking lots here.

DIRECTIONS

Southern entrance: From I-95, take Exit 74 to 45th St. (CR 702) westbound. Go a little more than 3 miles to end, passing Jog Road.

Northern entrance: Follow directions above to Jog Road, turn right onto Jog and go about 1.5 miles north to SWA Administration parking on left.

CONTACT

Palm Beach County Solid Waste Authority
7501 North Jog Road
West Palm Beach 33412
561-640-4000
www.swa.org/SWAGreen/swa_greenway
_trail_system.htm

28 Southern Glades Wildlife and Environmental Area

Facilities: Hiking and bicycling trails, no visitor facilities

Activities: Hiking, bicycling, wildlife viewing, hunting, fishing

Admission: Free

Hours: Day-use only

Pets: Allowed

South Florida Birding Trail: 105

Best Time of Year: October through April to catch the migrating and overwintering birds. From June to September, wildlife may use the levee roads as corridors, since everything else may be submerged. Be prepared for mosquitoes. Since this is a hunting area, wear bright clothing in the autumn and winter.

The southern Everglades includes much more than the area within Everglades National Park boundaries. One of the adjacent areas has been made available to hikers. The Southern Glades Wildlife and Environmental Area (SGWEA) is state-owned land under the administration of the South Florida Water Management District. It was purchased through the "Save Our Rivers" and "Conservation and Recreation Lands" programs for recreational use. The Florida Fish and Wildlife Conservation Commission enforces the hunting regulations, but the Florida Department of Environmental Protection and the South Florida Water Management District regulate other aspects.

The 32,000 acres contain canals and levees that were created long ago to drain the Everglades and provide flood protection. The dominant habitat is sawgrass marsh with bay heads and cypress domes interspersed.

The levees are excellent for wildlife viewing. With careful searching, you may see some of the endangered animals that have been reported in the SGWEA: Cape Sable seaside sparrows, snail kites, and wood storks. Also watch for the threatened crocodiles and eastern indigo snakes, bald eagles, least terns, and sandhill cranes. Other animals you may see are bobcats, river otters, white-tailed deer, limpkins, and roseate spoonbills.

Besides sawgrass, some trees and plants to look for are wax myrtles, redbay, sweet bay, coco-plum, paradise-tree, butterfly orchid, worm-vine orchid, and twisted air plant. Hunting, fishing, and frogging are permitted. Because this is not a true Wildlife Management Area but an area created for controlled multiple recreational and educational uses, there are more hunting regulations.

Northern Access Trail

A 13-mile shellrock trail called the Southern Glades Trail allows hikers, bicyclists, and equestrians. No hunting is allowed along the trail. The trail is on a levee and follows the C-111 canal south to US 1. Bring plenty of drinking water. For more information, call The Redlands Conservancy at 305-740-9007 or see www.miamidade.gov/greatparksummit/library/MPO_bp_sdgn_southernglades.pdf.

Southern Access Trails

Two trails, totaling 16 miles, are atop the levees paralleling the canals. The levees were built with the dredge material from the canals and are used as access to maintain the canals. Thus, no trails were cut to provide this recreational opportunity. The levees are 4–5 feet above the surrounding marsh, affording an open view and dry footing. The easternmost levee was leveled in 1996 as mitigation for the widening of US 1, so the trail that it formerly supported no longer exists.

The first trail can be found by driving west on SW 424th Street 1.8 miles from US 1. After a mile, the road is unpaved and rather narrow and rough. The trail is five miles long and suitable for all-terrain bicycles. The canal banks are overgrown, so the view is limited. The trail can also be reached from the southern end by driving on US 1 to MM 116.4 and turning east into the C-111 canal area (north side of the canal). Walk under the bridge and follow the canal west to the beginning of the trail. You may see a crocodile along this canal. The second trail, 4 miles long, is approximately 2 miles west of the first trail on SW 424 Street. The trails connect at their southern ends.

DIRECTIONS

Northern access: From US 1 in Florida City go west on SR 9336 for about 6.3 miles to left turn on SW 232 Ave. (Aerojet Road); go 0.8 miles south to "South Dade Greenway Network" sign.

Southern access: From SW 344th St. in Florida City go 5 miles south on US 1. Turn right on SW 424th St. (Work Camp Road).

CONTACT

Florida Fish and Wildlife Conservation Commission
561-625-5122
www.myfwc.com/recreation/WMASites_SouthernGlades_index.htm; or

South Florida Water Management District
866-433-6312
www.my.sfwmd.gov/portal/page/portal/pg_grp_sfwmd_landresources/pg_sfwmd_landresources_recopps_se_sglade

Stormwater Treatment Areas

New and unusual wildlife observation locations have been created in the Everglades since the 1990s. These Stormwater Treatment Areas, or STAs, are a group of marshes created as part of the Everglades restoration. The STA project was initiated in response to a lawsuit filed in 1988 by acting U.S. Attorney Dexter Lehtinen. Lehtinen sued the State on behalf of downstream federal waters (Everglades National Park and Loxahatchee National Wildlife Refuge), claiming that the State of Florida was ignoring its own water quality standards, particularly for the nutrient phosphorus. Excess phosphorus, originating from the fertilizer used on sugarcane and other crops on agricultural land south of Lake Okeechobee, was flowing into the Everglades. Excess phosphorus in the water causes an overgrowth of aquatic plants, which then shade out sunlight and steal oxygen from the water, thus suffocating fish.

Governor Lawton Chiles settled the case in 1991. The settlement required that six marshes be built to filter out the phosphorus and that farmers use less phosphorus or keep it from flowing downstream.

The STAs are situated downstream from the canals that carry water from the farm fields. The marshes were planted with cattails and other wetland plants that are known for absorbing phosphorus. As the water flows through the marshes, nutrients are reduced to a level more normal for the Everglades. The STAs, which mostly look like typical marshes, attract wading birds, shorebirds, frogs, alligators, turtles, snakes, bobcats, deer, and other wildlife. The STAs vary in their public access.

The STAs have no entrance fees, but there are few visitor facilities. For more information on all STAs call the South Florida Water Management District recreation line at 866-433-6312, in Florida 800-432-2045; or see www.sfwmd.gov/recreation. Only the STAs that are open for daily use are included here.

29 | STA 1 East
(6,562 acres)

Located in Wellington, Palm Beach County, northeast of A.R.M. Loxahatchee National Wildlife Refuge. From SR 7, go west on Southern Boulevard for about 9 miles to sign on left for C-51.

Public access for bicycling, hiking, wildlife observation, composting toilet. Open Friday, Saturday, Sunday, and Monday from sunrise–sunset. This STA is former agricultural land. On top of the levees are 5 miles of trails.

30 | STA 1 West
(6,670 acres)

Located in Wellington, Palm Beach County, northwest of A.R.M. Loxahatchee National Wildlife Refuge. From SR 7, go west on Southern Boulevard (SR 80) for 11.4 miles to CR 880. Turn left (south), cross green metal bridge, and continue south. Access entrance is on CR 880, 2.4 miles beyond the bridge. Look for brown recreation road signs.

Bicycling, paddling, hiking, wildlife viewing, 200-foot boardwalk, managed waterfowl and alligator hunts on certain weekends in fall, composting toilet. Open Friday, Saturday, Sunday, Monday from sunrise–sunset (except during hunting season—last weekend in September to November 15—when the area is closed to the public one day per weekend). There is a three-mile levee trail for hiking and bicycling. This STA is more marshlike than STA 1 East. Look for fulvous whistling ducks, roseate spoonbills, and wintering waterbirds. SFBT #48.

31 | STA 3 and 4
(16,772 acres)

Located in southwestern Palm Beach County. From US 27, go either 14 miles north of I-75 or 25 miles south of South Bay to a small paved road on the west side of US 27 at the L-5 Canal levee. Go west for 5 miles on the small road to the Harold A. Campbell Public Use Area on right.

Bicycling, paddling, hiking, wildlife viewing, boating, composting toilet. Open Friday, Saturday, Sunday, and Monday from sunrise to sunset. Boat ramp open 7 days a week. Follow the footbridge across the canal to 27 miles of perimeter canals. Paddlers should watch for motorboats. Bicyclists have about 4 miles of levee. These adjacent marshes are the largest constructed wetlands in the world. Note that this area is far from any developed areas.

Roseate Spoonbill in marsh at Harold A. Campbell Boat Launch in STA 3 and 4.

Water Conservation Areas

Around 800,000 acres of the historic Everglades outside of Everglades National Park are owned by the South Florida Water Management District as Water Conservation Areas (WCAs) 1, 2 and 3. A.R.M. Loxahatchee National Wildlife Refuge, which is managed by the U.S. Fish and Wildlife Service, contains Water Conservation Area 1 (147,000 acres); see **A.R.M. Loxahatchee National Wildlife Refuge** for more information. WCA 2 (134,400 acres) lies just south of Loxahatchee Refuge, and WCA 3 (584,700 acres) lies between WCA 2 and **Everglades National Park**. The conservation areas were created in the 1950s and 1960s by building levees and canals around them to control the surface water. They are now managed for multiple uses, including water storage and flood control, habitat protection, recreation, and hunting. WCAs 2 and 3 are managed by the Florida Fish and Wildlife Conservation Commission (FWC) as the Everglades and Francis S. Taylor Wildlife Management Areas. Hunting, frogging, and off-road vehicles are permitted. For more information, contact FWC at 561-625-5122.

Hiking, bicycling, and wildlife viewing are allowed on the levees. For example, hikers and bicyclists can travel the levee across WCA 2 from Sawgrass Recreation Area for 10.6 miles to the other side of the WCA at L-36. From L-36, hikers and bicyclists can then either go north for 8.8 miles on the L-36 levee to S-38 or south for 8.7 miles to Markham Park along the L-35A levee. People can leave a vehicle at either Sawgrass Recreation Area or Markham Park and do the trip one way. The levees have no shelter, so hiking long distances is not suggested in hot weather.

Boating and levee accesses are found at ramps along Alligator Alley, Tamiami Trail, and US 27. Some boat ramp locations along the eastern boundary:

34 **WCA 2:**

- At the west end of Loxahatchee Road (CR 827) in Palm Beach County (same area as Hillsboro Recreation Area of A.R.M. Loxahatchee NWR);
- Markham Park in western Broward County (I-595, Exit 1B, then west on SR 84);
- Sawgrass Recreation Area (entrances 2 miles and 6 miles north of SR 84 on SR 27).

35 **WCA 3:**

- Holiday Park in Broward County (concession) at west end of Griffin Road, off US 27, about 6 miles south of I-75 (954-434-8111);
- Milton E. Thompson Park and Campground in Miami-Dade County, 16665 NW 177 Ave., Miami 33178; 305-821-5122. 2 miles south of the intersection of US 27 and NW 177th (SR 997).

VI NATURAL AREAS OF SOUTHWESTERN FLORIDA

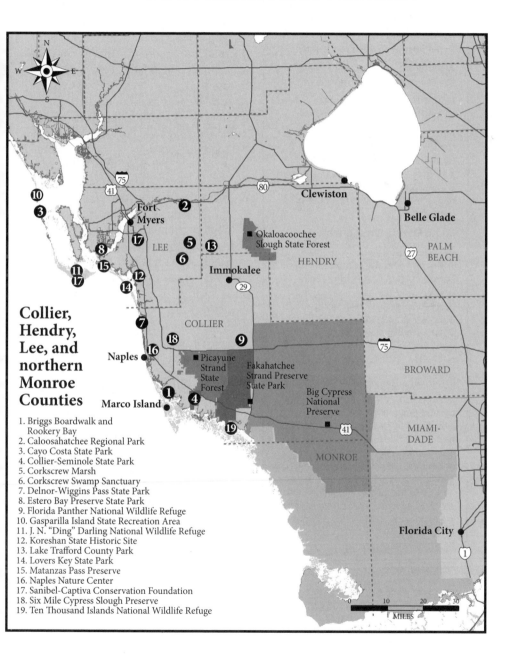

Collier,
Hendry,
Lee, and
northern
Monroe
Counties

1. Briggs Boardwalk and
   Rookery Bay
2. Caloosahatchee Regional Park
3. Cayo Costa State Park
4. Collier-Seminole State Park
5. Corkscrew Marsh
6. Corkscrew Swamp Sanctuary
7. Delnor-Wiggins Pass State Park
8. Estero Bay Preserve State Park
9. Florida Panther National Wildlife Refuge
10. Gasparilla Island State Recreation Area
11. J. N. "Ding" Darling National Wildlife Refuge
12. Koreshan State Historic Site
13. Lake Trafford County Park
14. Lovers Key State Park
15. Matanzas Pass Preserve
16. Naples Nature Center
17. Sanibel-Captiva Conservation Foundation
18. Six Mile Cypress Slough Preserve
19. Ten Thousand Islands National Wildlife Refuge

Big Cypress National Preserve

Facilities: Visitor center, scenic drives, hiking trails, interpretive programs, campgrounds

Activities: Hiking, paddling, camping

Admission: Free entrance; free primitive campsites, fee for most campsites

Hours: Visitor center open daily 9 am to 4:30 pm, closed Christmas

Pets: Not allowed on any hiking trails; must be leashed and may not be left unattended anywhere; allowed in campgrounds, picnic areas, and pullouts along the paved scenic drives; may be walked on roads or in parking lots

South Florida Birding Trail: 77

Best Time of Year: Hiking the Florida Trail is better in the winter and spring (January–April). The summer rains usually flood the trail, and hiking is reduced to slogging through mosquitoes with nary a dry spot to pitch a tent. Wildlife viewing from a car is good year-round on the Loop Road, but heavy rainfalls cause some road flooding in summer. Hunting seasons (waterfowl, small game, turkey, archery) run from September to April, but the main big game season (deer and feral hog) occurs during the period from mid-November to January 1 and is not a good time to wander around the preserve. Many hunters park their cars along the Loop Road and set out from there. Call the visitor center in advance for local trail flooding conditions and hunting seasons. If you hike during deer season, wear bright orange clothing.

Other: Because this is a national preserve, visitor facilities are intentionally minimal. No lodging or food facilities; nearest food service is at Ochopee (21 miles west).

Although Big Cypress is part of the National Park Service, it is a national preserve, and thus has fewer restrictions than a national park. The preserve was established partly as a buffer to Everglades National Park and partly for its own ecological and recreational value. An immense international airport and satellite city were almost built on this land in the early 1970s to ease the burden on Miami International Airport. Cypress logging, cattle ranching, and oil drilling added to the pressures. Environmentalists blocked the original plan but had to settle for a training airport north of Tamiami Trail, the Dade-Collier Training Airport (where commercial pilots practice take-offs and landings).

The National Park Service acquired 570,000 acres in 1974 but had to make concessions to landowners. Concessions included owner-retained hunting camps, off-road vehicle access (such as airboats and swamp buggies), hunting, and environmentally safeguarded mining and oil-drilling. The preserve now totals 729,000 acres.

The name "Big Cypress" refers to the extent of the cypress strands, rather than the size of the trees. Most of the preserve consists of bald-cypress, and very little is old-growth. Pinelands and marshes comprise much of the remaining preserve.

Most people see the preserve only from the pavement of Tamiami Trail or Alligator Alley, both of which bisect it. The **Florida Trail**, an unpaved hiking trail that stretches for 1,400 miles across the state (but not yet completed), has its southern terminus here. Six species of endangered animals can be found within the preserve: wood stork, snail kite, red-cockaded woodpecker, Cape Sable seaside sparrow, West Indian manatee,

Cypress-lined Florida Trail in Big Cypress National Preserve

and Florida panther. The preserve is the last stronghold in extreme south Florida for the red-cockaded woodpecker and the panther, both of which still breed there.

Visitor Center

At the Oasis Visitor Center, you can obtain backcountry information for camping (permits not required), permits for off-road vehicles (required and available here), and hiking information. Nature books and videos are sold. An observation deck overlooks alligators, wading birds, and other marsh wildlife. A butterfly garden is maintained.

Camping

The Park Service maintains three campgrounds along US 41: from east to west, they are Midway, Monument Lake (closed mid-April to late August), and Burns Lake. Self-sufficient camper vehicles and tents are suitable, and the maximum stay is 10 days. Burns Lake is primitive (not even water); call the park for months that it is open. Along Loop Road are two primitive campgrounds. A dump station and potable water are found at Dona Drive on Tamiami Trail (fee charged). Reservations are not accepted for any campsite.

Tent camping is allowed along the Florida Trail. The safest way to ensure having a dry place to sleep is to carry a lightweight string hammock. The two primitive campsites designated on the official map are on higher ground, but they have no shelter or cooking grill. Campfires are permitted using deadwood found on the ground. No source of drinking water is guaranteed along the trail, so bring your own potable water or methods to purify water.

Hiking Trails

The southern terminus of well-known Florida Trail that stretches northward to the Florida panhandle is at Big Cypress. Tamiami Trail (US 41) bisects the trail. The northern section of the trail (from Oasis north to I-75) is about 29.7 miles long (www.floridatrail.org/Trails/south-florida/BigCypressN.html). The southern section starts at Oasis and goes south to the Loop Road for 8.3 miles. The north section is wet until middle or late winter, the south section year-round. See www.floridatrail.org/Trails/southflorida/BigCypressS.html for more information on the Florida Trail.

From the Oasis Visitor Center, the northern section of the trail leads north through cypress, pinelands, marshes, and hardwood hammocks. Even in the dry season, parts of the trail can be wet. Off-road vehicles are permitted to cross the trail but may not traverse it. Watch for deer, feral hogs, bald eagles, swallow-tailed kites and Everglade snail kites, alligators, and possibly even a Florida panther. About four miles north of Oasis is a colony of endangered red-cockaded woodpeckers in a stand of pines. Two primitive campsites are available along the trail (see "Camping" above). One campsite is 6.9 miles north of Oasis. The other is 9.8 miles north of the first one. A loop day- or overnight-hike of 13 miles can be done from the visitor center to the first campsite. Let a ranger know your intentions if you're leaving your car parked overnight. You can also access this section of the trail at the north end and hike south; the access from I-75 is located at a rest area and recreation access point near mile marker 63. Coming from the north, the nearest campsite is 13 miles.

The southern section of the Florida Trail is on the south side of US 41, across from Oasis in an area known as the Loop Road Unit. Look directly across from the eastern entrance to the visitor center parking lot to find this narrow trail. This 8.3-mile section is better for day hikes because off-road vehicles are not permitted anywhere in the Loop Road Unit. This beautiful section of trail is resplendent with bromeliad-festooned bald-cypress trees shading the way.

Scenic Drives
Loop Road
Another way to see the southern part of the Preserve is by driving the Loop Road—a 26-mile stretch of narrow road between Forty-Mile Bend (near the Tamiami Ranger Station) and Monroe Station on the Tamiami Trail. The nine easternmost miles (east of the Environmental Education Center) are paved and gentle on city cars. West of there, however, the road is pockmarked with potholes and occasional puddles, so expect to average about 15 mph. That means it may take over an hour to drive the unimproved section. Add a little extra time for stopping to view wildlife.

Although the Loop Road is entirely within preserve boundaries, it is a county road (the only Monroe County road on the mainland—the rest are on the Keys), and you will see homes of people that live along the road. Please respect their privacy.

Aside from the homes, the road goes through some wild country, and you may see otters, bobcats, wild turkeys, snakes, wading birds, purple gallinules, sandhill cranes, and rarely, a panther. Just west of Pinecrest is an environmental education center for Everglades National Park. Its main function is to teach local school children, so there is nothing of interest to the drop-in visitor.

The short Hammock Nature Trail (on the north side of the road, opposite the education center gate) leads to an old whiskey still and is open to visitors. The trail can be covered in a leisurely 15 minutes (not handicapped-accessible). Look for strap fern, white stopper, and gumbo-limbo.

This road is worth the trip if you have the time and a car that can take potholes. In the summer, the road may be flooded, so call ahead to the visitor center for conditions. At any time of the day or night you'll probably see something interesting. If you go at night, make sure your car is in good operating condition.

Turner River Road
This unpaved, graded county road (CR 839) is worth driving for wildlife viewing. It is located 14.5 miles west of the visitor center and 4.1 miles east of Big Cypress Headquarters (turn north at the H.P. Williams Roadside Park). It runs straight north for about 18 miles, and a borrow canal, which provided the fill for the road, runs parallel the entire length. This road is not likely to flood but can get dusty or muddy. White ibises roost in the trees beside the canal. Panthers still roam this area, and the lucky person may catch a glimpse of one. An alternate loop route (also unpaved) is to drive north from Tamiami Trail for 7.1 miles, turn left at Upper Wagonwheel Road (CR837) for 3 miles, then left at Birdon Road (CR 841). This brings you back to Tamiami Trail.

Paddling
(also see Paddling under **Everglades National Park** – Everglades City)

Turner River
This river can be canoed or kayaked downstream for 8.5 miles to Chokoloskee Island. The roadside launch is at the bridge on Tamiami Trail, 0.5 miles west of H.P. Williams Roadside Park. You can launch on the east side of the bridge. Because of the lack of parking, it's best to park your vehicle at the Roadside Park.

The river winds through a variety of habitats, from freshwater cypress swamps to saltwater mangroves, including tunnel-like mangroves. Because of the many twists, turns, and tributaries, use of a nautical chart is recommended, or at the least, a map from the visitor center or ranger station. The trip downstream takes 5–6 hours. Although the current is generally slow, many people opt to do the trip one way and park a vehicle in Chokoloskee.

Halfway Creek Canoe Trail
This 7.5-mile trail starts at the canoe launch at the Preserve Headquarters on Seagrape Drive (off of US 41, about 2.5 miles east of SR 29) and ends at Everglades National Park's Gulf Coast Visitor Center. The first mile or so is on a canal, then mangroves close in on Halfway Creek and alternate with open sawgrass, gradually changing to brackish water. The creek emerges onto the open water of Chokoloskee Bay for a short distance. A loop around the Barron River is an option for returning to the canoe launch without going to the bay. This trail has markers to accompany the map, so obtain the map at the visitor center.

DIRECTIONS
The Oasis Visitor Center is on Tamiami Trail (US 41), 37 miles west of Krome Avenue (SR 997) and 21 miles east of SR 29. The preserve headquarters is on US 41 in Ochopee, 18 miles west of the visitor center. The eastern preserve boundary is 25 miles west of Krome Avenue on US 41 and the western boundary is at SR 29.

CONTACT
Big Cypress National Preserve
33100 Tamiami Trail East
Ochopee 34141
239-695-2000
www.nps.gov/bicy

Visitor Center:
239-695-1201

Briggs Boardwalk and Rookery Bay

Facilities: Environmental learning center, nature trails, boardwalk, guided paddling and boat tours, interpretive programs, boat ramp

Activities: Paddling, hiking, wildlife viewing

Admission: Free for walking and paddling trails; entrance fee for learning center

Hours: Learning center open Monday–Saturday 9 am-4 pm, closed Saturday from May through October; boardwalk, trails, and boat ramp area open dawn to dusk

Pets: Not allowed on boardwalk or in learning center

Best time of year: November to April

Other: Due to the location of Briggs Boardwalk within Rookery Bay National Estuarine Research Reserve, these entries are combined. Briggs Boardwalk is owned by The Conservancy of Southwest Florida.

When the estuary between Naples and Everglades National Park was threatened by development in 1964, a local conservation movement saved it temporarily. In 1977, the conservationists' efforts were rewarded when Rookery Bay was included in the National Estuarine Sanctuary Program. The 110,000-acre reserve is administered by NOAA and managed by the Florida Department of Environmental Protection.

Nestled within the Rookery Bay National Estuarine Research Reserve is a concentrated land access for public use. Most of this area is managed by the Reserve's Environmental Learning Center. Briggs Boardwalk is owned by The Conservancy of Southwest Florida.

The protected mangrove estuary is vital to the growth of sport fish, commercial fish, shrimps, crabs, oysters, and spiny lobsters. This estuary supports some of the most stable wading bird colonies remaining in south Florida. Visitors can see some of the reserve from the trails and from the water.

Rookery Bay
Environmental Learning Center
The 16,500-square-foot learning center houses exhibits, classrooms, laboratories, and an auditorium. A highlight is the 2,300-gallon aquarium of local estuary life. Special programs, lectures, and events are offered. The gift shop has environmental items.

Trails
Three short walking trails (each about 0.5 miles) are located at the end of Shell Island Road. Gopher tortoises and yellow rat snakes may be seen along the road to the trails. See the kiosk at trail heads for trail map. The Monument Trail starts behind a gate on the left side of the boat ramp and follows a roadbed to a monument dedicated to local conservationists. There are no interpretive signs and much of the roadside vegetation is nonnative, the result of human disturbance. The Catclaw Trail turns off near the beginning of the Monument Trail. Trees you'll see are saffron-plum, white stopper, white indigo-berry, red mangrove, and catclaw (for which the trail was named). The Shell Mound Trail starts on the right side of the boat ramp.

The 0.5-mile Snail Trail opened in 2011. It is accessible from the learning center on Tower Road or from the trails at the end of Shell Mound Road. The trail crosses Henderson Creek on a 440-foot-long pedestrian bridge completed in 2009. From the bridge, you may see manatees, sharks, and large fish.

Free guided walks on some of these trails are offered from November to May. Meet at the Rookery Bay Field Station, 0.25 miles before the end of Shell Island Road on the right (see sign "Guided Walks Meet Here"). Park there or by the boat ramp.

Paddling

Shell Island Road ends at a small boat ramp, where you can launch a canoe or kayak to paddle around the mangroves (between Shell Mound Trail and Monument Trail). The 2-mile, marked Shell Point Canoe Trail loop has a map and interpretive guide (see Rookery Bay's website). Guided paddling trips (kayaks provided) are offered for a fee several days a week from November to April. The trail goes through a lagoon and past shell mounds that were made by the Calusa Indians who formerly inhabited the region and depended on shellfish as staple foods. The shells were discarded over centuries to become the mounds (middens) along the way.

The Conservancy

Briggs Boardwalk

The 0.5-mile boardwalk starts at the right of the building. This self-guided loop passes through six ecosystems: oak scrub, wet hammock, brackish pond, fringe mangrove, fringe marsh, and pine flatwoods. A covered observation platform overlooks a brackish pond. You may see Florida scrub-jays which were probably not native to this area, but the scrub habitat is suitable and little re-mains elsewhere. Allow an hour for the boardwalk. From November to April, volunteers provide guided tours between 9 am and noon. Proceed at your own risk; maintenance is minimal. The future of the boardwalk is uncertain and may close within a few years of this printing.

Boat Tours

Sunset pontoon cruises are available most evenings from January to April around the mangrove islands. Volunteer guides are on board for these 2-hour trips. You may see dolphins, manatees, pelicans, and many species of herons and egrets.

DIRECTIONS

From Naples, take US 41 south for about 8 miles to SR 951 and turn right. Turn right again in 0.75 miles (Tower Road) for Rookery Bay Environmental Learning Center; or turn right in 2.8 miles to Shell Island Road. From here, the parking lot for Briggs Boardwalk is one mile; boat ramp, boat tour, paddling and hiking trails are at 2.5 miles.

CONTACT

For Briggs Boardwalk, pontoon boat tours:
The Conservancy of Southwest Florida
239-262-0304
www.conservancy.org.

For Rookery Bay Environmental Learning Center, hiking, canoeing:
300 Tower Road, Naples 34113
239-417-6310 x401
www.rookerybay.org

Cayo Costa State Park

Facilities: Tent sites and rental cabins, bicycle rentals, walking trails, beach

Activities: Tent camping, bicycling, hiking, paddling, swimming, snorkeling, shelling, picnicking

Admission: State Park fee; fee for ferry

Hours: 8 am to sunset

Pets: Not allowed overnight

South Florida Birding Trail: 27

Best Time of Year: Summer for boating and swimming, late summer for migrating birds, winter for shelling and camping

Put your walking shoes on, because you can't drive to or around this park. No roads span the Pine Island Sound to the 2,426-acre pristine park, which still resembles its appearance 500 years ago. The park includes parts of three islands: LaCosta, North Captiva, and Punta Blanca. LaCosta contains the docks, campground, and trails. Shelling is popular on the nine miles of sandy beaches as it is on all the barrier islands in the area. The habitat includes pines, oak-palm hammocks, and mangroves. This is a popular stop for southbound shorebirds in August and September.

Five walking trails lace the north end of the main island. Sea turtles nest in summer on the beaches. The campground contains tent sites and 12 rustic cabins. Reservations are accepted for the cabins. Look for black skimmers, American oystercatchers, magnificent frigatebirds, ospreys, and smaller birds in the trees. Cayo Costa is a marked stop on the **Great Calusa Blueway** Paddling Trail.

DIRECTIONS
Park is accessible only by private boat or ferry. Commercial ferries include Tropic Star of Pine Island, Pineland Marina, 13921 Waterfront Drive, Pineland 33945; 239-283-0015; and Kingfisher Cruise Lines in Punta Gorda; 941-639-0969.

CONTACT
Cayo Costa State Park
880 Belcher Road
Boca Grande 33921
941-964-0375
www.floridastateparks.org/cayocosta

Collier County Parks

For more information on Collier County Parks contact Collier County Department of Parks and Recreation, 15000 Livingston Road, Naples, FL 34109; 239-252-4000; www.colliergov.net/Index.aspx?page=112.

---

13 **Collier County Parks**

Lake Trafford County Park

Facilities: Boat launch, picnic tables, pier

Activities: Canoeing, kayaking, picnicking

Admission: Free; no boat launch fee

Hours: 8 am to sunset

Pets: Allowed on leash

Best Time of Year: Winter and spring for weather and wildlife viewing

---

This park exists as access to Lake Trafford north of Immokalee. Since the shores of this large lake, almost four square miles, are relatively undeveloped, paddlers should find it a pleasant trip.

DIRECTIONS
From Immokalee, take SR 29 north 2 miles, turn left (west) on CR 890 (Lake Trafford Road), go to end (3.2 miles).

CONTACT
Lake Trafford County Park
6001 Lake Trafford Road
Immokalee 34142
239-252-4000

Ospreys may be seen at Lake Trafford, as well as other lakes and along the coasts.

---

4 Collier-Seminole State Park

Facilities: Self-guided nature trail, hiking and bicycling trails, interpretive center, canoe rentals, boating and boat ramp, guided boat tours, campground

Activities: Hiking, bicycling, paddling, boating, primitive camping

Admission: State Park fee; fees for camping, boat tours, and canoe rentals

Hours: 8 am to sunset

Pets: Allowed in campground

South Florida Birding Trail: 74

Best Time of Year: November to April (the nonmosquito season)

Everywhere you turn in this part of the state you encounter the Barron Collier name. Barron Collier owned a million local acres in the 1920s. Part of his holdings included a rare stand of native royal palm trees. Collier reserved this stand for a park that became a state park in 1947. Before Collier owned the land, it was the home of the Seminole Indians. Some still live nearby. The park's name partly honors these Native Americans.

An impressive historical feature is the enormous "walking dredge" displayed near the entrance station. The dredge was used to dig the Tamiami Canal in the 1920s. The 60-foot-long machine had legs that spanned the width of the yet-to-be-dug canal. The dredge would scoop the ground between its legs, then "walk" along, scooping as it went. The dredged material would be placed alongside the canal and sculpted into a road. Other walking dredges were used to build other canals in south Florida.

The park's 7,271 acres contain diverse habitats: tropical hardwood hammocks, mangroves, cypress swamps, salt marshes, and pine flatwoods; thus, the wildlife is also diverse. Some of the rare species that have been seen here are the bald eagle, wood stork, brown pelican, red-cockaded woodpecker, crocodile, manatee, black bear, and mangrove fox squirrel.

The tropical hardwood hammock contains trees typical of the coasts of the West Indies and Mexico's Yucatan Peninsula. Royal palms, which may reach 100 feet tall, grow in this hammock. The mangroves are mostly found in a 4,760-acre wilderness preserve within the state park. This relatively untouched preserve can be explored by canoe and kayak.

The 120 campsites are split into two areas, one popular for tenting and one for recreational vehicles. Bathrooms have hot showers.

One-hour guided pontoon boat tours through the mangroves on the Blackwater River are run year-round. Some ranger-led programs are available only during the winter. Paddleboats can be rented for use in the boat basin. From the ramp at the boat basin, motorboats can run the Blackwater River to the Ten Thousand Islands.

Interpretive Center

The interpretive center is a tiny building that is of more interest than the exhibits it houses. The building is a cypress log block house, a replica of the type used locally during the Seminole Wars by the defending whites. Its six sides were made of limestone rocks on the first floor and cypress logs on the second. The interpretive exhibits on local natural and human history are located in the small room downstairs. Open 10 am–5 pm daily.

The Royal Palm Nature Trail

This 0.9-mile self-guided walking trail wanders through tropical and temperate hardwoods. Large royal palms, Jamaica dogwoods, and gumbo-limbos grow along the trail. The cabbage palms are hosts for the epiphytic golden polypody and rare shoestring ferns. The trail is partly boardwalk and partly hardpacked dirt (not wheelchair accessible). Interpretive signs line the trail. A dead-end spur of boardwalk leads to a small observation platform overlooking the salt marsh. During the winter, songbirds that migrated from the north use the hammock for foraging.

Bicycling Trail

The 3.5-mile Mountain Bike and Hiking Trail allows hiking and off-road biking through marsh, hammock, and pine flatwoods.

Collier-Seminole Hiking Trail

This trail starts on US 41, 0.7 miles east of the park entrance. The small gate is unmarked because hikers must first register at the entrance station to gain access through the locked gate. The 6.5-mile loop trail passes primarily through pine flatwoods and cypress swamps. A primitive backpackers' campsite is placed about halfway around. Carry at least a gallon of drinking water per person for an overnight stay.

Blackwater River–Royal Palm Paddling Trail

The mangrove Wilderness Preserve is accessible by paddling along the Blackwater River, one of the Florida Designated Paddling Trails (www.dep.state.fl.us/gwt/guide/designated_paddle/BlackwaterRPH_guide.pdf). The trail is a 13.5-mile loop and has a primitive campsite at "Grocery Place" on a small strip of higher ground suitable for an overnight stay. Because of the tides, winds, and tricky navigation, intermediate skill or more is suggested; however, beginners may choose to stay around the quiet backwaters away from the bay. In the winter, rangers lead three-hour guided canoe trips to Mud Bay, part way along the canoe trail. Manatees are occasionally seen and wading birds are common.

DIRECTIONS

Park is located on US 41, 17 miles south of Naples, near Marco Island; 8.4 miles east of SR 951, 15.6 miles west of SR 29.

CONTACT

Collier-Seminole State Park
20200 E. Tamiami Trail
Naples 34114
239-394-3397
www.floridastateparks.org/collierseminole

5 Corkscrew Marsh

Facilities: Hiking trails, guided hikes, primitive camping (by permit), observation tower

Activities: Hiking, birding, limited bicycling, hunting

Admission: Free

Hours: Daily sunrise–sunset

Pets: Allowed on leash

South Florida Birding Trail: 41

Best Time of Year: Dry season (trails can be flooded in wet season); spring good for wildflowers, autumn for migrating birds

The Corkscrew Regional Ecosystem Watershed (CREW) Trust is a private, nonprofit organization committed to protecting the watershed around Corkscrew Marsh. It purchases and manages lands within the watershed in cooperation with the South Florida Water Management District. This tract of 6,825 acres was purchased in 1990 by SFWMD and contains uplands as well as the headwaters and wetlands of Corkscrew Marsh. Approximately 5 miles of trails in several loops are maintained for hikers.

Corkscrew Marsh Trails

The trails (about 5 miles total) in this area are Marsh Loop, Pine Flatwoods Loop, Pop Ash Slough Loop, and Hammock Trail. The first skirts the edge of Corkscrew Marsh, where plains of sawgrass stretch off to the south. The Pine Flatwoods Trail goes through a slash pine community. The Hammock Trail visits a community of live and laurel oaks, red maples, cabbage palms, and ferns. The Marsh Loop goes to the observation tower. Look for tracks of raccoons, bobcats, armadillos, and other animals along the trail.

Cypress Dome Trails

The Green and Orange Loop Trails offer approximately 5 miles of trails through pine flatwoods, seasonal marshes, and around two cypress domes. Hiking, bicycling, and horseback riding (by permit only) are permitted at this trail system.

DIRECTIONS

Park is located at 4600 Corkscrew Road, between Estero and Immokalee.

From Immokalee: Go north on SR 29 to SR 82 (passing turnoff for Lake Trafford boat ramp at Lake Trafford Road), turn left and go 5.5 miles to CR 850, turn left and go 1.4 miles to entrance on left.

From Fort Myers: Take SR 82 south, right onto CR 850, go 1.5 miles to entrance on left to Corkscrew Marsh Trails section. To get to the Cypress Dome Trails section, continue south on CR 850 about 3.5 miles to trailhead on left.

From Estero: Cypress Dome is 13.7 miles east on Corkscrew Road from I-75, Exit 123.

CONTACT
CREW Trust, Inc.
23998 Corkscrew Road
Estero 33928
239-657-2253
www.crewtrust.org/corkmarsh.html

Typical habitat at Corkscrew Marsh—saw palmetto understory with cabbage palms (center) and pines (background).

6

Corkscrew Swamp Sanctuary

Facilities: Boardwalk nature trail, birding and wildlife observation, nature store, educational displays, nature programs

Activities: Birding, wildlife viewing

Admission: Entrance fee

Hours: 7 am–7:30 pm April 11–September 30, 7 am–5:30 pm October 1–April 10; store closes at 5:30 pm year-round

Pets: Not allowed

South Florida Birding Trail: 42

Best Time of Year: The famous wood stork colony starts forming (if it forms) any time from December to March. Nesting should be going strong from February through May. You are likely to see storks during this time. In the winter, decreasing water levels concentrate wading birds, alligators, and snakes. Summer visitors will find much of the wildlife dispersed and rainstorms frequent, but many plants are flowering and the vegetation is lush. Mosquitoes are mild.

Corkscrew is owned and managed by the National Audubon Society and is one of the jewels of its sanctuary system. The sanctuary's 11,000 acres protects the largest remaining stand of old-growth bald-cypress in North America. Some of the trees are more than 500 years old. The U.S. Department of the Interior designated it a "Registered Natural History Landmark" in 1964. In 2010, the sanctuary received the prestigious designation as a Ramsar Wetland of International Importance.

The sanctuary would be valuable enough just for protecting the trees, but the real claim-to-fame of the swamp is the wood stork colony that forms almost every year. The colony has historically been the largest stork colony in the United States. However, the loss of wetlands in the southeastern United States has greatly reduced the wood storks' habitat. Although the size of the colony has decreased over the years and varies considerably from year to year, it is still possible to see 1,000 pairs of storks nesting at the sanctuary in good years. In 1961, 17,000 wood stork chicks fledged from this swamp, but from 1980 to 2010, the highest number was 3,162 chicks (in 2002). In many years, no chicks hatch, although the adults may still attempt to nest. Nesting depends on water levels in the area; these may fluctuate by up to 4.5 feet between the wet and dry seasons. Alligators are an intimate part of this swamp and are frequently seen. More than 200 species of birds have been found here.

Visitor Center

The visitor center contains exhibits and a nature store that sells an excellent variety of natural history books, binoculars, wildlife clothing, note cards, wildlife art prints, gear, and so forth. Small selection of snacks available December–April (otherwise, the nearest food is at a convenience store seven miles

Wood storks nest at Corkscrew Swamp nearly every year.

away).

Pick up an illustrated self-guided tour booklet at the visitor center before you head out for the boardwalk. The chalkboard at the trailhead lists recent sightings of animals. Also ask for the bird checklist and spend a few minutes in the butterfly garden.

Boardwalk

The boardwalk at Corkscrew is world-famous to birders. This 2.25-mile-long serpentine path has given hundreds of thousands of people the opportunity to view a pristine swamp without damaging it (a shortcut is only a mile long). The boardwalk traverses many habitats: bald-cypress, pine flatwoods, hammocks, willows, wet prairies, marshes, ponds, and lettuce lakes. Orchids, ferns, epiphytes, sawgrass, lichens, palms, and hardwoods are among the many plants you'll find here. In June, the wild hibiscuses bloom, including the world's only known wild variety with white flowers.

Alligators, Carolina anoles, southeastern five-lined skinks, and cottonmouth snakes are among the many reptiles found here. Mammals include otters and white-tailed deer. Numerous wading birds, warblers during migration, and other birds can be found. Barred owls and limpkins are seen regularly. Many animals become accustomed to humans and walk on the boardwalk themselves.

At the halfway point is an observation platform that overlooks the central prairie—a beautiful view and a good photographic spot. During the stork nesting season, groups of stork nests can be seen in the cypresses surrounding the prairie.

DIRECTIONS

From Immokalee: Take CR 846 south then west for 14 miles to Sanctuary Road.
From I-75: Take Exit 111, east then north on CR 846 (Immokalee Road) for 15 miles to Sanctuary Road.

CONTACT

Corkscrew Swamp Sanctuary
375 Sanctuary Road
Naples 34120
239-348-9151
www.corkscrew.audubon.org

White ibises are often seen in the cypress trees of Corkscrew Swamp.

7

Delnor-Wiggins Pass State Park

Facilities: Boat ramp, occasional nature walks

Activities: Swimming, picnicking, paddling

Admission: State Park fee

Hours: 8 am to sunset

Pets: Not allowed on beaches

South Florida Birding Trail: 68

Best Time of Year: No preference

A mile-long beach is the main draw to this 166-acre park on the Gulf Coast. Paddlers can float around the estuary and beach at this relatively undeveloped area.

DIRECTIONS

Park is about 10 miles north of Naples. Go north on US 41 to Immokalee Road (CR 846), turn left; turns into Bluebill Ave., turn right onto Gulfshore Dr.

CONTACT

Delnor-Wiggins Pass State Park
11135 Gulfshore Drive
Naples 34108
239-597-6196
www.floridastateparks.org/delnorwiggins

Sea oats help to stabilize the beach dunes.

8

Estero Bay Preserve State Park

Facilities: No visitor facilities, information kiosk has trail maps

Activities: Hiking

Admission: Free

Hours: 8 am to sunset

Pets: Allowed

Best Time of Year: Winter and spring for weather and wildlife viewing

Other: Park on grass

The preserve encompasses 9,000 acres, with about 600 acres of pine flatwoods, salt flats, and tidal marshes at Winkler Point (the public land access). This is a buffer area for Estero Bay. The Orange trail is 1.13 miles, Yellow is 1.57 miles, and Blue is 2.28 miles. Management for invasive species is ongoing. Waterfowl and wading birds are easily seen at the water's edge.

DIRECTIONS

On Winkler Road in Estero. From Summerlin Road (CR 869) between Pine Ridge Road and Gladiolus Drive, go south on Winkler Road to end (about 2 miles).

CONTACT

Managed by Koreshan State Historic Site
239-992-0311
www.floridastateparks.org/esterobay/default.cfm

Trailhead at Winkler Point

Fakahatchee Strand Preserve State Park

Facilities: Boardwalk, scenic drive, hiking trails, guided walks and canoe trips (reservations required)

Activities: Hiking, bicycling, birding, paddling

Admission: Free

Hours: Daily 8 am–sunset

Pets: Not allowed on the Big Cypress Bend boardwalk; allowed elsewhere on a 6-foot leash

South Florida Birding Trail: 75

Best Time of Year: February–April for the driest conditions on the tram roads; November–April for Big Cypress Bend (best concentration of wildlife)

Other: This preserve is not developed with facilities for visitors (limited to bathroom at Headquarters, chemical toilet at Big Cypress Bend). Write in advance for the vertebrate checklist (birds, mammals, amphibians, and reptiles).

Fakahatchee Strand Preserve is a priceless addition to the state park system. It extends from Alligator Alley at the north end to Everglades National Park and the Ten Thousand Islands at the south end. The strand, approximately 20 miles long and 3 to 5 miles wide, is part of the Big Cypress Swamp. The 74,000-acre preserve, the largest unit in the Florida park system, contains the largest stand of native royal palms and the greatest variety of native epiphytic orchids, bromeliads, and ferns in North America. Many rare plants are found; there are 38 native ferns, 44 native orchids, and 14 native bromeliads.

Although the strand is now one of the wildest areas left in Florida, traces of old logging operations that ended in the 1950s are evident. The old roads used for logging cypress trees are called "trams" now by the locals. The only old-growth cypresses left in the preserve are at Big Cypress Bend. Natural plant communities in the preserve include mixed hardwood swamps, swamp lakes, wet prairies, cypress forests, pine rocklands, oak-palm islands, freshwater marshes, saltwater marshes, and mangrove swamps. Because of this diversity, about 140 bird, 21 mammal, 24 reptile, and 14 amphibian species have been documented in the preserve. Fakahatchee Strand is one of the last strongholds for the Florida panther. Black bears, Everglades mink, bald eagles, swallow-tailed and Everglade snail kites, and wood storks also live in the preserve. During the dry season, you can easily spend a day hiking the trams and walking the Big Cypress Bend boardwalk.

Fakahatchee Strand is included in the Comprehensive Everglades Restoration Plan, a major program to restore the ecology of south Florida by filling and plugging canals, removing levees and pumping stations, filtering pollutants from the water, and so on.

White ghost orchid in Fakahatchee Strand, known for its orchids. It is illegal to remove or relocate any wild orchid in Florida.

Big Cypress Bend

This 2,000-foot (one way) boardwalk is an impressive addition to the state park system, rivaling Corkscrew Swamp Sanctuary's boardwalk on a smaller scale. If you are in the area to see Everglades City, for example, Big Cypress Bend is well worth a stop. The area has been designated a National Natural Landmark. The boardwalk ends at a central slough with deeper water. Interpretive signs along the way describe the slough over which the boardwalk passes, the massive old growth cypress trees, the abundant and fascinating epiphytes, other plants, and wildlife. Preserve brochures are available at this location also. Handicapped-accessible.

W.J. Janes Memorial Scenic Drive

Janes Scenic Drive is a graded gravel road about 11 miles long. Unless you really know your way around the abandoned roads at the far end (formerly part of the Golden Gate Estates, now **Picayune Strand State Forest**), consider the road a dead end. The speed limit is 30 mph to protect the wildlife, such as black bears, deer, panthers, foxes, turtles, and snakes. The limited vehicular traffic makes Janes Drive a good road for mountain bikes.

Hiking

The trams (old dirt logging roads) are scattered at intervals along Janes Drive. They are marked by locked gates, preventing vehicular passage. Most of the trams are overgrown and difficult to hike. In the summer, many trails are partly or all wet. Seven of the 20 trams have been partially cleared of regrowth for at least the first few miles, and passage by foot is easy. The cleared trams and their lengths are Gates 2 (1.5 miles), 7 ("West Main," 2.25 miles), 12 ("East Main," 10.5 miles, goes to I-75), 15 (1.5 miles), 16 ("Mud Tram," 2.25 miles), 19 (many trails heading north, including a dry fire road), and 20 (dry fire road). Even on the uncleared trams, the trails are obvious, since they are higher than the surrounding land. For specific information on the cleared trams, call the preserve headquarters.

The trams pass through many types of habitats, such as hardwood hammocks and swamps. Some of the more picturesque, such as Gate 7 (4.4 miles from the headquarters), open onto wet prairies. Because of the variety of habitats, it's possible to see many types of wildlife.

Guided Walks

The giant preserve is understaffed, leaving a paucity of natural history programs in this fascinating region. Also, conditions are often too hot and buggy in summer to lead walks. From November to February, rangers lead walks through the strand. Call in advance for reservations. Be prepared for some wet slogging—you may find yourself in waist-high water!

East River Canoe Route

Paralleling the Tamiami Trail is a canal that was created by "borrowing" fill to build the road. Occasionally, more fill was needed and large pits were dug. The pits have filled with water and become ponds. One such pond is in Fakahatchee Strand Preserve State Park. To find it, drive on US 41 for 5.2 miles west of the intersection with SR 29. A small brown sign for the preserve indicates the dirt turnoff on the left (south side).

The pond is brimming with alligators. During April to June, tricolored herons and snowy egrets may be seen in the mangroves. They are visible from the water's edge with a spotting scope and provide a good photographic opportunity. You can launch a canoe or kayak for the East River Canoe Route, which enters **Everglades National Park** part way to Fakahatchee Bay. It passes through mangrove tunnels and lakes before becoming a tidal river (East River). The trail is 11.6 miles to Everglades City. It is not marked, but the Gulf Coast Visitor Center in Everglades City has a route map.

DIRECTIONS
There are two main accesses.
Big Cypress Bend: On US 41, 7 miles west of SR 29 (next to Indian Village).

Headquarters and Janes Scenic Drive: From US 41, go north on SR 29 for 2.5 miles to CR 837 in Copeland; turn left for 1.1 miles, bear sharply right at the fork, to small building on the right. If office is closed, pick up a brochure outside and continue up the road. Almost immediately the road becomes Janes Scenic Drive.

CONTACT
Fakahatchee Strand Preserve State Park
137 Coastline Drive
Copeland 34137
239-695-4593
www.floridastateparks.org/
fakahatcheestrand/

9 Florida Panther National Wildlife Refuge

Facilities: Hiking trails, guided tours by reservation for small groups (call a few weeks ahead), special events for "Save the Panther Week" in March, chemical toilets

Activities: Hiking, wildlife observation

Admission: Free

Hours: Day use only

Pets: Not allowed

Best Time of Year: Winter and spring; trails may be flooded in summer

The National Wildlife Refuge system was established first and foremost to protect wildlife and their native habitats. A secondary goal is to allow public access where it is compatible with the primary goal. Thus, some refuges are not accessible to the general public or are barely so. Florida Panther is one of those. The 26,400-acre refuge was established in 1989 to protect the Florida panthers. However, the staff has found a way to share the refuge while preventing disturbance to the big cats. Only a small portion of the southeast corner of the refuge is open to the public on designated hiking trails. Refuge staff offer guided education tours in other areas to small groups on a limited basis.

The refuge encompasses the northern end of Fakahatchee Strand, which consists of cypress and subtropical hardwoods. It shares its eastern boundary with Big Cypress National Preserve. The flatness of the terrain, like so much of south Florida, allows most of the refuge to have standing water during the wet season from several inches to three feet. Slight rises in the limestone substrate allow for variations in vegetation communities—wet prairies, mixed hardwood hammocks, slash pines, and palmettos.

The refuge staff is actively involved in the recovery of the panther. The refuge forms the core of several panthers' home ranges. Some panthers travel across the refuge between Big Cypress National Preserve and Fakahatchee Strand Preserve State Park. Other species of special interest at the refuge are the Florida black bear, Everglades mink, fox squirrel, Florida grasshopper sparrow, wood stork, and indigo snake.

Rare orchids and bromeliads thrive in the refuge. A refuge priority is to restore populations of these plants.

Hiking Trails

The Leslie M. Duncan Memorial Trail is a 0.3-mile wheelchair-accessible loop through a hardwood hammock of ancient oak trees and tropical vegetation. A small boardwalk and overlook allow visitors to view a restored, seasonal pond.

The 1.3-mile unpaved loop trail is easier to navigate in winter when it is drier and mowed; it often floods from summer to early winter, and tall vegetation may obscure the trail. Hikers will enjoy the variety of habitats including hardwood hammocks, pine flatwoods, and wet prairies. The chance of seeing a panther is remote because they are secretive, but you may find their tracks.

Call the refuge office ahead to check the status of the trails and special tours in winter.

DIRECTIONS

The Refuge entrance is approximately 20 miles east of Naples at the northwest corner of the intersection of I-75 (Exit 80) and SR 29. The gate is 0.25 miles north of I-75 on SR 29.

CONTACT

Florida Panther National Wildlife Refuge Headquarters
3860 Tollgate Boulevard, Suite 300
Naples 34114
239-353-8442
www.fws.gov/floridapanther/

Most of the refuge is off-limits to the public to give Florida panthers undisturbed space.

10 Gasparilla Island State Park

Facilities: Lighthouse museum and nature center, beach

Activities: Swimming, snorkeling, shelling, shorebirding, fishing

Admission: State Park fee

Hours: 8 am to sunset

Pets: Not allowed on beaches

Best Time of Year: Autumn and during outgoing tides for shorebirds; summer for swimming; after a storm in winter for shelling

Development has squeezed much of the life out of this beautiful barrier island. All that remains of the original habitat are some beaches and dunes. The wildlife that is left survives out of instinct and luck, not because of any assistance given by the park service. During the fall, migrations of shorebirds, raptors, and other birds follow the coastline and end up at Gasparilla temporarily. Shellers try their luck here, although it's not as productive as Sanibel Island. The sugar-white sands are dazzling.

Gasparilla was named for the pirate Gaspar (actually, "Little Gaspar"), who supposedly hid on the island between attacks. Charlotte Harbor was and still is excellent for shipping because of its depth.

Boca Grande Lighthouse and beach at Gasparilla Island State Park

The town of Boca Grande reflects this fact in its name, which means "Big Mouth" in Spanish, referring to the deep port.

Part of the interest of coming to this park is the drive to the island. Along the causeway, mud flats harbor shorebirds and wading birds, especially when the tide is out. White pelicans winter on the bay side. Watch for magnificent frigatebirds over the ocean.

Several sections of bathing beaches are located periodically along the road to the end of the island, each one with portable toilets. Check each place for birds and shells.

The lighthouse (built in 1890) at the southern end of the island houses a small interpretive center with exhibits of shells, sea life, butterflies, and local history. It is only open the last Saturday of each month.

DIRECTIONS

Gasparilla Island, located in Lee County, is accessible by land via the Boca Grande Causeway at the island's north end; take either CR 771 or 775 to the causeway (private toll) at Placida, then follow Gulf Boulevard south to the park.

CONTACT

Gasparilla Island State Park
880 Belcher Road
Boca Grande 33921
941-964-0375
www.floridastateparks.org/
gasparillaisland

11 J.N. "Ding" Darling National Wildlife Refuge

Facilities: Wildlife Drive (auto route), visitor center; concession: tram tour; guided paddling tours; bicycle, pontoon boat, canoe, and kayak rentals

Activities: Wildlife observation, bicycling, paddling

Admission: Wildlife Drive is U.S. fee area. The rest is free.

Hours: Sunrise to sunset; Wildlife Drive gate opens at 7:30 am and closes a half-hour before sunset; closed on Fridays; visitor center core hours are 9 am–4 pm, closed Fridays and federal holidays

Pets: Allowed on short leash, but visitors are *strongly* recommended not to bring pets because of risk that alligators may attack a pet even on leash; allowed in vehicles if attended

South Florida Birding Trail: 28

Best Time of Year: Winter is best for wintering birds and weather; fall and spring are good for migrating shorebirds, raptors, warblers, and so on; summer is best to see manatees off Tarpon Bay and Wildlife Drive

One of the greatest tributes a conservationist can receive is to have a national wildlife refuge named after him. Thus, the great conservationist J.N. "Ding" Darling, founder of the National Wildlife Federation, has become immortalized in a refuge he helped create through his initiation of the federal "Duck Stamp" program.

The 6,390-acre refuge protects several tracts of land. The largest (Darling Tract) consists of mangroves and mud flats on San Carlos Bay. Migratory and wading birds frequent the two brackish impoundments within this tract. Over half of the Darling Tract is designated a Wilderness Area. The popular Wildlife Drive goes through part of the Darling Tract. The 100-acre Bailey Tract in the interior of the island is a freshwater wetland. Native dune plants thrive on the three-acre Perry Tract on the Gulf side of Sanibel Island. The 176-acre Buck Key offers canoeing around shallow mangrove flats. The refuge attracts around 850,000 visitors each year.

Birders from all over the continent come to "Ding" Darling, touted as one of the greatest birding hotspots in the country. Such birds as the magnificent frigatebird, white pelican, reddish egret, roseate spoonbill, mottled duck, black skimmer, American oystercatcher, and bald eagle are common. Alligators are commonly seen, and occasionally a crocodile is found. This is the northern limit for crocodiles on the Gulf coast. West Indian manatees regularly visit the refuge in the winter and eastern indigo snakes are seen occasionally year-round. Atlantic loggerhead turtles and Atlantic Ridley turtles dwell in the adjacent marine waters.

Visitors to the refuge should allow a day for driving or bicycling the auto route, canoeing, and hiking the short trails.

The island of Sanibel has a beach resort atmosphere and scenic charm. It is

Snowy Egret at Ding Darling

considered one of the best shelling places in the world. The island is popular with tourists in winter, so expect crowds and reserve your lodging accommodations well in advance. The crowds are gone in summer.

The refuge also manages several other undeveloped national wildlife refuges accessible only by boat: Pine Island (548 acres, 16 islands), Matlacha Pass (512 acres, 23 islands), Caloosahatchee (40 acres, 3 islands), and Island Bay (20 acres, 5 islands). They are bird nesting areas and have visitor restrictions. Contact "Ding" Darling's office for more information or see www. fws.gov/dingdarling/.

Wildlife Drive

This is the main visitor access to view wildlife. The self-guided auto route is 5 miles long through salt marshes, mangroves, brackish and fresh water impoundments, and mud flats. The best time to see foraging birds is at low tide. An observation tower provides a good photography vantage.

Almost 240 species of birds have been seen on the refuge, and many can be seen along this route. Bald eagles and peregrine falcons are occasionally seen. Wading birds such as reddish egrets, snowy egrets, great egrets, white ibises, great blue herons, little blue herons, tricolored herons, roseate spoonbills (especially in spring), and wood storks can be seen. Ospreys are year-round residents (look for nests high up in open areas). Peregrines are fall and winter visitors. Waterfowl (such as mottled ducks, blue-winged and green-winged teal, northern pintails, northern shovelers, American widgeons, hooded and redbreasted mergansers) are found from December to April. Many species of shorebirds overwinter and are residents.

Visitors can take a 2-hour guided tour of Wildlife Drive by tram. The tram operates from the concession at Tarpon Bay Recreation Area on Tarpon Bay Road, just east of the refuge visitor center. The tram reduces the number of cars using Wildlife Drive. It does not run on Fridays.

Walking Trails

The Indigo Trail is two miles one way, starts at the visitor center, and runs along a dike through mangroves. The Shell Mound Trail is a 0.3-mile interpretive loop trail to an Indian shell midden and is located at far end of Wildlife Drive.

The Bailey Tract is a 100-acre freshwater wetland area offering a network of 1.75 miles of hiking trails. Alligators and wading birds may be seen. To find it, take Tarpon Bay Road south from Periwinkle Way (opposite direction from the concession) for 0.25 miles; parking lot on the right.

The Perry Tract is a 3-acre tract that features native dune vegetation on the Gulf of Mexico side of Sanibel Island. Long stretches of pristine beach are accessible from here. To reach it from the causeway, take Periwinkle Way west, turn left onto Casa Ybel Road, then left onto Algiers Road.

Visitor Center

This fine center offers exhibits, a short video program, and an excellent selection of natural history books and gifts. Rangers and volunteers offer many types of programs (ask at desk for schedule).

Bicycling

Bicycles are allowed on Wildlife Drive. Indeed, this is a wonderful way to see some of the more shy creatures. The concession rents bicycles.

Paddling Trails

The Commodore Creek Trail is a 2-mile loop trail reached by the Tarpon Bay Recreation Area at the northern end of Tarpon Bay Road. From the boat launch, paddle west along the shore of Tarpon Bay for 0.75 miles to the trailhead. The trail winds through beautiful red mangroves and seagrass and mud flats, offering views of wading birds, shorebirds, fish, crabs, and other wildlife.

The Buck Key Trail is a 4-mile marked loop trail on Captiva Island. To reach a launch, drive west on Sanibel-Captiva Road to Captiva Island, about 9 miles past Tarpon Bay Road. The access is 'Tween Waters Marina (private), which also rents canoes and kayaks. From the marina, paddle southeast about 0.25 miles to Buck Key. Sections of the trail follow canals that were dug for mosquito control. The island is heavily vegetated with mangroves along the shore and hammocks in the interior. Avoid travel during low tide because the canoe trail may be impassible.

Visitors may also launch non-motorized boats from the right side of Wildlife Drive (the bay side) at marked locations.

DIRECTIONS

Visitor Center: From I-75, take Exit 131 and go west on Daniels Parkway (which becomes Cypress Lake Dr.). Turn left onto McGregor Blvd. (CR 867) and follow to Sanibel Island by crossing Sanibel Causeway (toll). On Sanibel, turn right onto Periwinkle Way, right onto Tarpon Bay Rd., and left onto Sanibel-Captiva Rd. Visitor center is 2 miles on right.

Concession (at Tarpon Bay): Follow directions above onto Tarpon Bay Rd., then straight north to Tarpon Bay.

CONTACT

J.N. "Ding" Darling
National Wildlife Refuge
Visitor Center:
1 Wildlife Drive
Sanibel 33957
239-472-1100
www.fws.gov/dingdarling

CONCESSION:

900 Tarpon Bay Road
Sanibel Island 33957
239-472-8900
www.tarponbayexplorers.com

Koreshan State Historic Site

Facilities: Nature trail, campground, canoe rentals, naturalist programs, historic site

Activities: Camping, paddling, hiking, picnicking

Admission: State Park fee

Hours: 8 am to sunset

Pets: Allowed

Best Time of Year: Winter for paddling and camping. Insects are rare in winter, making it a popular time to visit Koreshan. Even in the summer, insects aren't as prevalent here as they are at other coastal parks.

Nature lovers come to this park to canoe on the Estero River. The 305-acre park was actually preserved for its historic merit. In 1894, Cyrus Teed preached his religion of "Koreshanity" (the belief that the universe exists within a hollow sphere) to a group of followers who settled with him here. Teed's religion did not catch on, and the last four followers deeded part of their property to the state in 1961. Visitors can stroll around the restored village. The Estero River is designated a **Florida Canoe Trail** and makes a relaxing canoeing day trip. It is also a section of the **Great Calusa Blueway**.

Hiking

A 0.25-mile self-guided loop nature trail along the Estero River goes through pine flatwoods and scrub oak. Look for gopher tortoises. Ask for the park's vertebrate list.

Historic structure at Koreshan State Historic Site.

A jogging trail hugs the park's boundary.

Paddling

Visitors can rent canoes and kayaks at the ranger station or launch their own at the boat ramp and head downstream to Estero Bay (about 3 miles). Ask for the canoe map at the entrance station. Then you can follow all the curves of the Estero River, through subtropical hammocks and mangroves and out to the bay. Once in the bay, you'll see Mound Key, the large island to the southwest (3.5 miles from ramp). Mound Key is an Indian shell mound that is a State Archeological Site. If you paddle to the west side of Mound Key, you can pull into a cove and find a walking trail that crosses the island. Less experienced canoeists should return to Koreshan from Mound Key. The current is slow enough to permit round-trip travel. Make sure you memorize the way downstream, so you don't get confused by side channels on your return. Along the way, watch for manatees, dolphins, roseate spoonbills, black-whiskered vireos, and mangrove cuckoos.

The river is part of the **Great Calusa Blueway.** Only experienced canoeists with navigation equipment should attempt to cross Estero Bay, and then only on a relatively calm day. You can explore around other mangrove islands and return to Koreshan, or you can pull out at the ramp at **Lovers Key State Park** (about 3 more miles south).

Camping

The campground has 60 sites with water and electricity. Twelve sites along the Estero are designated for tents only. From December to April the campground is usually full every day. Reservations are recommended. The park has no concession store, but wood and ice are sold at the ranger station. Naturalist programs are held at the amphitheater on the bank of the Estero.

DIRECTIONS

From Fort Myers or Naples, take I-75 to Exit 123. Go west on Corkscrew Road, cross US 41, to entrance.

CONTACT

3800 Corkscrew Road
Estero 33928
239-992-0311
www.floridastateparks.org/koreshan

Lee County Parks

For more information on Lee County parks contact Lee County Parks & Recreation, 3410 Palm Beach Blvd., Fort Myers 33916; 239-533-7275; www.leeparks.org.

2

Lee County Parks

Caloosahatchee Regional Park and Hickey's Creek Paddling Trail

Facilities: Hiking, bicycling, and equestrian trails, kayak rentals (reserve in advance), tent campground

Activities: Hiking, mountain bicycling, horseback riding, paddling, camping

Admission: Small parking fee

Hours: 7 am–dusk year-round

Pets: Not allowed

South Florida Birding Trail: 40

Best Time of Year: No preference

Along the banks of the Caloosahatchee River, this 768-acre park opened in 1999. The habitat is pine flatwoods, cypress swamps, and oak hammocks. This park is a good launch site for Hickey's Creek and is part of the **Great Calusa Blueway**.

Hickey's Creek

Hickey's Creek is accessible several places along the Caloosahatchee River, about 15 miles east of Fort Myers. Half of this paddling trail is on the Caloosahatchee River (wide and open, exposing paddlers to wind, waves, and motorboats) and half is on Hickey's Creek (narrow and sheltered). From the campground, paddle west (downstream) about 1.5 miles to the creek entrance on the left (south) bank. Paddle up the creek for about 2 miles. The creek flows under SR 80 and ends at Hickey's Creek Mitigation Area (a wildlife and environmental area; SFBT #39), with a short loop hiking trail and a small picnic area. Hickey's Creek flows gently through a subtropical hammock. Look for crested caracaras, bald eagles, ospreys, scrub-jays, wild turkeys, and wading birds. 7–8 miles paddling roundtrip. Call a day or more ahead for launching and kayak rentals. For more information, see www.dep.state.fl.us/gwt/guide/designated_paddle/Hickey_guide.pdf.

DIRECTIONS
From Fort Myers, take SR 80 (Palm Beach Blvd.) east to SR 31, turn left (north), cross the Caloosahatchee River, and turn right (east) onto SR 78 (N. River Rd.). Drive about 7.1 miles; the park is on the right. Call for directions and access to kayak launch gate.

CONTACT
Caloosahatchee Regional Park
18500 North River Road
Alva 33920
239-693-2690
www.leeparks.org/facility-info/facility-details.cfm?Project_Num=0253

Lee County Parks

Matanzas Pass Preserve

Facilities: Hiking trails, canoe launch

Activities: Hiking, paddling

Admission: Free

Hours: Dawn to dusk daily

Pets: Not allowed

South Florida Birding Trail: 34

Best Time of Year: Winter and spring for weather and wildlife viewing

The preserve's 60 acres protect native flora and fauna on Estero Island, part of Fort Myers Beach. The 1.25 miles of easy hiking trails along Estero Bay provide a quiet oasis of maritime oak habitat in this otherwise developed area. Red, white, and black mangroves grow unusually close together here. A portage of about 0.25 miles on a boardwalk leads to the canoe access for Matanzas Pass on Estero Bay (canoe portage wheels useful). This site is number 7 on the **Great Calusa Blueway**.

DIRECTIONS
From Fort Myers, take CR 865 across bridge to Estero Island, go south on Estero Blvd. (CR 865) for 1 mile to Bay Road on left.

CONTACT
Matanzas Pass Preserve
199 Bay Road
Fort Myers Beach 33931
239-533-7444 or 239-229-0649
www.leeparks.org/facility-info/facility-details.cfm?Project_Num=0202

Lee County Parks

Six Mile Cypress Slough Preserve

Facilities: Interpretive boardwalk, interpretive center, amphitheater, picnic area, observation decks, guided walks

Activities: Birding, wildlife viewing, picnicking

Admission: Small parking fee

Hours: Boardwalk open dawn to dusk; interpretive center open November to April: Tuesday–Friday 10 am–4, Saturday 10 am–2 pm, Sunday 12–4 pm; May–October: Tuesday–Sunday 10 am–2 pm

Pets: Not allowed

South Florida Birding Trail: 38

Best Time of Year: Winter for more bird activity

Other: Trail map: www.leeparks.org/maps/Overview_maps/new_six_mile_map.html

DIRECTIONS

From Fort Myers: Take I-75 south to Exit 136, west on CR 884 (Colonial Blvd.), turn left onto Six Mile Cypress Parkway (Ben C. Pratt Parkway), go 3 miles to entrance on left.

From Naples: Take I-75 north to Exit 131, west on Daniels Parkway (CR 865), turn right on Six Mile Cypress Parkway (Ben C. Pratt Parkway) and go 2 miles north to entrance on right.

CONTACT

Six Mile Cypress Slough Preserve
7751 Penzance Crossing
Fort Myers 33966
239-533-7550
www.leeparks.org/sixmile/

Part of the preserve was purchased by the South Florida Water Management District under Save Our Rivers Program. The preserve is managed by Lee County. The 2,500 acres encompass a long, narrow cypress strand, about 9 miles long and 0.75 miles wide. The slough drains a 57-square-mile watershed and empties into Estero Bay. The 1.2-mile-long boardwalk goes through cypresses, pine flatwoods, hardwoods, and several ponds. Many wetland species can be seen, such as river otters, Florida panthers (not likely), wading birds, snakes, and alligators. The 11,000-square foot interpretive center offers a wide range of displays and educational programs.

14 Lovers Key State Park

Facilities: Nature trail, boat and canoe launches, canoe, kayak and bicycle rentals

Activities: Beach activities such as shelling and swimming (beware of strong currents while swimming), paddling, birding

Admission: State Park fee (includes tram from parking lot to beach)

Hours: 8 am to sunset

Pets: Not allowed on beach; allowed on trails and elsewhere

South Florida Birding Trail: 36

Best Time of Year: Winter and spring for birding

Along the barrier islands from Naples to Fort Myers are many public beaches. Lovers Key is one of the quietest, least developed, and least crowded. The 1,616 acres encompass Black Island, Lovers Key, Inner Key, and Long Key. Sea-grapes dominate the woody vegetation. A canoe launch (no motors) provides access to quiet red mangrove lagoons around Estero Bay for hours of exploring. Bottlenose dolphins and manatees are occasionally observed near shore. Wading birds (including reddish egrets and roseate spoonbills) and shorebirds can be seen in the lagoon at low tide.

The 2.5 miles of undeveloped sandy beaches are accessible by a courtesy tram from the parking lot and by two foot bridges. Loggerhead sea turtles nest in summer. Paddling is popular in the mangrove waterways and along Estero Bay and the Gulf of Mexico. The **Great Calusa Blueway** passes through this park. A 3-mile hiking trail traverses a maritime hammock on Black Island. Bicycling is permitted on 5 miles of trails and Black Island.

This is an excellent birding area, especially around the mud flats at low tide. Ospreys, eagles, snowy plovers, piping plovers, and least terns nest here.

DIRECTIONS
Park is located on CR 865 (Estero Blvd.) between Fort Myers and Bonita Beaches, about 6 miles south of Fort Myers Beach and 7 miles north of Bonita Beach.

CONTACT
Lovers Key State Park
8700 Estero Boulevard
Fort Myers 33931
239-463-4588
www.floridastateparks.org/loverskey

Concession:
239-765-7788

Naples Nature Center

Facilities: Nature Discovery Center Museum, nature trails, boat tours, kayak rentals, self-guided paddling trail, wildlife rehabilitation center, aviary, butterfly garden, nature store, and environmental education programs

Activities: Nature walks, paddling

Admission: Entrance fee includes boat tour

Hours: Monday to Saturday 9 am–4:30 pm year-round; Sundays 12–4 pm, November 1–April 30. Boat tours November–April: Monday–Saturday 10 am–3 pm, Sunday 12:30–2:30 pm; May–October: Monday–Saturday 10 am–12 pm

Pets: Not allowed

South Florida Birding Trail: 69

Best Time of Year: Although naturalist programs are reduced in the summer, boat tours and other programs are provided. The museum, trails, and gardens are worth a visit any time.

In the heart of Naples lies a quiet refreshing break from city life. The Naples Nature Center, located on a 21-acre sanctuary, is owned and operated by The Conservancy of Southwest Florida (The Conservancy), a private nonprofit conservation organization active in the Naples area. The Naples Nature Center was completed in 1981 and has since been serving Collier County with educational programs. The Conservancy's extensive schedule of quality programs is enhanced by the dedication of several hundred well-trained volunteers.

The Nature Center Complex contains the Nature Discovery Center museum, auditorium, nature store, wildlife rehabilitation center, classrooms, and nature trails. Altogether, it is one of the best examples in south Florida of a complete environmental education and conservation center. Because their programs encompass all ecosystems of south Florida, The Conservancy encourages people to visit the nature center before exploring natural areas such as the ones described in this book. Then they will have a good understanding of all they are seeing.

Surrounding the nature center complex are special conservation plantings. A xeriscape demonstration plot shows which garden plants don't require supplemental watering. A screened-in butterfly garden contains both the plants that attract butterflies and the live butterflies that feed on them. The aviary, which houses injured birds, can be seen from the outside. There is much to see and do in the nature center. School groups and children's summer camps are nature center specialties. Call ahead for a schedule of tours and programs.

Nature Discovery Center

Just about every aspect of south Florida natural history is represented in the exhibits: hydrology, habitats, wildlife, early Indians, and so on. Exhibits in this 5,000-square foot interactive museum include a life-sized diorama of part of a cypress swamp and its bird life, a rare shell collection, and a 2,300-gallon marine aquarium. The live serpentarium houses virtually every species of non-venomous snake found locally. You will want to spend at least an hour looking around.

Walking Trails

Three self-guided interpretive trails radiate from the nature center complex. All three are short (about 10 minutes). The wide, wood-chipped trails are carefully maintained. The numbered markers correspond to the guide booklet available at the Nature Store. Characteristic of everything The Conservancy does, the booklet is thorough and excellently prepared. Guided walks are also available. The Hammock Trail goes through a typical hardwood hammock. Bromeliads and ferns are abundant in the live oaks. The Arboretum Trail displays a variety of native plants, including those suitable for xeriscaping. The Peninsula Trail takes you to the edge of a tidal lagoon, where you may see an alligator or a manatee. More than 140 species of birds have been found on the property.

Boat Tours

The Conservancy offers electric boat tours from the nature center every morning (except Sundays from May to October); included with admission. Reservations must be made in person on the day of the tour. The boat seats five to six people. The trip lasts 45 minutes and cruises through a tidal lagoon to the Gordon River. Mangroves line the water, with mangrove plantings along the way that are the result of a mitigation agreement by a developer who destroyed the original mangroves. Mangroves are protected by state law; for every one destroyed, five must be planted. Wading birds, like yellow-crowned night-herons, can be viewed along the way. You'll find it hard to believe you're still in the middle of Naples when you take this tour. You may even see a manatee.

Kayaking

Kayak and canoe rentals are available for additional fees. A 2-hour guided tour is available on the Gordon River or paddle on your own.

Nature Store

If you are looking to buy nature-related items, this store has an exceptional selection. Among the thousands of items for sale are jewelry, tee-shirts, nature art prints, children's educational toys, bird feeders, field guides, children's books, hard-to-find regional books, and other natural history books.

DIRECTIONS

From the south: From the intersection of SR 29 and US 41, go west on US 41 about 23 miles to CR 851 (Goodlette Rd.), then right (north) about 2 miles, right onto 14th Avenue North and go a short distance to end of the street.

From the north: Get onto CR 851 either from CR 886 (Golden Gate Parkway) or US 41, then south on Goodlette to 14th Avenue North, then left and go short distance to end.

CONTACT

The Conservancy of Southwest Florida
1450 Merrihue Drive
Naples 34102
239-262-0304
www.conservancy.org

Okaloacoochee Slough State Forest

Facilities: Hiking, bicycling, and equestrian trails; primitive campsites (no potable water)

Activities: Wildlife observation, hunting, hiking, bicycling, horseback riding, camping

Admission: Nominal fees for day use and camping

Hours: Open year-round

Pets: Allowed on leash

South Florida Birding Trail: 45

Best Time of Year: Winter and spring for weather and wildlife viewing; to avoid hunting seasons, January, February, and April are best

Other: Access to Okaloacoochee Slough is available through honor fee pay stations located along CR 832. Seven informational kiosks show the locations of pay stations, gates, trails, and designated roads.

Okaloacoochee Slough State Forest (or "OK Slough") is 32,039 acres. The slough (13,382 acres) is oriented north-south and provides water for Big Cypress and Faka-hatchee Strand to the south. Although OK Slough was previously logged, it remains in relatively pristine condition. Hiking and wildlife observation are the highlights of this area. The land is managed for multiple uses, which include ecosystem restoration; recreation; and management for silviculture, wildlife, archeology, cultural resources, and watersheds. Thirty-nine miles of trails and unimproved roads are available for hiking, bicycling, and horseback riding from six access points along CR 832. Some unimproved roads can be driven to look for wildlife. This area provides habitat for Florida panthers and crested caracaras. Swallow-tailed kites are common in spring and summer.

DIRECTIONS

State Forest is located approximately 30 miles east of Fort Myers in Hendry and northeast-ern Collier counties. From the junction of SR 29 and CR 846 in Immokalee, go north on SR 29 for 13.1 miles, turn right on CR 832 (Keri Road) for 6.4 miles to headquarters on right. Trailheads are scattered along CR 832 (on both sides of the road, starting at 3.5 miles and ending at 8.5 miles).Three desig-nated parking areas are located along CR 832 with additional parking areas in various areas of the Forest.

CONTACT

Okaloacoochee Slough State Forest
6265 County Road 832
Felda 33930
863-612-0776
www.fl-dof.com/state_forests/
okaloacoochee.html

Picayune Strand State Forest

Facilities: Hiking, bicycling, and equestrian trails; primitive campground

Activities: Hiking, bicycling (with sturdy bicycles), horseback riding, picnicking, camping

Admission: Small entrance fee for day use (sunrise to sunset)

Hours: Open year-round and all hours

Pets: Allowed on leash

South Florida Birding Trail: 71

Best Time of Year: Winter and spring for weather and wildlife viewing; to avoid hunting seasons, January, February, and April are best

The 78,615-acre Picayune Strand State Forest in western Collier County had a lively beginning. First the cypresses were logged in the 1940s and 1950s. Then a developer purchased 57,000 acres to create the largest subdevelopment in the country. The developer built roads and drainage canals criss-crossing the land and advertised 2.5-acre retirement and vacation lots. In a clever scheme, the lots were shown during the dry season or sold over the telephone, and 29,000 were sold. However, the land flooded in the summer and could not be built upon. This scam eventually became known as the "swampland in Florida" scam. The land was eventually abandoned until the state and federal governments stepped up to restore the habitat.

Under the Save our Everglades program, the lots were purchased back from 17,000 owners. Few houses had been constructed because of the flooding and a lack of utilities. The land is now being restored by filling in some of the 45 miles of canals and removing some of the 227 miles of roads to restore sheet flow of water to the Ten Thousand Islands, downstream of Picayune Strand. Picayune is a Cajun word that means "little," referring to the smaller size of this strand compared to its larger neighbor, Fakahatchee Strand, to the east.

Forest managers are encouraging the native vegetation to grow. The cypress trees that remain here were too small to be logged several decades earlier. Because of the ongoing restoration, roads can disappear and flood, so it is best to stick to the main preserve roads. The land is waterlogged in the summer.

Aside from the 52nd Avenue entrance, there are no visitor facilities. The Belle Mead Tract has a 22-mile equestrian trail. Sabal Palm Trail is a 3.2-mile hiking trail (with several shorter loops), accessed from Sabal Palm Road. The north access is the

Trail at Picayune Strand State Forest

main one. From here, you can hike on a network of trails. The longest (Blue Trail) is 8.3 miles one way; the far end of this trail meets the Beck Road entrance, so you can hike one-way if you leave a car at Beck Road. The south entrance on Sabal is on a rough, unimproved road. Use care, because it's all wild land. This is a good place to just drive slowly or bicycle (with off-road bikes) to look for wildlife. Wood storks, red-cockaded woodpeckers, Florida panthers, black bears, gopher tortoises, and indigo snakes may be found here.

DIRECTIONS

The State Forest is about 2 miles east of Naples and there are three entrances.

Northern access: Main entrance, restroom facilities, campground, and trailheads are located at 2225 52nd Ave. SE, Naples 34117. Exit 101 off I-75, go north on CR 951 (Collier Blvd.) to Golden Gate Blvd., then right (east) for 8.8 miles, right on Everglades Blvd. S (south) for 6 miles, then right on 52nd Ave. SE for 1 mile to Forestry Headquarters.

Middle access: Just south of I-75 on CR 951 (Collier Blvd.) is Beck Road on the east. Turn down Beck Road and follow all the curves to the end to small parking area (about 2.5 miles).

Southern access: From the junction of US 41 and CR 951 (Collier Blvd.) go north on CR 951 for 2.4 miles to Sabal Palm Road. Turn right for 3.2 miles to trailhead.

CONTACT

Picayune Strand State Forest
239-348-7557
www.fl-dof.com/state_forests/
picayune_strand.html

<table>
<tr><td>

17

Sanibel-Captiva Conservation Foundation

Facilities: Nature center, educational programs, hiking trails, native plant sales, butterfly house

Activities: Hiking, birding

Admission: Entrance fee

Hours: Monday–Friday 8:30 am–4 pm, October–May; and 8:30 am–3 pm, June–September; Saturday 10 am–3 pm December–April; closed Saturdays May–October

Pets: Not allowed

Best Time of Year: Spring and fall for warbler migrations; summer is hot, but many plants in flower and fruit, attracting birds

</td></tr>
</table>

The Sanibel-Captiva Conservation Foundation (SCCF) was founded in 1967 to protect the sand dunes, lush hammocks, and wildlife on and around Sanibel and Captiva Islands. This nonprofit group owns and protects almost 1,800 acres in several parcels. SCCF's primary function is the acquisition, restoration, and management of wildlife habitat. SCCF is active in environmental research, education, sea turtle nest protection, native plant propagation, and removal of nonnative plants. The Barrier Island Research Laboratory at Tarpon Bay is operated by SCCF under a cooperative agreement with the U.S. Fish and Wildlife Service and Iowa State University.

Nature Center Complex

The nature center houses excellent exhibits of local natural history. Guided programs are provided for exploring the beaches and trails. The staff also narrates the boat tours that are run by an independent operator (Captiva Cruises at 239-472-5100). In the enclosed butterfly house, SCCF raises butterflies to be released into the wild, similar to a fish hatchery. Tours of the butterfly house are on Tuesdays at 10 am.

The Nature Shop carries a large selection of nature-related books for all ages, as well as gifts and handicrafts. The native plant nursery specializes in the retail selling of hard-to-find south Florida plants.

Hiking

Four and a half miles of short loop trails lace the 250-acre area around the nature center. They span hammocks and wetlands along the Sanibel River. Many of the native plants are labeled, making this an excellent destination for botanists. Ask for the "Walk in the Wetlands" trail guide. Some plants you can see are Jamaica dogwood, snowberry, Christmas berry, paurotis palm, coontie, shoestring fern, mastic, sawgrass, myrsine, and white indigo-berry. Gopher tortoise burrows are evident. Short 15-minute loops can be taken or longer hikes of several miles.

A 0.25-mile hike on the Center Road trail leads to a 40-foot high observation tower overlooking the Sanibel River, an excellent place for observing wildlife. Along this trail is evidence of the battle SCCF wages with Brazilian pepper and other invasive plants, which they have treated with herbicides, flooding, and fire. From the tower an artificial nesting platform for ospreys is visible and usually occupied.

A 0.6-mile trail is in a nearby tract in the Periwinkle Blue Skies Preserve. After Hurricane Charlie hit in 2004, intensive restoration was undertaken to remove Australian-pines and encourage live oaks and mastics to become the canopy. Access this trail by foot, near the gazebo, which is across the street (and a little to the west) from Sanibel Community Church.

DIRECTIONS

Located adjacent to J.N. Ding Darling NWR. From I-75, take Exit 131 and go west on Daniels Parkway (which becomes Cypress Lake Dr.). Turn left onto McGregor Blvd. (CR 867) and follow to Sanibel Island by crossing Sanibel Causeway (toll). On Sanibel, turn right onto Periwinkle Way, right onto Tarpon Bay Rd., and left onto Sanibel-Captiva Rd. Drive to 3333 Sanibel-Captiva Road, one mile west of Tarpon Bay Road.

CONTACT

Sanibel-Captiva Conservation Foundation
P.O. Box 839
Sanibel 33957-0839
239-472-2329
www.sccf.org

Ten Thousand Islands National Wildlife Refuge

Facilities: Hiking and paddling trails; boat ramps; observation tower

Activities: Hiking, paddling, camping, wildlife viewing

Admission: Free

Hours: Marsh Trail parking lot is for day-use only

Pets: Allowed on leash

Best Time of Year: No preference

The 35,000-acre Ten Thousand Islands National Wildlife Refuge is part of a large area of mangrove islands of the same name on the Gulf Coast near Everglades City. The refuge connects the water flow from Picayune and Fakahatchee Strands to the Gulf of Mexico. The estuary abounds with wildlife, both above and under water. The uplands of the mangrove-fringed islands support hardwood hammock trees, such as gumbo-limbo and Jamaica-dogwood. The refuge was acquired in 1996 but didn't have any visitor facilities until 2009, when a hiking trail, several boat ramps, and paddling trails were opened. Before that, access was by boat from existing public ramps. The refuge manager from **Florida Panther NWR** also oversees this unstaffed refuge.

Hiking

The Marsh Trail is a 1-mile flat hiking trail across the marsh and upper estuary. An observation tower is a 0.25-mile walk on a paved section of the trail. The rest of the trail is unpaved. Excellent views of waterbirds and other salt marsh wildlife abound.

Boating and Paddling

At the same parking lot for the Marsh Trail on US 41 is a ramp for canoes and motorboats. This ramp allows for motors up to 25 hp, but the water may be only 18 inches deep or less, and thereby impassable. Along US 41 are four paddling launches, although only the Marsh Trail ramp is well marked on the road as of this printing. Trail 2 (for boats) starts at the Marsh Trail parking lot and totals 2.1 miles roundtrip. You can continue onto Trail 3 at the end of Trail 2 for an additional 1.4 miles roundtrip. Trail 1 is 1.6 miles to the end and back and Trail 4 is 3.0 miles to the end and back; however, these trailheads are not marked and are difficult to find. Paddlers may see roseate spoonbills, manatees, and loggerhead sea turtles, which frequent this area.

DIRECTIONS

Refuge is located about 20 miles southeast of Naples, on the south side of US 41. Most of the refuge is best accessed by boat. Public ramps are located in Goodland on SR 92 (5 miles west of US 41) and Port-of-the-Islands Marina on US 41 (5 miles south of SR 82). The Marsh Trail parking lot (hiking trail and boat ramp) within the refuge is on the south side of US 41, 2.7 miles southeast of CR 92. Three other canoe launches are along this same stretch of US 41 but are not marked and have no parking.

CONTACT

Florida Panther National Wildlife Refuge
3860 Tollgate Boulevard, Suite 300
Naples 34114
239-353-8442
www.fws.gov/floridapanther/
TenThousandIsland/

Observation platform at Ten Thousand Islands National Wildlife Refuge

Coconut palms grace the beach at Bahia Honda. The newer bridge through the Keys is on the horizon.

VII NATURAL AREAS OF THE FLORIDA KEYS

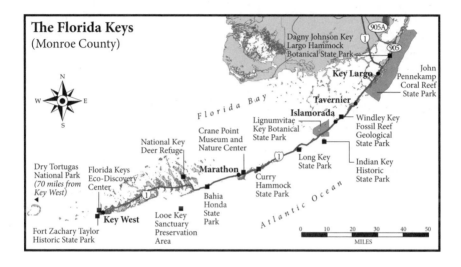

The Florida Keys
(Monroe County)

Dagny Johnson Key
Largo Hammock
Botanical State Park

Key Largo

John
Pennekamp
Coral Reef
State Park

Florida Bay

Tavernier

Islamorada

Lignumvitae
Key Botanical
State Park

Windley Key
Fossil Reef
Geological
State Park

Crane Point
Museum and
Nature Center

National Key
Deer Refuge

Long Key
State Park

Indian Key
Historic
State Park

Dry Tortugas
National Park
*(70 miles from
Key West)*

Florida Keys
Eco-Discovery
Center

Marathon

Curry
Hammock
State Park

Atlantic Ocean

Key West

Looe Key
Sanctuary
Preservation
Area

Bahia
Honda
State
Park

Fort Zachary Taylor
Historic State Park

0   10   20   30   40   50
MILES

Bahia Honda State Park

Facilities: Nature trail, nature center, campground, boat ramp, marina, cabins, kayak and snorkel rentals

Activities: Birding, swimming, snorkeling, picnicking, camping, boating, paddling

Admission: State Park fee

Hours: 8 am to sunset

Pets: Allowed in limited areas

South Florida Birding Trail: 112

Best Time of Year: March, April, and September–November for migrating raptors, shorebirds, and warblers; December–April for wintering birds; April–November for diving and snorkeling

The Spanish influence in this area is obvious by the name of the park, which means "deep bay." Indeed, the channel at the west end is one of the deepest natural channels in the Florida Keys. The bridge that spans it is correspondingly high, since the deeper the water, the higher the waves will be. The 635-acre park encompasses lagoons, beach dunes, coastal berms, mangroves, submerged marine habitats, and tropical hardwood hammocks. Several rare and unusual plants are protected here: satinwood, manchineel, key thatch palm, and the endangered small-flowered lily thorn (or spiny catesbaea). Many of the plant species are of West Indian origin, including one of the largest remaining stands of silver palm.

Flagler's railroad passed through Bahia Honda, and remnants of the hurricane-torn tracks still rise above the park. Because of its height above the water, the old bridge is a good scenic observation spot.

The Sand and Sea Nature Center introduces visitors to sea turtles, corals, and other sea life. The shallow water along the beach is excellent for snorkeling, especially for beginners. Corals, conchs, and many fish can be seen. Green, hawksbill, and loggerhead turtles can be seen and may nest on the beach starting in April.

In the autumn, Bahia Honda is a good place to watch for migrating birds. The birds fly south along the chain of keys, resting, feeding, and searching for a way to cross the Gulf of Mexico.

The Silver Palm Trail is a short loop trail, about a 15-minute walk through mangroves, hammocks, and dunes near the swimming beach on the Atlantic side. A printed trail guide follows the numbered posts, explaining the hammock and dune ecology. Watch the vegetation change with slight changes in elevation. The shrubby silver palms, named for the silvery

Bahia Honda State Park

undersides of the fronds, are common here because they are protected in the park. Elsewhere, silver palms are stolen from their natural settings to be planted in peoples' yards and have become rare.

Other plants along the trail, such as bay-cedar and black-torch, are typical of Keys beaches. Sea oats and sea-grape, seen along the beach, are state-protected dune stabilizers. Animals include land crabs and white-crowned pigeons (summer) in the hammock and wading birds in the lagoon.

There are three camping areas with 80 sites for trailers and tents. Six cabins can accommodate eight people each; linens and utensils are provided. Swimming and snorkeling are excellent from the beaches on the ocean and bay sides. The concession runs daily snorkel trips to the coral reef at **Looe Key**, part of the Florida Keys National Marine Sanctuary. At the marina, charter boats and fishing guides are available for hire. The concession store sells marina supplies and limited groceries.

DIRECTIONS
From Florida City, take US 1 South to MM 36.9 on Bahia Honda Key; the park is 12 miles west of Marathon.

CONTACT
Bahia Honda State Park
36850 Overseas Highway
Big Pine Key 33043
305-872-2353
www.floridastateparks.org/bahiahonda/

Nature Center:
305-872-9807

Concession:
305-872-3210

Crane Point Museum and Nature Center

Facilities: Adult and children's museums, artificial lagoon, self-guided walking trail, gift shop

Activities: Birding, botanizing

Admission: Entrance fee

Hours: Monday–Saturday 9 am–5 pm, Sunday 12–5 pm

Pets: Not allowed

South Florida Birding Trail: 111

Best Time of Year: Any time of year for museum. The trail is beautiful year-round, with plenty to see, but it may be buggy and muggy in the summer. October, November, March, and April are good months to see migrating warblers and raptors.

A major victory for conservation in the Florida Keys came when the Florida Keys Land and Sea Trust acquired the 63.5-acre Crane Point Hammock in Marathon in 1989. The Florida Keys Land and Sea Trust is a private, nonprofit organization that acquires natural areas in the Keys to protect habitats and cultural history. It was a prime site for development on the crowded land-starved island of Key Vaca. The area did not escape development by accident. The Crane family members, who bought the property in 1949, were ardent conservationists.

This hammock contains probably the last intact virgin thatch palm hammock left in North America. The hammock supports 160 native species of plants, and artifacts of pre-Columbian native people have been found here. Allow about a half day for your tour of the museum and a walk on the nature trail.

Museum

The main attraction is the museum housing 20 major exhibits and additional rotating displays of cultural and natural history. In the main building is the "adult" museum, which boasts a 600-square-foot walk-through replica of a coral reef cave. It extends 30 feet above you as you walk through, and you will see mounts of many fish common and not-so-common to the Florida Keys reefs.

Also in the museum is a Key deer exhibit that features a two-day-old fawn that drowned in a ditch dug years ago for mosquito control. Many ditches remain in the Keys, a hazard for deer that drown when they try to cross the ditch and cannot climb the steep sides. Strategically placed near the mother and fawn in the exhibit is a taxidermy bald eagle that cleverly shows how diminutive the deer really are.

Exhibits in the main museum depict the 5,000-year human history of the Marathon area. Highlights include rare and unusual artifacts of cultural history, some dating back 5,000 years. Other exhibits include a 600-year-old dugout canoe, a tree snail display, and displays about the ship-wrecking business.

An outdoor walkway passes over an artificial lagoon, where live sharks, snappers, barracudas, parrotfish, and angelfish may be seen swimming around as they might just offshore from the hammock.

The walkway leads to the children's museum, a one-room building created for inquisitive children. Here children can handle the objects in the touch tank and study the fish in the 200-gallon saltwater tanks. The museum is a regular field trip destination for local school classes.

Behind the main building is the beginning of the nature trail, a 1.5-mile self-guided loop that runs through tropical Crane Point Hammock and ends at a lookout on Florida Bay. It explains the ecology of the hammock and some of the native trees you'll see. Many trees along the trail have identification tags. You'll see the Key (or brittle) thatch palm, Florida thatch palm, wild dilly, black ironwood, Jamaica dogwood, and paradise-tree. All the poisonwood trees are labeled so you'll know not to touch them. Also along the trail are a butterfly meadow and the Marathon Wild Bird Rehabilitation Center. Many birds end up here as the victims of fish hooks and monofilament line.

For history buffs, the Adderly House is open to the public. This restored house, built in 1903, is on the National Register of Historic Places and is the oldest house in the Keys outside of Key West. It was built by a Bahamian with home-made concrete and has withstood every hurricane that threatened its threshold.

Call ahead for the schedule of programs. Group tours and programs are available if arranged in advance.

DIRECTIONS
From Florida City, take US 1 South to MM 50.5 in Marathon. Look for a small sign on the bay side.

CONTACT
Crane Point Museum and Nature Center
5550 Overseas Highway
Marathon 33050
305-743-9100
www.cranepoint.net/

Curry Hammock State Park

Facilities: Hiking trails, kayak rentals, campground, beach

Activities: Paddling, hiking, birding, wildlife viewing, swimming, snorkeling

Admission: State Park fee

Hours: 8 am to sunset

Pets: Allowed in limited areas

South Florida Birding Trail: 110

Best Time of Year: Winter and spring for weather and birding

The more than 1,000 acres on five islands encompass hardwood hammocks, mangroves and seagrass beds. The largest remaining U.S. population of Florida thatch palms is found here. Thatch palms are so named because the fan-shaped leaves form almost a complete circle and are therefore often used to cover shelters. The species, which is native to south Florida, the West Indies, the Bahamas, and Central America, may grow to 30 feet. Two miles of the **Florida Keys Overseas Heritage Trail** pass through the park.

A 1.5-mile hiking trail winds through hardwood hammock, with a spur to the bay shore; the trailhead is on US 1, one mile southwest of the park entrance on the bay side. The surface is rough, so wear sturdy shoes. Snorkeling is excellent in shallow seagrass beds, as is kayaking along the miles of shoreline and mangrove inlets. The 28 campsites fill quickly in the winter; they have water and electricity.

Birders gather from mid-September to early November for spectacular hawk migration watches, including large numbers of peregrine falcons. Observers can get a good aerial view from the bat tower. White-crowned pigeons are frequently seen in summer. Reddish egrets and magnificent frigatebirds are often seen. The Florida Keys Birding and Wildlife Festival is held annually in September. Manatees and dolphins may be seen from the shore. A subspecies of the familiar raccoon—the Key Vaca raccoon *Procyon lotor auspicatus*—may be seen here and elsewhere in the Middle and Lower Keys.

DIRECTIONS
From Florida City, go south on US 1 to MM 56.2 in Marathon.

CONTACT
Curry Hammock State Park
56200 Overseas Highway
Marathon 33050
305-289-2690
www.floridastateparks.org/curryhammock

Dagny Johnson Key Largo Hammock Botanical State Park

Facilities: Self-guided walking trails, occasional guided walks

Activities: Birding, botanizing, bicycling

Admission: Small entrance fee

Hours: Daily 8 am to 5 pm

Pets: Allowed in picnic areas, along sea wall, bike trails, and hiking trails

South Florida Birding Trail: 107

Best Time of Year: Winter for better weather, fall–spring for birding, year-round for plants, spring and summer for flowers

This 2,421-acre remnant of West Indian hardwood hammock on the northern third of Key Largo protects many rare species of plants and animals. It has more than six miles of trails for self-guided walks and birding. One trail partly coincides with a small road that is part of the abandoned condominium development that also left traces of walls and foundations around. The Department of Environmental Protection manages this land, which is much larger than the area they allow the public to access. For the serious birder or botanist, this park is a must-see.

This area of the Keys contains the most species of trees found anywhere in the United States, and most of them are West Indian. Some trees and shrubs you'll encounter include snowberry, mahogany, velvetseed, Jamaica dogwood, poisonwood, paradise-tree, willow bustic, and lancewood. Many passerine birds feed and rest here during spring and fall migrations. This is an excellent area for botanists and birders. The native plants have regrown and have identification tags. A 0.5-mile self-guided trail is paved and bicycling is permitted. An additional 6 miles of trails, mostly coral substrate, are open to the public, but first obtain a backcountry permit from nearby Pennekamp State Park.

Migrating birds stop over primarily in October on their way south, resting and feeding before heading over the ocean; a smaller migration event occurs in April with northbound birds. Warblers and raptors are prominent. Breeding residents include white-crowned pigeons, black-whiskered vireos, gray kingbirds, and mangrove cuckoos. Butterfly-attracting plants are abundant and support Schaus' swallowtails, silver-banded hairstreaks, hammock skippers, and mangrove skippers. The hammock also supports crocodiles and Key Largo woodrats.

DIRECTIONS

From Florida City, go south on US 1 to upper Key Largo, turn left on SR 905 and go 0.4 miles east to parking lot on right.

CONTACT

John Pennekamp Coral Reef State Park (Dagny Johnson Park is unstaffed)
Key Largo
305-451-1202
www.floridastateparks.org/
keylargohammock

Coral rock substrate in a hardwood hammock

Dry Tortugas
National Park

Facilities: Campground, historical fort, visitor center, self-guided walking tour, ranger-led programs

Activities: Birding, swimming, snorkeling, camping

Admission: U.S. fee area and small fee for camping

Hours: Ft. Jefferson on Garden Key and Loggerhead Key are open year-round during daylight hours; Bush Key hours are subject to change; Hospital and Long Keys are closed year-round and visitors should remain 100 feet offshore; Middle and East Keys are closed April 1–October 15 for turtle nesting

Pets: Allowed only on Garden Key, but not in Fort Jefferson

South Florida Birding Trail: 116

Best Time of Year: For birding, April to September for nesting terns, spring and autumn for migrants; year-round for sea birds; for snorkeling, water warmest and calmest in summer

Other: See **DIRECTIONS** for access to this island park. Tours for guided birding and other wildlife viewing, scuba diving, and fishing are available from Key West vendors. Those with Park Service permits to operate in the park are posted at www.nps.gov/drto/planyourvisit/.

Visitors must bring all their own provisions. This includes drinking water and food; no fresh water available (however, toilets are available). No lodging available; overnight stays on land require tent camping. All garbage must leave with you. The fort, visitor center, and campground are on Garden Key.

Flung far out into the Gulf of Mexico are the rest of the Florida Keys. Few visitors realize that the Keys don't end at Key West—just the road does. Almost 70 miles farther west, and another world away, is a small cluster of seven coral islands known as the Dry Tortugas. Fort Jefferson, the "Gibraltar of the Gulf," is located on one of these islands.

Ponce de León found the islands in 1513. He named them Las Tortugas (Spanish for "The Turtles") because of the many sea turtles he found. The adjective "Dry" was added later to warn mariners that the islands had no fresh water. Located strategically in the shipping path between Central America and the United States, the islands became the sanctum of pirates for centuries. When Florida became part of the United States in 1821, so did the Dry Tortugas.

In 1846, the U.S. Corps of Engineers began to build the fort (named after Thomas Jefferson) on 16-acre Garden Key. Although construction continued for three decades, the fort was never completed. Still, it was the largest seacoast fortress from Maine to Texas at that time, with a perimeter of a half mile. The 8-foot-thick, 45-foot-high walls contain 16 million hand-made bricks. During the Civil War, Fort Jefferson became a military prison for army deserters. The most famous political prisoner was Dr. Samuel Mudd, who set the broken leg of Abraham Lincoln's assassin, John Wilkes Booth. Although sentenced to life imprisonment for conspiracy, Mudd was pardoned after saving the army garrison from a yellow fever epidemic. The Navy took over the fort for a refueling station in 1889. President Franklin D. Roosevelt proclaimed the fort and adjacent islands a national monument (known as Fort Jefferson National Monument) in 1935 for their historic and educational values. In 1992, the monument achieved national park status in recognition of its exceptional natural resources.

Now let's talk about birds. Just as the

Fort Jefferson moat and campground

islands are located in the middle of the shipping lanes, so they are also located in the middle of the migration flyways between North and South America. For as long as the lonely coral islands have poked their heads above the water, sea birds and land-dwelling migrants have found a haven on them. Nesting birds start arriving in March, and by April, up to 100,000 terns have laid eggs on Bush, Hospital, and Long Keys. Most are sooty terns, but brown noddies and roseate terns also nest here. Gulls, other terns, shorebirds, raptors, frigatebirds, boobies, and accidentals from the West Indies can all be found most of the year. In 1832, John James Audubon visited the Tortugas to study the spectacular bird life.

Not to be outdone, the underwater scene is equally spectacular. Excellent snorkeling and scuba diving sites abound. The clear shallow waters are perfect for the growth of coral and associated reef fish. Elkhorn and staghorn corals were listed as federally threatened in 2006. Four endangered species of sea turtles— the hawksbill, green, Kemp's Ridley, and leatherback—as well as the threatened loggerhead, have been found here.

In 2001, the Tortugas Ecological Reserve was established in the waters northwest and southwest of the park. Boaters entering these waters may need permits. Call Florida Keys National Marine Sanctuary for details (305-809-4670; www.floridakeys.noaa.gov/welcome.html). In 2007, the Park Service established a 46-square-mile Research Natural Area in the Park that is a no-take marine ecological preserve. This means that fishing and anchoring boats are not permitted. Still allowed throughout the Park are boating to the islands, swimming, snorkeling, and diving. Fifty-four percent of the Park is outside of the Research Natural Area.

If you don't mind primitive camping, this is the place to do it. This small cluster of islands has so much to see. It's farther from a road than anywhere else in Florida.

Visitor Center

The visitor center (on Garden Key) contains historical exhibits, an interpretive program, and books for sale. Ranger-led programs are offered in the winter; check the center for the schedule. Ask for the bird checklist here; it's thorough because this is a serious birder's haven. Snorkel equipment can be borrowed at the visitor center.

The Fort

The half-mile self-guided tour treads around the historic fort. Interpretive signs guide you inside and outside the brick fortress, through bastions and narrow stairwells, past the ammunition magazine, and even into Mudd's spartan cell. Calcified water percolates through the ceiling in places, creating mini-stalactites and corresponding stalagmites inside the building. The fort was never completed because of the invention of the rifled cannon, which could penetrate even the 8-foot-thick walls. Old and new cisterns can be seen. The old ones cracked from settling, letting in salt water. The original lighthouse stands defunct. From the roof of the fort (accessible by stairs), the view across the water and other islands is spectacular.

Entirely surrounding the fort is a brick seawall constructed as added protection to the fort, much as the coral reefs protect the islands. Between the fort and the seawall is a moat containing quiet, sheltered water. You can walk on top of the seawall for its entire length and see into the clear water on both sides. Nonswimmers will be treated to a view of marine life almost as good as a snorkeler's view if the water is calm. Bring a strong flashlight if you're staying at night, and try looking into the moat after dark. The wind often dies down after dusk, making the water calmer. The nocturnal creatures emerge, and wonderful views of active conchs, lobsters, crabs, shrimp, moray eels, urchins, and sea stars can be seen.

Loggerhead Key

About two miles west of Garden Key is the largest of the seven islands. Boaters are permitted to land at Loggerhead and climb the 180 steps to the top of the functioning lighthouse. It affords a glorious view of the Dry Tortugas. The island was named for the loggerhead turtles that nest on the sandy beaches in the summer. The nests are carefully protected by park rangers.

Birding

Birders from around the country and many other countries come to the Dry Tortugas to view seabirds and migrating land birds; 285 species are known to occur here. Many are accidentals from far away, appearing briefly after getting blown off course from a cold front or tropical storm. The late winter cold fronts blow flocks of weary migrants onto the islands. The exhausted birds perch listlessly on branches, recovering strength enough to feed. This is when binoculars just get in the way. The metaphor "the trees were dripping with warblers" is appropriate after cold fronts.

From March to October, tens of thousands of sooty terns and brown noddies can be watched from Garden Key. Most nest on Bush and Long Keys, only a few hundred yards from Garden Key. A strong spotting scope will give an impressive view of the nest islands from Garden Key.

In October and November, the north winds bring migrations of raptors (such as merlins, peregrine falcons, sharp-shinned hawks, and broadwings), warblers, and shorebirds. All are hoping to rest, feed, and store up energy for the remaining marathon flight across the havenless water to Cuba and beyond.

Snorkeling and Swimming

Snorkeling and swimming are exceptional around the outside of the seawall on Garden Key. Snorkelers will find a rich variety of marine life in a mere three or four feet of water. Colorful fish, lobsters, sea cucumbers, conchs, corals, and so on, are all easily visible. Look for loggerhead and hawksbill sea turtles feeding in the seagrasses. Scuba divers must bring their own diving equipment, but snorkeling equipment can be borrowed at the visitor center.

Boating

Many sailboaters find the Dry Tortugas a great destination from cities on both coasts of Florida. Motor boaters usually embark from Key West. If you bring your own boat to the islands, make sure you have the Dry Tortugas NOAA Chart #11438 to navigate safely around the shallow reefs. Also check the Park's website for regulations on where to anchor. The waters between Key West and the Tortugas can become rough during the winter or during summer thunderstorms, so check the forecast before casting off. No fuel or provisions of any type are available at the islands; you must be completely self-sufficient. The islands have no overnight slips. Mooring at the dock on Garden Key is limited to two hours during daylight. Boats must be anchored in designated places at night. Water skiing and jet skiing are not permitted.

From February through September, nesting and fledging birds have priority on Bush Key, and the island is closed to human visitation. Also, because sea turtles nest on East, Middle, Bush, and Loggerhead Keys, these islands are closed from sunset to sunrise from May through September. Hospital and Long Keys are closed year-round.

Campground

A more peaceful, picturesque, relaxing setting for camping can't be found in Florida. Your tent is pitched under a palm tree, birds "drip" from the trees, and with a mere two skips you're slipping into the warm coral reef waters. Camping is permitted only in the designated camping area on Garden Key. Picnic tables, grills, and saltwater toilets are provided; no showers. Camping is on a first-come, first-served basis for the limited number of sites (10 sites plus an overflow area). Groups of 10 or more must obtain a permit in advance. All supplies must be packed in and all trash must be packed out. Campers arriving by concession ferry or seaplane should check the vendor's restrictions on carrying stove fuel—it is generally not allowed on their boats and planes (self-starting charcoal is allowed).

DIRECTIONS

The Park is accessible only by boat (private, chartered boat, ferry) or seaplanes. There is no Park Service transportation for the public. Tour boats take 2 or more hours each way; seaplanes 45 minutes from Key West. Half day, all day, overnight, and snorkeling tours can be arranged. Several private concessions fly seaplanes from the Keys and southern Florida cities to Garden Key. Occasionally it is too rough for seaplanes to land. The standard seaplane trips are half-day or full-day, but overnight trips can be negotiated. The concessions below were approved by the Park Service.

Boats from Key West:
Sunny Days
800-236-7937 or 305-292-6100

Yankee Freedom
800-634-0939 or 305-294-7009
www.yankeefreedom.com or
www.drytortugas.com

Seaplanes from Key West:
Key West Seaplane Adventures
305-942-9777
www.keywestseaplanecharters.com

CONTACT

Dry Tortugas National Park
P.O. Box 6208
Key West 33041
305-242-7700
www.nps.gov/drto/

Florida Keys Eco-Discovery Center

Facilities: Nature center, gift shop

Activities: Indoor learning experience

Admission: Free

Hours: Tuesday–Saturday 9 am–4 pm; closed Thanksgiving and Christmas, and Sundays and Mondays

Pets: Not allowed

Best Time of Year: No preference

The 6,400-square-foot nature center opened in 2007. World-class exhibits interpret the ecology of the Florida Keys National Marine Sanctuary as well as the national wildlife refuges and national parks of the Florida Keys by using interactive displays, underwater cameras, and aquaria to explain the terrestrial, shoreline, and underwater habitats. A 2,500-gallon state-of-the-art living reef contains live corals, fish, and other marine life.

DIRECTIONS
From the north, take US 1 (Overseas Highway) to Key West, almost to the end. Where US 1 turns right on Whitehead Street, continue a few blocks to left turn on Southard Street, then straight to the Center on right. Located across from **Fort Zachary Taylor Historic State Park.**

CONTACT
Florida Keys Eco-Discovery Center
35 East Quay Road
Key West
305-809-4750
floridakeys.noaa.gov/eco_discovery.html

Developed by Mote Marine Laboratory, "The Living Reef" exhibit educates visitors about preserving coral reefs.

Fort Zachary Taylor Historic State Park

Facilities: Historic site, snorkel gear rentals

Activities: Birding, paddling, snorkeling

Admission: State Park fee

Hours: 8 am to sunset

Pets: Not allowed on beach or in fort

South Florida Birding Trail: 115

Best Time of Year: No preference

This is the southernmost park in the continental United States. It was designated a national historic landmark in 1973 for its military history (as a Civil War fort). Because it is the largest natural area in Key West, birds migrating in spring and fall often stop here to refuel before or after crossing the Gulf of Mexico. Warblers are prevalent in spring migrations and raptors in the fall. Other birds that may be seen are magnificent frigatebirds, roseate terns, white-crowned pigeons, gray kingbirds, Antillean short-eared owls, migrating songbirds, and Caribbean vagrants.

The two short walking trails are the Sand Hog Trail (goes through coastal habitat) and the Fort View Trail (goes through a tropical hardwood hammock to a view overlooking the fort and moat). Rent a mask and fins and go snorkeling from the beach (artificially created by filling with sand), and then watch the sun set over the water.

Paddlers must check in at the entrance station and launch at the eastern end of the beach. No rentals at the park. This is one end of the **Florida Keys Overseas Paddling Trail**. Paddle with care around the island, which is rife with boating and shipping traffic.

DIRECTIONS
Take US 1 (Overseas Hwy.) to the western end of Key West; US 1 becomes Roosevelt Blvd. Turn right onto Whitehead St. and left onto Southard Street for 0.2 miles to entrance (go through Truman Annex).

CONTACT
Fort Zachary Taylor Historic State Park
Southard Street
Key West 33041
305-292-6713
www.floridastateparks.org/
forttaylor/default.cfm

Indian Key Historic State Park

Facilities: Interpretive trails, guided tours, historic site, observation tower, day-use boat dock

Activities: Paddling, boating, snorkeling, swimming

Admission: Free

Hours: Island open from 8 am to sunset daily

Pets: Not allowed

Best Time of Year: November to April, the dry season, when mosquitoes are fewest (no artificial mosquito control)

Other: Robbie's Rent-A-Boat has motorboat, canoe, and kayak rentals

Indian Key is a 10-acre island on the ocean side of the Keys. Originally inhabited by Calusa Indians, it was bought in 1831 by Jacob Housman, who built a local empire with his wreck-salvaging business. Dr. Henry Perrine, an avid botanist, moved to the island in 1837 and imported tropical plants from Mexico for cultivation. The thriving town (it was the county seat for Dade) was destroyed by retaliating Calusas. All that remains are foundations, overgrown tropical plants, and old roads.

The island is still laid out with the old street pattern, although reverting to nature. Interpretive signs explain natural and cultural history. This is an interesting trip for a paddling destination, because it is about 0.5 miles from the public ramp (oceanside); slightly longer from Robbie's. Ranger-led tours are available twice a day Thursday through Monday.

The island is unstaffed and is part of the **Windley Key Fossil Reef Geological State Park** complex. Swimming and snorkeling are allowed from the shore or a boat.

DIRECTIONS
Park is located at MM 78.5 US 1 on the ocean side and is accessible only by water. There is a public boat ramp on Indian Key Fill at MM 78.5 US 1 bayside. Concession tour boat leaves from Robbie's Marina at MM 77.5 on US 1.

CONTACT
Windley Key Fossil Reef Geological State Park
Islamorada 33036
305-664-2540
www.floridastateparks.org/indiankey

Tour boat reservations:
Robbie's Rent-A-Boat
305-664-9814
www.robbies.com/statetours.htm

John Pennekamp Coral Reef State Park

Facilities: Scuba diving instruction, rentals, guided trips; snorkeling rentals and guided trips; swimming and snorkeling area; glassbottom boat trips; campground; canoe and kayak rentals; nature trails; visitor center and seaquarium; snack bar; gift shop; dive shop; boat ramp and fuel; boat rentals

Activities: Scuba diving, snorkeling, swimming, camping, paddling, picnicking

Admission: State Park fee

Hours: 8 am to sunset. Visitor center open 8 am–5 pm daily. Concession open 8 am–5 pm daily

Pets: Not allowed on beach, in buildings, or at group campsite

South Florida Birding Trail: 108

Best Time of Year: The water temperature from November to April is 70–75°F at the surface. Except during cold fronts, snorkeling is comfortable. Scuba divers usually wear wet suits since the deeper water is colder. In the winter, cold fronts can cause strong winds, occasionally canceling scheduled boat trips. From May to October, the surface temperature is 80–85°. Starting in June, thunderstorms and tropical storms can make water-related activities hazardous. The most reliable months for good weather, migrating birds, few crowds, and few biting insects are April and May.

Appropriately, the nation's first undersea preserve is mostly under water. The park protects part of the only living coral reef in the continental United States. Within this marine sanctuary live 40 species of corals and 650 species of fish. The coral reef is shallow in places, providing excellent snorkeling and scuba diving opportunities. The park's concession services make it easy for almost everyone to see the colorful reef, either by snorkeling, diving, or glassbottom boating. Other water-related activities are available here, including canoeing, fishing, and swimming. Land-bound facilities include camping and interpretive trails.

The park is named for the late John Pennekamp, a Miami Herald editor, who was instrumental in getting Everglades National Park established. The original plan for the national park called for the boundary to extend south of Florida Bay, across Key Largo, and into the Atlantic Ocean, thus including the reef. Opposition from Florida Keys residents, whose homes would be within the new park boundaries, convinced officials that the only way to get the Everglades preserved was to exclude Key Largo and the reef. Fortunately, the reef was made into a state park shortly after.

Because of the intensive human usage of the reef, this glorious ecosystem is showing signs of stress and declining health. Among the culprits are careless anchoring, propellers striking bottom in shallow water, silting of coral by propeller wash, touching of coral by divers, littering, spilling fuel and oil, bilge pumping, and polluting from land sources. The reef is still beautiful, so please do your part to keep it that way.

Visitor Center

The star attraction is the 30,000-gallon saltwater aquarium, called "The Patch Reef Tank," that recreates a coral reef. Visitors can view the tank from all sides. Although

Porkfish on reef at Key Largo

the corals are not alive, the fish don't seem to notice. The live occupants include large lobsters, queen and gray angelfish, ocean surgeons, foureye butterflyfish, hogfish, parrotfish, and yellowtail snapper. Lining the visitor center walls are many smaller tanks, including "The Seagrass Community," "The Spiny Lobster," "Threats to the Reef," "The Reef Fish Community," and "The Outer Reef." Static displays explain natural storm protection from the reef and the mangrove community. This is an excellent small seaquarium for all ages and is included with admission into the park.

Swimming and Snorkeling from Shore

The park has three designated swimming areas. The main swimming area, near the main parking lot and the visitor center, is somewhat sheltered from the open ocean. It is a roped-off area with an artificial wreck of a Spanish galleon in shallow water. The wreck attracts grunts, barracuda, hogfish, gray snapper, and other fish, all easy for the beginning snorkeler to see. In fact, this is one of the few places in the Keys to go snorkeling from shore and see something interesting. Because of the proximity of the swimming area to the muddy mangrove bottoms, upside-down jellyfish flourish here. They are so named because they swim mouth-downward, but flip over when resting on the bottom, exposing their fluttery mantle containing photosynthesizing cells. They can grow to one foot across and can give irritating stings, but they are not a serious problem.

The two other swimming areas are away from the main parking lot. One is more open-ocean where the scuba classes go; the other is a sheltered area.

Reef Snorkeling and Scuba Diving

You can't see the coral reef by snorkeling from shore. The concession at the dive shop can set you up with everything you need for snorkeling or diving on your own. The concession also offers guided snorkeling and diving trips several times daily, weather permitting. You should call ahead to make a reservation and check the weather forecast. The calmest water is usually in the morning—windier in afternoon. The light is best at noon because it is from directly overhead, revealing all the colors just below the water's surface. You can rent or purchase all types of snorkeling and diving equipment at the dive shop.

In a typical 30-minute dive, snorkel, or glassbottom boat trip, you may see as many as 100 species of fish. These are the fish that are the most abundant and active in the daytime. Many other species are present but are less likely to be seen on a short trip. Some of the common ones are blue tangs, trumpetfish, angelfish, damselfish, parrotfish, barracuda, grunts, butterflyfish, and snappers. Moray eels are common but nocturnal, and stingrays camouflage themselves with the sea bottom. Please don't touch the coral.

Glassbottom Boat

A good way for nonsnorkelers and nondivers to see the coral reef is on the 65-foot glassbottom high-speed catamaran. The scenery is excellent on this 2.5-hour

trip. Reservations are suggested. The natural light is best at noon, when the sun's rays are most direct. Trips leave three times daily from the concession.

Boating

Motorboats and sailboats are available to rent. Don't anchor a boat on coral—it is illegal and extremely damaging to the reef. Anchor on sand patches.

Paddling

The park has 2.5 miles of marked mangrove trails. From the canoe launch by the Mangrove Trail (see "Hiking Trails" below), paddlers can wind through narrow mangrove channels or paddle out to the ocean. Another place to launch is at the concession, where you can rent canoes and kayaks. Paddling is a good way to see the park. During the winter season (November to March or April) ranger-naturalists lead paddling trips.

Hiking Trails

One short trail goes through mangroves and two go through a hardwood hammock. The Mangrove Trail is actually a boardwalk, a leisurely 15-minute self-guided walk with interpretive signs. The 10-foot-tall observation tower is just tall enough to view across the tops of the red mangroves.

The Tamarind Trail (near the entrance station) is a leisurely 20-minute walk through a tropical hardwood hammock. The narrow trail is rough with roots and coral rocks and is unmarked. It is best to go with a ranger for a guided tour. You will see such trees as pigeon-plum and gumbo-limbo, plus the wild-tamarind for which the trail was named. Some commonly seen birds are warblers (palm, prairie, blackpoll, yellow-throated, and redstarts) and indigo buntings. The Grove Trail starts at the visitor center and goes to a tropical fruit grove that replicates what early settlers grew.

Ranger-naturalists lead daily walks in the winter (end of November to March or April). During the off-season, no guided trips are scheduled, but you can often find a ranger to give you a tour on request. Special group tours can be arranged year-round. Ask at the visitor center for the bird list, which contains 198 species.

Camping
The 47 tent and recreational vehicle sites are small but full-facility. Available by reservation only (800-326-3521) up to 11 months in advance. At one end of the campground is a lagoon-type pond that often has white ibises, great white herons, terns, and other water birds feeding.

DIRECTIONS
From Florida City, go south on US 1 to MM 102.5 oceanside.

CONTACT
John Pennekamp Coral Reef State Park
102601 US 1
Key Largo 33037
305-451-1202
www.floridastateparks.org/pennekamp/

Concession:
Coral Reef Park Company
305-451-6300
www.pennekamppark.com/

Lignumvitae Key Botanical State Park

Facilities: Guided nature walk and tour of historical house, day-use boat dock; Robbie's Rent-A-Boat has motorboat, canoe, and kayak rentals; not all facilities are handicapped accessible

Activities: Paddling, botanizing, birding

Admission: Free

Hours: Island open from 9 am to 5 pm; closed Tuesday and Wednesday; Matheson House open Friday, Saturday, Sunday

Pets: Not allowed

Best Time of Year: November to April, the dry season, when mosquitoes are fewest (no artificial mosquito control here).

Other: Private boats may dock free and passengers may join the 10 am or 2 pm guided walks, held Friday, Saturday, and Sunday. This island is unstaffed and part of the Windley Key Fossil Reef Geological State Park complex.

The 280-acre Lignumvitae Key is a mile cruise across Florida Bay from the nearest road. Although it has some of the highest (and safest) ground in the Keys (up to 16.5 feet above sea level), it has miraculously escaped development. The Florida Department of Environmental Protection (DEP) took over maintenance of the island in 1971. DEP has preserved the flora in its natural state, making it one of the best remaining examples of a West Indian tropical hammock. DEP staff and volunteers painstakingly removed nonnative vegetation that had escaped cultivation from the original residents' landscaping. A few nonnative plants have been left around the building for historical value. The park boundary includes the surrounding waters of Lignumvitae Key, Shell Key, and Indian Key, totaling 10,838 acres. Collecting of sponges and tropical fish is banned in these waters. The use of boat motors is prohibited where the water depth is three feet or less.

The island's name comes from a small tree, the lignum vitae. Lignum vitae, Latin for "wood of life," is native to Central America, the Antilles, the Bahamas, and extreme southern Florida (mostly the Keys, rarely the mainland). "Wood of Life" was the name dubbed by 16th-century Europeans who thought it was a cure for syphilis and other diseases. The wood, the densest used commercially, does not float. It is so loaded with resins (about 30 percent of the weight of the wood) and is so self-lubricating that it was once in demand by the shipping industry to make propeller shaft bearings.

Truly blue flowers, such as those borne by the lignum vitae, are uncommon in native North American plants; most of our blue flowers were introduced. The flowers appear in spring and early summer. The tree is small, up to 33 feet tall, and gnarled. The opposite, evenly pinnate compound leaves are evergreen. Lignum vitae trees may grow to be 1000 years old, but they are not common enough to be used commercially any more. In fact, they are on the state's endangered species list.

For botanists, Lignumvitae Key is well worth the trip from the mainland and the limited opportunities to get to the island. It is perhaps the most pristine example of native tropical hardwoods left in the continental United States. The historical aspects (such as the tour of the house) are also fascinating.

Matheson House

This picturesque house was built of coral rock and Dade County (slash) pine in 1919 by William J. Matheson, who also donated the original land for **Matheson Hammock Park**. The house is furnished with original and period furniture and now serves as a ranger station and museum. The windmill that provided power to the residents still stands next to the house; now a generator does that job. Fresh water was, and still is, obtained from cisterns. Cisterns are tanks that are filled with rainwater falling on the roofs of buildings. The rainwater is funneled through gutters to the tanks. From the tanks, the water is pumped to a modern plumbing system. Water that collects during the summer rainy season is usually enough to last through the winter dry months. Be sparing on your restroom flushes here. Once the water is depleted in the reservoir tank, no more will be available until the next heavy rain. Lignumvitae is one of the few places left in the Keys still using cisterns because aerial spraying for mosquitoes contaminates the water elsewhere; spraying is not permitted over Lignumvitae. The Matheson house was built with the hot tropical climate in mind, and the design reflects careful usage of architectural features that take advantage

of the cooling breezes.

Trails

Although there are several trails on the island, visitors must remain with a tour guide when on any trail. The tour guides are knowledgeable about the native plants. Some of the trees you may see are mastic, lancewood, white stopper, saffron-plum, pigeon-plum, wild coffee, sapodilla, and satinleaf. From May to October, white-crowned pigeons are easily seen in the canopy feeding on the fruits of the pigeon-plum, poisonwood, and native fig trees.

The trails are wide and level enough for wheelchairs. The tour, including the boat ride, takes up to three hours. Long sleeves and pants are recommended.

Paddling

Canoes and kayaks are ideal for spotting wildlife in the shallow waters of nearshore Florida Bay while minimizing damage to the seagrass beds. From the launch ramp at MM 78.5 or Robbie's Marina, it's about 1.5 miles to the dock on the island's east side. Be careful of winds, tides, and motorboats.

Boat Tours

Robbie's Marina is the concession that runs scheduled boat trips to the island. Tours are held on Friday, Saturday, and Sunday and depart a half-hour before the 10 am and 2 pm guided walks at the Lignumvitae dock.

DIRECTIONS

The Park is accessible only by water (tour boat, private motorboat, or paddling). There is a public boat ramp on Indian Key Fill at MM 78.5 US 1 bayside. Concession tour boat leaves from Robbie's Marina at MM 77.5 on US 1.

CONTACT

Windley Key Fossil Reef Geological State Park
Islamorada 33036
305-664-2540
www.floridastateparks.org/
lignumvitaekey

Tour boat reservations:
Robbie's Marina
305-664-9814
www.robbies.com/statetours.htm

Buttonwood trees, like this solitary one, are a type of mangrove common in the Florida Keys.

Long Key State Park

Facilities: Hiking trails, canoe rentals, campground

Activities: Hiking, paddling, camping, picnicking, swimming, snorkeling, birding

Admission: State Park fee, except Layton Trail is free

Hours: 8 am to sunset

Pets: Not allowed on beaches, along the natural shoreline, in buildings

South Florida Birding Trail: 109

Best Time of Year: Winter and spring for birding

Perched atop vestiges of an-

cient coral reefs, Long Key is rich in West Indian vegetation and marine life. Realizing the natural resource and recreational values of the area, the state began to protect it in 1961, and by 1973 it had acquired 965 acres for the park; 116 acres are submerged.

Local saltwater fishing was an attraction that brought world-wide attention when Henry Flagler (builder of the overseas railroad to Key West) established the Long Key Fishing Club in 1906 after the first bridge was completed. Fishing continues to attract people to the ocean and bay waters around Long Key.

The park has walking and paddling trails that bring the nature-seeker close to the shallow lagoons where birds feed on the varied marine fish and invertebrates.

Along the oceanside are natural sandy beaches, accessible only by boat. In the summer, these narrow beaches are reserved for nesting sea turtles. Because sandy beaches are rare in the Keys, this is one of the few places around where sea turtles can lay their eggs.

Walking Trails
Golden Orb Trail
This is a 1-mile interpretive loop trail around a lagoon and beach. An observation tower provides a panoramic view of Long Key and is popular for fall hawk watches. Mangrove cuckoos, gray kingbirds, and white-crowned pigeons may be seen anywhere in the park.

Layton Trail
Layton Trail is difficult to find because it's outside the park entrance, a few hundred yards north of MM 68 on US 1 bayside. Look for a green historical marker sign "Long Key Fishing Club" and the small "Layton Trail" sign next to it. Park on the shoulder of the road. If you are driving down the Keys and want to take a break to stretch your legs, this is just the place. The short, shady loop

trail takes about 15 minutes to walk. The habitat is a tropical hardwood hammock, rich with native Keys plants, such as wild-lime, Jamaica dogwood, buttonwood, and seven-year apple (trees are labeled). The trail opens onto the rocky shore of Florida Bay.

Paddling Trail

The Long Key Lakes Canoe Trail is a 1.3-mile, self-guided paddling trail in a lagoon. It takes about an hour to paddle the loop around the mangroves, seagrass patches, and soft corals. Rent a canoe here or bring your own. The trail is suitable for novices.

DIRECTIONS

From Florida City, take US 1 south to Long Key. Park entrance is at MM 67.6 on US 1 oceanside.

CONTACT

Long Key State Park
67400 Overseas Highway
Long Key 33001
305-664-4815
www.floridastateparks.org/longkey

Kayak on Long Key at low tide. Kayaking and canoeing around the Florida Keys are excellent ways to see both land and water.

Looe Key Sanctuary Preservation Area

Facilities: No visitor facilities

Activities: Scuba diving, snorkeling, boating

Admission: Free

Hours: Day trips for snorkeling and diving

Pets: Not applicable

Best Time of Year: Weather for diving and snorkeling is generally warmer and calmer spring through fall

Other: Accessible only by tour or private boat. See **Bahia Honda State Park** for tours

Looe Key is a coral reef located about 6 miles south of Big Pine Key. Its name comes from a ship—the *HMS Looe*—that wrecked on the reef in 1744. The reef is about 200 yards long and 800 yards wide, but it is one of the best areas in the Keys to snorkel or dive. In 1981, it became part of the Florida Keys National Marine Sanctuary, which encompasses the third largest barrier reef in the world. The national marine sanctuary program was created by Congress to manage ecological, historical, recreational, and esthetic resources. The sanctuary preservation area (sometimes called Looe Key National Marine Sanctuary) is a small area around Looe Key.

DIRECTIONS
Area is located in the Atlantic Ocean, about 6 miles south of Big Pine Key. Looe Key is accessible from boat launches and guided trips at **Bahia Honda State Park** as well as resorts and dive shops in the vicinity of Big Pine Key.

CONTACT
Managed by National Oceanic and Atmospheric Administration (NOAA)
305-292-0311
floridakeys.noaa.gov/research_monitoring/looe_key.html

National Key Deer Refuge

Facilities: Walking trails, wildlife observation area, a few visitor displays in headquarters building

Activities: Wildlife viewing, birding, hiking

Admission: Free

Hours: Headquarters building open weekdays

Pets: Pets allowed on leash. However, even dogs on a leash are a major threat to the deer, because the deer become accustomed to their presence and lose their fear of unleashed dogs. Therefore, it is preferable to not bring dogs.

South Florida Birding Trail: 113

Best Time of Year: Deer are present year-round; winter and spring for birding

Other: If you arrive after hours, obtain a refuge map outside the office door or at the trail entrance. The map will show the most likely places to see the deer.

The diminutive Key deer (the smallest subspecies of white-tailed deer) had reached the perilously low population size of about 50 individuals when protection came in the form of a refuge created specifically for them. The islands had never supported great herds of deer, and human interference had whittled the numbers down further from hunting, habitat destruction, automobile collisions, and other hazards. With the establishment of the refuge in 1957 came protection from hunting, reduced speed limits, and regulations preventing harassment. The population has partially recovered, largely due to the persistent efforts of Jack Watson, the first warden of the refuge. Watson tirelessly and fearlessly pursued poachers and succeeded in getting them convicted. The deer population is now estimated at 800, scattered on about 30 islands.

The small size of these deer can be attributed to island living. Since the islands provide limited food and fresh water, the smaller deer thrive. Key deer bucks weigh about 80 pounds and does average about 64 pounds, the size of large dogs. Other than that, they resemble their larger mainland cousins.

Most of the 84,352 acres of refuge is submerged in the Gulf of Mexico. Limited visitor facilities exist. The Watson Trail and Blue Hole wildlife observation spot are all that were created for visitors. The deer may be found wandering anywhere on Big Pine or No Name keys. With patience and careful looking, you will see these delicate animals.

A special word of caution: drive very slowly and carefully around Big Pine and No Name keys to protect the deer. Many are killed by cars. Also, do not feed or entice the deer. Besides the improper diet they might receive, they learn to associate humans (and thus houses and cars) with food. Besides, there's a hefty fine. A sign on US 1 near the refuge keeps a grim tally of the year's

Young buck Key deer by red mangroves

deer mortality. Ten to fifteen percent of the population may be killed by cars in a single year. Free-ranging dogs are also deadly.

Observe the deer quietly from a distance, and you will be rewarded by seeing more natural behavior. The deer are visible any time of the year. Wander around the local roads in early morning or late afternoon and evening and you'll have a good chance of seeing a deer.

Several other undeveloped refuges in the Keys are managed out of Key Deer: Crocodile Lake, Great White Heron, and Key West. These are primarily shallow water areas with mangrove islands that serve as vital habitat for seabirds, wading birds, sea turtles, and many other animals. Access is restricted or prohibited in most areas. Call Refuge office for information.

Blue Hole Observation Area

Formerly a limestone quarry mined for local road construction, this gaping hole now contains fresh water, a rare commodity in the Keys. The water (from rainfall), which sits atop a layer of salt water (from seepage), attracts many terrestrial animals that come to drink, including the deer. Freshwater aquatic animals, uncommon elsewhere on the Keys, may be found here. These include alligators (rare in the Keys), frogs, soft-shelled turtles, and largemouth bass. It's a good place to photograph (you need only lug your equipment a few yards from your car) or just sit and watch the wildlife parade. You can also walk around the pond (0.25 miles).

Watson and Manillo Trails

The Watson Trail was named for Jack Watson, the first refuge manager, and is about 0.6 miles long. As the name of the island (Big Pine Key) suggests, the island is wooded with slash pines (*Pinus elliottii* var. *densa*), and so is this trail. The varietal name refers to the density of the wood. Enough light gets through the canopy to allow the understory hardwoods to outcompete the pines. Under natural conditions, that doesn't happen, since wildfires suppress the hardwoods.

Under the pines are saw palmetto, wax myrtle, sawgrass, blackbead, buttonwood, key thatch palm, silver palm, and sweet acacia, to name some species along the trail. From May to October, expect to see white-crowned pigeons flying around. They feed on mast (fruit) from fig and poisonwood trees in Watson's Hammock, which the trail passes near. Also look for old, small ditches cut through the limestone years ago and stocked with mosquito-fish for mosquito control. The ditches are treacherous to Key deer fawns that drown while trying to cross them.

The Manillo Trail is an 800-foot, flat trail, surfaced with a thin layer of gravel, and is suitable for a wheelchair. An observation deck overlooks a freshwater wetland, a rarity in the Keys.

DIRECTIONS

Headquarters: From Florida City, go south on US 1 to traffic light on Big Pine Key at MM 30.5 (Key Deer Boulevard). Turn bayside (right) and go 0.1 miles on Key Deer Boulevard to shopping plaza on right; refuge office is on south side of shopping plaza.

Blue Hole: Go north on Key Deer Boulevard 3.2 miles to sign "Blue Hole Observation Pool Entrance." Parking lot on left.

Watson and Manillo Trails: Go 0.3 miles past Blue Hole on Key Deer Blvd. Look for small sign "Wildlife Trail Entrance." Parking lot is on left.

CONTACT

National Key Deer Refuge
179 Key Deer Boulevard
Big Pine Key 33043
305-872-2239
www.fws.gov/nationalkeydeer

Windley Key Fossil Reef Geological State Park

Facilities: Walking trails, guided walks, visitor center

Activities: Botanizing, geologic study, hiking

Admission: Small entrance fee

Hours: Visitor center open Friday–Sunday 8 am–5 pm; park closed Tuesday and Wednesday

Pets: Allowed

Best Time of Year: Winter and spring for weather and birding

Windley Quarry was a commercial quarry from which rock was obtained for building the Overseas Railroad and later, the Overseas Highway. The unique feature of this site is that visitors can descend into the quarry and examine layers of ancient petrified coral formations. Five trails totaling less than 2 miles bring visitors through the tropical hardwood hammock, where interpretive signs explain the vegetation, wildlife, and geology. The Alison Fahrer Environmental Education Center features exhibits about the area's history, biology, and geology. If you're in the Upper Keys, this small park is worth the small entrance fee and a few hours of your time.

It is part of a complex of local state parks. Information about Ligumvitae Key Botanical State Park and Indian Key Historic State Park can also be found here.

DIRECTIONS
From Florida City, take US 1 south to MM 84.9 on US 1 bayside.

CONTACT
Windley Key Fossil Reef
Geological State Park
MM 84.9 US 1
Islamorada 33036
305-664-2540
www.floridastateparks.org/windleykey

Paddling in interior south Florida is often encumbered by spadderdock, water-lilies, and other aquatic vegetation, especially in summer.

VIII Trails: Blueways And Greenways

○ **Hiking and Bicycling Trails** ---
   1. Florida Trail
   1A. Lake Okeechobee Scenic Trail
   2. Florida Keys Overseas Heritage Trail

● **Paddling Trails** ——
   1. Great Calusa Blueway (longer sections)
   2. Paradise Coast Blueway
   3. Wilderness Waterway
   4. Florida Keys Overseas Paddling Trail
   5. Loxahatchee River

Paddling Trails

Florida Recreational Trails

The Florida Recreational Trails Act of 1979 authorized the state to establish recreational, scenic, and historic trails for the public. One network of trails is for canoeing and kayaking (paddling). Forty such trails exist in the state trail system. The rivers and creeks were chosen for their scenic quality, variety of habitats, and distribution around the state. Five trails are within the geographic area covered by this book and described in park entries above. They are: Great Calusa Blueway (Estero River segment) under **Koreshan State Historic Site**; Blackwater River–Royal Palm Hammock under **Collier-Seminole State Park**; Oleta River under **Oleta River State Park**; Hickey's Creek under **Caloosahatchee Regional Park**; and Loxahatchee River under **Riverbend County Park**. The Loxahatchee River is also designated a National Wild and Scenic River.

The state trail designation does not mean that they are the only waterways worth paddling. For example, lakes and larger rivers are not included but may be excellent for canoeing. Also not covered in the book is the Florida Circumnavigational Saltwater Paddling Trail covering 1,500 miles around the entire coast.

Nor does the designation mean that they are only for paddling; for example, motorboats are permitted. The waterways are publicly owned but often flow through private property, meaning that the stream banks are privately owned. Paddlers must take care that they don't trespass. Water conditions vary with weather and season. After heavy rains, current flow may increase dramatically. During the dry season, water levels may be low enough to cause short portages.

For more information on state designated paddling trails, contact the Department of Environmental Protection, Office of Greenways and Trails at 850-245-2052; for a downloadable map: www.dep.state.fl.us/gwt/PDF/FL_Paddling_Trails.pdf.

1 **Great Calusa Blueway**

This 190-mile network of marked paddling routes encompasses three regions in Lee County on inland tributaries and coastal waters. One segment includes Matlacha Pass and Pine Island Sound, one includes the Caloosahatchee River, and one is through Estero Bay. The Estero Bay segment includes some stops at places highlighted in this book: **Matanzas Pass Preserve, Lovers Key State Park**, **Koreshan State Historic Site**. For more information, call Lee County Parks and Recreation at 239-533-7275 or see www.calusablueway.com for trail maps.

2 **Paradise Coast Blueway**

Collier County has its own group of trails. Like the Great Calusa Blueway, they are mostly coastal with some inland tributaries. Launch sites include **Collier-Seminole State Park**, **Everglades National Park** at Gulf Coast Visitor Center, and **Big Cypress National Preserve** at Turner River. The Goodland-to-Everglades City segment is approximately 16 miles, mostly along exposed coastline. Port-of-the-Islands to Panther Key is about 8 miles and mostly sheltered through mangrove islands. Chokoloskee to Rabbit Key is about 6 miles through mangrove islands and open

Kayaking in the Turner River

waters. Shorter segments and loops are available. See www.paradisecoastblueway.com for more information.

3 **Wilderness Waterway (see page 109)**

4 **Florida Keys Overseas Paddling Trail**
This 110-mile section of the Florida Circumnavigational Saltwater Paddling Trail lies between **John Pennekamp Coral Reef State Park** and **Fort Zachary Taylor Historic State Park,** paralleling the Overseas Highway. Paddlers can choose either the bayside or oceanside, so the total distance may vary. Allow 9–10 days for one way. Florida Department of Environmental Protection created this trail. Camping may be found at the state parks listed elsewhere in this book or private campgrounds. Short sections can be done for day trips. For more information, including maps, see www.dep.state.fl.us/gwt/paddling/Segments/Segment15/Segment%2015.htm.

5 **Loxahatchee River (see Riverbend Park, pages 133–134)**

Lake Okeechobee Scenic Trail

Hiking and Bicycling Trails

1 Florida Trail

The Florida Trail, one of eight National Scenic Trails in the United States, extends 1,400 miles from Pensacola in northwestern Florida to **Big Cypress National Preserve** in southern Florida. Side trails, designated by "FT" signs, extend the system farther. For more information, see www.floridatrail.org or call 877-HIKE-FLA.

See **Big Cypress National Preserve** for information on hiking the southern end of the Florida Trail.

1A Lake Okeechobee Scenic Trail ("LOST")

Several access points on the southern half of the lake are: Moore Haven Recreation Area—off of US 27 in Moore Haven, one section west of the Caloosahatchee River Canal and one section east of the canal; Pahokee Recreation Area—near the intersection of US 441 and SR 715 in Pahokee; Port Mayaca Recreation Area—off US 441 in Port Mayaca, on the north side of the St. Lucie Canal. South Bay Access Area: off of US 27, just northwest of South Bay. For more information: Florida Trail Association, www.floridatrail.org; 352-378-8823 or 877-HIKE-FLA; South Florida Water Management District, www.sfwmd.gov; 561-686-8800 or 1-800-432-2045 (Florida only).

Activities include hiking, bicycling, camping, and wildlife observation. Pets are allowed if under control. The best time of year is winter, because of the cooler weather and lack of thunderstorms.

To some hikers, reaching the summit of a mountain is the ultimate challenge. For Floridians, who have no mountains in their state, the challenge is met by circum-hiking Lake Okeechobee. The 110-mile circle trail is situated on the Hoover Dike (hence the trail's other name of Lake Okeechobee Hoover Dike Trail), the levee that surrounds the 750-square-mile lake (the third largest lake entirely within U.S. borders). It is one of the loop segments of the Florida Trail and is designated a Florida National Scenic Trail.

The dike was named for President Herbert Hoover, who ordered construction of the dike after the 1926 and 1928 hurricanes killed around 2,000 people. They drowned when a wind-driven wall of water overflowed the natural bank of the lake, flooding Belle Glade. Since then, the dike and its associated water control structures have been used to control water levels in the lake, and the lake has been maintained at a lower level. Because of the reduced water levels, a once-familiar landmark to boaters—the "Lone Cypress"—guides no more. Its distinctive spreading crown now shades a roadside historic marker a half-mile from the lake. The South Florida Water Management District maintains the dike and the water control structures.

Short segments of trail are plentiful, all with great vistas of South Florida, but this trail provides an unusual opportunity for a 110-mile circuit hike. Of the approximately 50 access areas, half are listed on the SFWMD recreational guide. Primitive camping is permitted along the levee at designated campsites or hikers may stay at fish camps. The mostly treeless, unpaved trail is 30-35 feet above the surrounding land, offering dry footing and wide vistas of the surrounding countryside. If it hasn't been mowed in a while, the grasses may be tall. The lake, marshes, cattle ranches, and citrus groves comprise parts of the view.

The lack of shade necessitates a warning to all trail users; bring ample drinking water and sun protection, even in the winter. Winter temperatures can be difficult to predict, so prepare for anything—from 40° to 80°. Before embarking on a long hike or bicycle ride, obtain the "South Florida Water Management District Recreation Guide to Lake Okeechobee" brochure and map from SFWMD (my.sfwmd.gov/portal/page/portal/common/pdf/lakeo_trail_waterway.pdf), which lists camping sites and facilities; water and grocery availability; and access points and parks.

Hiking
The LOST trail is open to the public year-round. The Florida Trail Association sponsors an annual trek around the lake, dubbed the "Big O Dike Hike," held the week of Thanksgiving to allow for the 9 days the trip takes. The FTA makes all the necessary arrangements. Contact them for more information.

Bicycling
Bicycling is also permitted on the entire trail and is an excellent alternative to hiking. Mountain bikes would be appropriate, since the levee may be rough. With a bicycle, you can easily leave the trail and wander into one of the small lakeside towns for

food, lodging, or just exploring. Plan around three days for a comfortable trip.

2 **Florida Keys Overseas Heritage Trail**

This multi-use trail is under development between Key Largo (MM 106) and Key West (MM 0), parallel to US 1. The trail provides a safer location for bicycling, walking, in-line skating, and access for swimming, snorkeling, fishing, and so on. More than 60 miles are complete. When complete, it will provide recreational access to the state parks and national wildlife refuges of the Keys. For more information, call 305-853-3571 or see www.dep.state.fl.us/gwt/state/keystrail/default.htm.

IX ADDITIONAL INFORMATION

WILDLIFE CHECKLISTS

The following checklists are intended to include all the known native and some of the more common nonnative vertebrates (except fish) found in south Florida. Species of unknown status, accidentals, or those numbering only a few individuals may not be included. Obscure subspecies, particularly in the Florida Keys, may be excluded.

Population status is given in relative terms as follows:
abundant—likely to be seen in the right habitat, population dense
common—often seen in the right habitat, population numerous
uncommon—infrequently seen, population low
rare—not likely to be seen, population very small or endangered

Geographic areas may be defined as follows:
Mainland—Florida mainland, excluding the Florida Keys
Keys—on or around the islands of the Florida Keys
Everglades—the freshwater marsh system from Lake Okeechobee to Florida Bay

Explanation of other symbols:
+ = known breeder in south Florida (bird checklist only)
* = nonnative species (breeds locally)
E = federally endangered under Endangered Species Act
T = federally threatened under Endangered Species Act
I = federally listed as injurious under Lacey Act (nonnative invasive species)

BIRD CHECKLIST

The following list of 356 bird species includes some that have occurred rarely in the south Florida region but that may be expected to occur in the future. At least 75 other naturally occurring species reported in the region are less likely to be found in the future and have been omitted. More than 100 nonnative species having uncertain reproductive success in southern Florida have been omitted. The following list was compiled predominantly by the late William B. Robertson Jr. and P. William Smith and revised by the author for this edition. Another excellent resource is *Florida's Birds: A Field Guide and Reference, Second Edition*, by David S. Maehr and Herbert W. Kale, available through Pineapple Press, Inc., P.O. Box 3889, Sarasota, FL 34230.

Loons and Grebes

☐ **Common loon** (*Gavia immer*)—variably common migrant and winter visitor; ocean and bays

☐ **Red-throated loon** (*Gavia stellate*)—uncommon winter visitor; oceans and bays

☐ **Red-necked grebe** (*Podiceps grisegena*)—uncommon visitor; oceans and bays

☐ **+Pied-billed grebe** (*Podilymbus podiceps*)—common migrant and winter visitor; some resident; fresh water

☐ **Least grebe** (*Tachybaptus dominicus*)—uncommon winter visitor; Keys

☐ **Horned grebe** (*Podiceps auritus*)—uncommon winter visitor; bays

☐ **Eared grebe** (*Podiceps nigricollis*)—uncommon visitor; generally fresh water

Shearwaters and Storm-petrels

☐ **Cory's shearwater** (*Calonectris diomedea*)—uncommon summer and fall migrant; pelagic

☐ **Greater shearwater** (*Puffinus gravis*)—uncommon late spring and summer migrant; pelagic

☐ **Sooty shearwater** (*Puffinus griseus*)—rare, chiefly spring migrant; pelagic

☐ **Audubon's shearwater** (*Puffinus lherminieri*)—fairly common; pelagic

☐ **Wilson's storm-petrel** (*Oceanites oceanicus*)—uncommon late spring and summer migrant; pelagic

☐ **Band-rumped storm-petrel** (*Oceanodroma castro*)—uncommon migrant; pelagic

☐ **Leach's storm-petrel** (*Oceanodroma leucorhoa*)—uncommon migrant; pelagic

Pelicans and Allies

☐ **White-tailed tropicbird** (*Phaethon lepturus*)—rare, chiefly spring and summer visitor; Dry Tortugas and pelagic

☐ **+Masked booby** (*Sula dactylatra*)—uncommon resident at Dry Tortugas, rare elsewhere; pelagic

☐ **Brown booby** (*Sula leucogaster*)—uncommon visitor; pelagic and Dry Tortugas

☐ **Blue-footed booby** (*Sula nebouxii*)—accidental; pelagic

☐ **Red-footed booby** (*Sula sula*)—rare spring and summer visitor; Dry Tortugas

☐ **Northern gannet** (*Morus bassanus*)—common migrant and winter visitor; chiefly pelagic

☐ **American white pelican** (*Pelecanus erythrorhynchos*)—common in winter, some in summer; bays, rare in Keys

☐ **+Brown pelican** (*Pelecanus occidentalis*)—abundant resident; coasts and bays

Cormorants and Anhingas
☐ **Great cormorant** (*Phalacrocorax carbo*)—uncommon; mostly Atlantic coast

☐ **+Double-crested cormorant** (*Phalacrocorax auritus*)—abundant resident; coasts, bays, and deeper inland waters

☐ **+Anhinga** (*Anhinga anhinga*)—common resident; fresh water, mainland

Frigatebirds
☐ **+Magnificent frigatebird** (*Fregata magnificens*)—variably common resident, breeds Dry Tortugas; coast and bays

Herons, Egrets, and Other Waders
☐ **American bittern** (*Botaurus lentiginosus*)—fairly rare migrant and winter visitor; fresh water marshes

☐ **+Least bittern** (*Ixobrychus exilis*)—uncommon resident; fresh water marshes

☐ **+Great blue heron** (*Ardea herodias*)—common resident; shallow fresh and salt water

☐ **+Great white heron** (*Ardea herodias occidentalis*)—common resident; usually shallow salt water, mainly Florida Bay and Keys

☐ **+Great egret** (*Casmerodius albus*)—common resident; shallow fresh and salt water

☐ **+Snowy egret** (*Egretta thula*)—common resident; shallow fresh and salt water

☐ **+Little blue heron** (*Egretta caerulea*)—common resident; shallow fresh and salt water

☐ **+Tricolored heron** (*Egretta tricolor*)—common resident; shallow fresh and salt water

☐ **+Reddish egret** (*Egretta rufescens*)—uncommon resident; shallow salt water, mainly Keys and Florida Bay

☐ **+Cattle egret** (*Bubulcus ibis*)—abundant resident, less common in winter; agricultural fields and roadsides

☐ **+Green heron** (*Butorides virescens*)—fairly common resident; shaded shallow fresh and salt water shorelines

☐ **+Black-crowned night-heron** (*Nycticorax nycticorax*)—fairly common resident; shallow fresh and salt water, scarce in Keys

☐ **+Yellow-crowned night-heron** (*Nyctanassa violacea*)—common resident (less common in east); shallow salt and fresh water

☐ **+White ibis** (*Eudocimus albus*)—common resident; shallow fresh and salt water, agricultural fields and lawns

☐ ***Scarlet ibis** (*Eudocimus ruber*)—occasional escapees or hybrids from past introduction; shallow fresh and salt water

☐ **White-faced ibis** (*Plegadis chihi*)—uncommon; fresh water, Everglades

☐ **+Glossy ibis** (*Plegadis falcinellus*)—uncommon resident; shallow fresh water, mainland

☐ **+Roseate spoonbill** (*Ajaia ajaja*)—locally common resident; shallow salt water, Florida Bay and Ten Thousand Islands

☐ **+Wood stork** (*Mycteria americana*)—common resident; fresh water margins and swamps, mainland **E**

☐ **Greater flamingo** (*Phoenicopterus ruber*)—rare visitor or escapee (mainly fall and winter); bays (particularly northern Florida Bay)

Ducks and Geese

☐ **Canada goose** (*Branta Canadensis*)—uncommon visitor; coast

☐ **Brant** (*Branta bernicla*)—winter visitor; coast

☐ **Snow goose** (*Chen caerulescens*)—winter visitor; coast

☐ **Black-bellied whistling-duck** (*Dendrocygna autumnalis*)—uncommon visitor; fresh water

☐ **Fulvous whistling-duck** (*Dendrocygna bicolor*)—rare visitor; fresh water marshes; breeds L. Okeechobee area

☐ ***Muscovy duck** (*Cairina moschata*)—locally common resident; urban ponds

☐ **+Wood duck** (*Aix sponsa*)—rare resident; wooded swamps

☐ **Green-winged teal** (*Anas crecca*)—variably uncommon winter visitor; ponds and bays

☐ **+Mottled duck** (*Anas fulvigula*)—uncommon resident; ponds and marshes, chiefly mainland

☐ ***Mallard** (*Anas platyrhynchos*)—fairly common resident; urban ponds

☐ **American black duck** (*Anas rubripes*)—uncommon visitor from north; ponds and marshes

☐ **White-cheeked pintail** (*Anas bahamensis*)—rare winter and spring visitor, also some escapees; mangrove ponds

☐ **Northern pintail** (*Anas acuta*)—variably uncommon migrant and winter visitor; ponds and bays

☐ **Blue-winged teal** (*Anas discors*)—common migrant and winter visitor, some summer; ponds and bays

☐ **Cinnamon teal** (*Anas cyanoptera*)—uncommon visitor; ponds and bays

☐ **Northern shoveler** (*Anas clypeata*)—variably uncommon migrant and winter visitor; ponds and bays

☐ **Gadwall** (*Anas strepera*)—rare migrant and winter visitor; ponds and bays

☐ **American wigeon** (*Anas americana*)—fairly common migrant and winter visitor; ponds and bays

☐ **Eurasian widgeon** (*Anas penelope*)—uncommon; ponds and bays

☐ **Canvasback** (*Aythya valisineria*)—winter; ponds and lakes

☐ **Redhead** (*Aythya americana*)—uncommon winter visitor; ponds and bays

☐ **Ring-necked duck** (*Aythya collaris*)—fairly common migrant and winter visitor; mainly ponds

☐ **Greater scaup** (*Aythya marila*)—uncommon winter visitor; bays

☐ **Lesser scaup** (*Aythya affinis*)—variably uncommon migrant and winter visitor;

mainly bays, rare in east

☐ **Common eider** (*Somateria mollissima*)—uncommon winter visitor; bays

☐ **Long-tailed duck** (*Clangula hyemalis*)—uncommon winter visitor; ponds and bays

☐ **Surf scoter** (*Melanitta perspicillata*)—uncommon winter visitor; ponds and bays

☐ **Black scoter** (*Melanitta nigra*)—rare to uncommon migrant and winter visitor; ocean and bays

☐ **White-winged scoter** (*Melanitta fusca*)—uncommon winter visitor; ponds and bays

☐ **Common goldeneye** (*Bucehphala clangula*)—uncommon winter visitor; ponds and bays

☐ **Bufflehead** (*Bucephala albeola*)—uncommon winter visitor; ponds and bays

☐ **Hooded merganser** (*Lophodytes cucullatus*)—fairly rare migrant and winter visitor; ponds

☐ **Red-breasted merganser** (*Mergus serrator*)—common migrant and winter visitor, some summer; ocean and bays

☐ **Masked duck** (*Nomonyx dominicus*)—uncommon visitor; ponds or bays

☐ **Ruddy duck** (*Oxyura jamaicensis*)—variably uncommon migrant and winter visitor; ponds and bays

Hawks, Falcons, Kites, and Other Raptors

☐ **+Black vulture** (*Coragyps atratus*)—locally common resident; mainland

☐ **+Turkey vulture** (*Cathartes aura*)—abundant winter visitor, fewer resident; mainland and Keys

☐ **+Osprey** (*Pandion haliaetus*)—common resident; bays, canals, and ponds

☐ **+American swallow-tailed kite** (*Elanoides forficatus*)—common spring and summer visiting breeder; wet and dry woodlands

☐ **+White-tailed kite** (formerly black-shouldered) (*Elanus leucurus*)—rare resident; former sawgrass prairies that have dried out, mainland

☐ **+Everglade snail kite** (*Rostrhamus sociabilis plumbeus*)—variably uncommon resident; freshwater marshes **E**

☐ **Mississippi kite** (*Ictinia mississippiensis*)—rare migrant

☐ **+Bald eagle** (*Haliaeetus leucocephalus*)—fairly common resident; mainly bays

☐ **Northern harrier** (*Circus cyaneus*)—common migrant and winter visitor; agricultural fields and marshes

☐ **Sharp-shinned hawk** (*Accipiter striatus*)—common migrant, uncommon winter visitor

☐ **Cooper's hawk** (*Accipiter cooperii*)—fairly rare migrant and winter visitor

☐ **+Red-shouldered hawk** (*Buteo lineatus*)—common resident; woodlands and edges

☐ **Broad-winged hawk** (*Buteo platypterus*)—common migrant and variably uncommon winter visitor

☐ **+Short-tailed hawk** (*Buteo brachyurus*)—uncommon fall and winter visitor, rare in spring and summer; woodlands, usually near creeks

☐ **Swainson's hawk** (*Buteo swainsoni*)—variably uncommon migrant and rare winter visitor

☐ **+Red-tailed hawk** (*Buteo jamaicensis*)—uncommon migrant and winter visitor, rare in summer

☐ **+Audubon's crested caracara** (*Caracara cheriway audubonii*)—uncommon resident; prairies and cattle ranches north and west of Lake Okeechobee **T**

☐ **+American kestrel** (*Falco sparverius*)—common migrant and winter visitor (throughout), also former or rare breeder (northern mainland); fields and edges; *F. s. paulus* is resident

☐ **Merlin** (*Falco columbarius*)—fairly common migrant and uncommon winter visitor

☐ **Peregrine falcon** (*Falco peregrinus*)—fairly common migrant and uncommon winter visitor

Turkeys and Quails

☐ **+Wild turkey** (*Meleagris gallopavo*)—rare resident; undisturbed woodlands, mainland (except extreme southern)

☐ **+Northern bobwhite** (*Colinus virginianus*)—uncommon resident; mainly old fields, groves, and pine woods, mainland

Rails, Limpkins, and Cranes

☐ **Black rail** (*Laterallus jamaicensis*)—variably rare migrant and possible resident; extensive damp marshes

☐ **+Clapper rail** (*Rallus longirostris*)—uncommon resident; mangroves and salt marshes

☐ **+King rail** (*Rallus elegans*)—fairly common resident; fresh water marshes

☐ **Virginia rail** (*Rallus limicola*)—rare winter visitor; fresh water marshes

☐ **Sora** (*Porzana carolina*)—common migrant and uncommon winter visitor; fresh water marshes and concealed margins

☐ **+Purple gallinule** (*Porphyrula martinica*)—variably uncommon migrant and local resident; fresh water marshes

☐ **+Common moorhen** (*Gallinula chloropus*)—common resident; fresh water ponds and marshes

☐ **+American coot** (*Fulica americana*)—variably common migrant and winter visitor, uncommon in summer; bays, ponds, and marshes

☐ **+Limpkin** (*Aramus guarauna*)—locally uncommon resident; fresh water swamps and marshes, mainland

☐ **+Sandhill crane** (*Grus canadensis*)—uncommon resident; prairies on mainland

☐ **+Whooping crane** (*Grus americana*)—extremely rare; introduced into prairies of central Florida; occasionally wanders south **E**

Plovers, Sandpipers, and Other Shorebirds

☐ **Black-bellied plover** (*Pluvialis squatarola*)—common migrant and winter visitor, some summer; coastal and interior shallow water and fields

☐ **American golden-plover** (*Pluvialis dominica*)—rare migrant, chiefly fall; usually interior fields

☐ **+Snowy plover** (*Charadrius alexandrinus*)—rare winter visitor (Gulf coast and Keys), also former or rare breeder (Gulf coast); undisturbed sandy beaches

☐ **+Wilson's plover** (*Charadrius wilsonia*)—locally common resident; spoil banks, especially Florida Bay and Keys

☐ **Semipalmated plover** (*Charadrius semipalmatus*)—common migrant and winter visitor; coastal flats, sometimes inland

☐ **Piping plover** (*Charadrius melodus*)—uncommon migrant and winter visitor; salt water banks and pond edges, mainly Florida Bay and Keys **T**

☐ **+Killdeer** (*Charadrius vociferus*)—common resident; fields and fresh water margins, chiefly mainland

☐ **American oystercatcher** (*Haematopus palliatus*)—rare visitor (mostly winter); salt water flats, chiefly Gulf coast

☐ **+Black-necked stilt** (*Himantopus mexicanus*)—common resident, except uncommon and local in winter; mainly fresh water ponds and margins

☐ **American avocet** (*Recurvirostra americana*)—rare migrant and winter visitor; usually salt water ponds and flats

☐ **Greater yellowlegs** (*Tringa melanoleuca*)—common migrant, less common winter visitor; flats and margins

☐ **Lesser yellowlegs** (*Tringa flavipes*)—common migrant, less common winter visitor; flats and margins

☐ **Solitary sandpiper** (*Tringa solitaria*)—uncommon migrant, rare winter visitor; fresh water margins

☐ **+Willet** (*Catoptrophorus semipalmatus*)—common migrant and winter visitor, less common in summer; chiefly salt marshes and flats

☐ **Spotted sandpiper** (*Actitis macularia*)—fairly common migrant and winter visitor; margins, usually fresh water

☐ **Upland sandpiper** (*Bartramia longicauda*)—uncommon migrant; chiefly fields

☐ **Whimbrel** (*Numenius phaeopus*)—uncommon migrant and winter visitor; salt water flats

☐ **Long-billed curlew** (*Numenius americanus*)—rare winter visitor; salt water flats, chiefly Gulf coast

☐ **Marbled godwit** (*Limosa fedoa*)—abundant migrant and winter visitor; salt water flats, mainly Gulf coast and Florida Bay

☐ **Ruddy turnstone** (*Arenaria interpres*)—common migrant and winter visitor; beaches and rocky areas

☐ **Red knot** (*Calidris canutus*)—locally common migrant and winter visitor; salt ponds and flats, mainly Gulf coast

☐ **Sanderling** (*Calidris alba*)—common migrant and winter visitor; beaches

☐ **Semipalmated sandpiper** (*Calidris pusilla*)—common migrant, rare in winter; flats and margins

☐ **Western sandpiper** (*Calidris mauri*)—abundant migrant and winter visitor; flats and margins, chiefly salt water

☐ **Least sandpiper** (*Calidris minutilla*)—common migrant and winter visitor; flats and margins, chiefly fresh water

☐ **White-rumped sandpiper** (*Calidris fuscicollis*)—uncommon (especially in spring) migrant; beaches, flats, and margins

☐ **Baird's sandpiper** (*Calidris bairdii*)—rare migrant; usually fields and fresh water margins

☐ **Pectoral sandpiper** (*Calidris melanotos*)—common migrant; fields, flats, and margins (usually fresh water)

☐ **Purple sandpiper** (*Calidris maritima*)—rare winter visitor; rock jetties

☐ **Dunlin** (*Calidris alpina*)—abundant migrant and winter visitor; flats and margins (usually salt water)

☐ **Stilt sandpiper** (*Calidris himantopus*)—uncommon migrant, usually rare in winter; flats and shallow ponds (often fresh water)

☐ **Buff-breasted sandpiper** (*Tryngites subruficollis*)—rare migrant, chiefly fall; usually interior fields

☐ **Short-billed dowitcher** (*Limnodromus griseus*)—abundant migrant and winter visitor; chiefly flats and shallow salt ponds

☐ **Long-billed dowitcher** (*Limnodromus scolopaceus*)—variably common migrant and winter visitor; usually shallow fresh water ponds

☐ **Common snipe** (*Gallinago gallinago*)—fairly common migrant, less common in winter; fresh water margins, chiefly mainland

☐ **+American woodcock** (*Scolopax minor*)—uncommon winter visitor, rarely breeds; old fields, mainland

☐ **Wilson's phalarope** (*Phalaropus tricolor*)—rare migrant; fresh water margins

☐ **Red-necked phalarope** (*Phalaropus lobatus*)—rare migrant or winter visitor; usually pelagic, sometimes ashore

☐ **Red phalarope** (*Phalaropus fulicaria*)—rare migrant, may winter; usually pelagic, rarely ashore

Gulls and Terns

☐ **Pomarine jaeger** (*Stercorarius pomarinus*)—fairly common migrant, less common in winter; usually pelagic

☐ **Parasitic jaeger** (*Stercorarius parasiticus*)—fairly common migrant, some may winter; usually pelagic, sometimes coastal

☐ **+Laughing gull** (*Larus atricilla*)—abundant resident; chiefly coasts and bays, sometimes inland

☐ **Bonaparte's gull** (*Larus philadelphia*)—variably uncommon migrant and winter visitor; usually coasts and bays

☐ **Ring-billed gull** (*Larus delawarensis*)—abundant migrant and winter visitor, some summer; coasts, bays, and inland ponds and fields

☐ **Herring gull** (*Larus argentatus*)—uncommon winter visitor; coasts, bays, and ponds

☐ **Lesser black-backed gull** (*Larus fuscus*)—rare winter visitor; coasts, bays, and ponds

☐ **Glaucous gull** (*Larus hyperboreus*)—rare winter visitor; coasts, bays, and ponds

☐ **Great black-backed gull** (*Larus marinus*)—rare winter visitor; coasts, bays, and ponds

☐ **+Gull-billed tern** (*Sterna nilotica*)—local and uncommon resident and uncertain breeder; salt marshes and flats, chiefly mainland

☐ **Caspian tern** (*Sterna caspia*)—common migrant and winter visitor, some summer; coasts and bays, less common in east

☐ **Royal tern** (*Sterna maxima*)—abundant migrant and winter visitor, many summer; coasts and bays

☐ **Sandwich tern** (*Sterna sandvicensis*)—fairly common migrant and winter visitor, some summer; coasts and bays, less common in east

☐ **+Roseate tern** (*Sterna dougallii*)—variably common late spring and summer breeding visitor, rare at other seasons; coastal, chiefly lower Keys and Dry Tortugas **T**

☐ **Common tern** (*Sterna hirundo*)—fairly common migrant, rare in winter; coasts and bays, less common in east

☐ **Arctic tern** (*Sterna paradisaea*)—rare migrant (stops over during transcontinental migrations); coastal

☐ **Forster's tern** (*Sterna forsteri*)—common migrant and winter visitor, some summer; bays and ponds

☐ **+Least tern** (*Sterna antillarum*)—fairly common spring and summer visitor; bays, ponds, and urban rooftops

☐ **+Bridled tern** (*Sterna anaethetus*)—uncommon, probably resident, rare breeder; offshore, lower Keys

☐ **+Sooty tern** (*Sterna fuscata*)—abundant spring and summer visitor and breeder, common offshore except absent in late fall and winter; Dry Tortugas, pelagic when not breeding

☐ **Black tern** (*Chlidonias niger*)—locally common migrant, chiefly summer and fall; fresh water ponds and offshore

☐ **+Brown noddy** (*Anous stolidus*)—common spring and summer visitor and breeder, uncommon offshore except absent in late fall and winter; Dry Tortugas, pelagic

☐ **Black noddy** (*Anous minutus*)—rare spring visitor; Dry Tortugas

☐ **+Black skimmer** (*Rynchops nigra*)—locally common resident; flats, spoil islands

Doves and Pigeons

☐ ***Rock dove** (*Columba livia*)—common resident; urban areas

☐ **+White-crowned pigeon** (*Columba leucocephala*)—common summer resident, fewer in winter; tropical hardwood hammocks and mangroves, Keys and extreme southern mainland

☐ ***Eurasian collared-dove** (*Streptopelia decaocto*)—locally abundant resident; southern suburban areas, including Keys

☐ **+White-winged dove** (*Zenaida asiatica*)—locally common resident; groves and suburban areas

☐ **+Mourning dove** (*Zenaida macroura*)—common resident; open areas
☐ **+Common ground-dove** (*Columbina passerina*)—uncommon resident; fields
☐ **+Key West quail-dove** (*Geotrygon chrysia*)—rare visitor; Florida Keys

Parakeets (list not inclusive but none are native)
☐ ***Monk parakeet** (*Myiopsitta monachus*)—locally common resident; suburban areas
☐ ***White-winged parakeet** (*Brotogeris versicolurus*)—uncommon resident; Coconut Grove area of Miami
☐ ***Budgerigar** (*Melopsittacus undulatus*)—local resident; suburban areas

Cuckoos and Anis
☐ **Black-billed cuckoo** (*Coccyzus erythropthalmus*)—rare migrant; woodlands
☐ **+Yellow-billed cuckoo** (*Coccyzus americanus*)—common migrant and uncommon summer visitor and breeder; woodlands
☐ **+Mangrove cuckoo** (*Coccyzus minor*)—uncommon resident, seldom seen in fall and winter; tropical hammocks and mangroves, Keys and southern mainland
☐ **+Smooth-billed ani** (*Crotophaga ani*)—local and decreasing resident; brushy areas

Owls
☐ **+Barn owl** (*Tyto alba*)—uncommon permanent resident; chiefly mainland
☐ **+Eastern screech-owl** (*Otus asio*)—common resident; suburbs and woodlands, mainland and upper Keys
☐ **+Great horned owl** (*Bubo virginianus*)—uncommon resident; chiefly pine woodlands, mainland
☐ **+Burrowing owl** (*Speotyto cunicularia*)—locally common resident; airports, campuses, and other open grassy areas
☐ **+Barred owl** (*Strix varia*)—common resident; mesic woodlands, mainland
☐ **Short-eared owl** (*Asio flammeus*)—rare winter and spring visitor; chiefly Keys, Dry Tortugas; also grassy marshes and fields on mainland

Goatsuckers
☐ **Lesser nighthawk** (*Chordeiles acutipennis*)—rare spring migrant; chiefly Dry Tortugas
☐ **+Common nighthawk** (*Chordeiles minor*)—common migrant and summer breeding visitor; open areas and urban rooftops, chiefly mainland and upper Keys
☐ **+Antillean nighthawk** (*Chordeiles gundlachii*)—uncommon spring and summer breeding visitor; open areas and urban rooftops, chiefly lower Keys
☐ **+Chuck-will's-widow** (*Caprimulgus carolinensis*)—common migrant and uncommon winter visitor throughout, fairly common summer breeder; woodlands, mainland and upper Keys
☐ **Whip-poor-will** (*Caprimulgus vociferus*)—common fall and winter visitor; woodlands, chiefly mainland

Swifts
☐ **+Chimney swift** (*Chaetura pelagica*)—fairly common migrant throughout and uncommon summer breeder on suburban mainland

Hummingbirds
☐ **+Ruby-throated hummingbird** (*Archilochus colubris*)—common migrant and winter visitor throughout, rare breeding visitor on northern mainland; around flowering plants
☐ **Rufous hummingbird** (*Selasphorus rufus*)—rare migrant and winter visitor; around flowering plants

Kingfishers
☐ **Belted kingfisher** (*Ceryle alcyon*)—common visitor from late summer through early spring; canals and ponds

Woodpeckers
☐ **+Red-headed woodpecker** (*Melanerpes erythrocephalus*)—rare migrant throughout, resident in pine-oak woodlands, northern mainland
☐ **+Red-bellied woodpecker** (*Melanerpes carolinus*)—common resident; suburban and wooded areas
☐ **Yellow-bellied sapsucker** (*Sphyrapicus varius*)—fairly common migrant and uncommon winter visitor; suburban and wooded areas
☐ **+Downy woodpecker** (*Picoides pubescens*)—fairly common resident; suburban and wooded areas, mainland
☐ **+Hairy woodpecker** (*Picoides villosus*)—rare resident; pine woodlands, mainland
☐ **+Red-cockaded woodpecker** (*Picoides borealis*)—rare resident; pine woodlands, northern mainland **E**
☐ **+Northern flicker** (*Colaptes auratus*)—fairly common resident; suburban and wooded areas
☐ **+Pileated woodpecker** (*Dryocopus pileatus*)—uncommon resident; suburban and wooded areas, chiefly mainland

Flycatchers
☐ **Olive-sided flycatcher** (*Contopus borealis*)—rare migrant, chiefly fall
☐ **Eastern wood-pewee** (*Contopus virens*)—uncommon migrant, chiefly fall
☐ **Yellow-bellied flycatcher** (*Empidonax flaviventris*)—rare migrant, chiefly fall
☐ **Acadian flycatcher** (*Empidonax virescens*)—rare migrant, chiefly fall
☐ **Willow flycatcher** (*Empidonax traillii*)—rare migrant, chiefly fall
☐ **Least flycatcher** (*Empidonax minimus*)—uncommon migrant and winter visitor; second growth, edges
☐ **Eastern phoebe** (*Sayornis phoebe*)—common fall and winter visitor; suburban and wooded areas, chiefly mainland
☐ **+Great crested flycatcher** (*Myiarchus crinitus*)—common migrant and resident; suburban and wooded areas

☐ **Brown-crested flycatcher** (*Myiarchus tyrannulus*)—rare winter visitor; woodlands

☐ **La Sagra's flycatcher** (*Myiarchus sagrae*)—rare winter and spring visitor; coastal hammocks

☐ **Western kingbird** (*Tyrannus verticalis*)—locally uncommon migrant and winter visitor; open areas, fruiting trees

☐ **+Eastern kingbird** (*Tyrannus tyrannus*)—uncommon spring migrant and summer breeder, very common late summer migrant; woodland edges, only breeds on mainland

☐ **+Gray kingbird** (*Tyrannus dominicensis*)—uncommon migrant and summer breeder (local away from Keys); suburban and wooded areas

☐ **Scissor-tailed flycatcher** (*Tyrannus forficatus*)—locally uncommon migrant and winter visitor; open areas, around fruiting trees

☐ **Fork-tailed flycatcher** (*Tyrannus savana*)—rare visitor, chiefly summer; open areas, around fruiting trees

Swallows

☐ **+Purple martin** (*Progne subis*)—common winter and spring breeder, spring and fall migrant; open areas, only nests in man-made nesting structures on mainland

☐ **Tree swallow** (*Tachycineta bicolor*)—variably abundant visitor, late fall through early spring; marshy and open areas

☐ **Bahama swallow** (*Tachycineta cyaneoviridis*)—rare spring and summer migrant

☐ **+Northern rough-winged swallow** (*Stelgidopteryx serripennis*)—uncommon migrant throughout in open areas, rare summer breeder in holes near water on mainland

☐ **Bank swallow** (*Riparia riparia*)—uncommon spring, common late summer and fall migrant; open areas

☐ **Cliff swallow** (*Hirundo pyrrhonota*)—rare spring, uncommon late summer and fall migrant; open areas

☐ **+Cave swallow** (*Hirundo fulva*)—rare migrant throughout in open areas, locally uncommon breeder under highway bridges near water in southeast Miami area

☐ **+Barn swallow** (*Hirundo rustica*)—abundant migrant throughout in open areas, rare breeder under highway bridges in Keys

Jays and Crows

☐ **+Blue jay** (*Cyanocitta cristata*)—common resident; suburban and wooded areas, mainland and upper Keys

☐ **+Florida scrub-jay** (*Aphelocoma coerulescens*)—uncommon resident; scrub areas **T**

☐ **+American crow** (*Corvus brachyrhynchos*)—common resident; wilder wooded areas, chiefly mainland

☐ **+Fish crow** (*Corvus ossifragus*)—common resident; suburban areas, chiefly mainland

Titmice, Nuthatches, and Bulbuls
☐ **+Tufted titmouse** (*Parus bicolor*)—uncommon resident; chiefly cypress woodlands, northern mainland
☐ **+Brown-headed nuthatch** (*Sitta pusilla*)—locally rare resident; pine woodlands, northern mainland
☐ ***Red-whiskered bulbul** (*Pycnonotus jocosus*)—uncommon resident; suburbs, Kendall area **I**

Wrens
☐ **+Carolina wren** (*Thryothorus ludovicianus*)—common resident; woodlands, mainland and upper Keys
☐ **House wren** (*Troglodytes aedon*)—common migrant and winter visitor; suburban and brushy areas
☐ **Sedge wren** (*Cistothorus platensis*)—variably uncommon winter and spring visitor; damp grassy marshes, mainland
☐ **Marsh wren** (*Cistothorus palustris*)—variably uncommon winter and spring visitor; reedy marshes, mainland

Kinglets and Gnatcatchers
☐ **Ruby-crowned kinglet** (*Regulus calendula*)—uncommon winter visitor; woodlands, chiefly mainland
☐ **+Blue-gray gnatcatcher** (*Polioptila caerulea*)—common migrant and winter visitor throughout in suburbs and wooded areas, local breeder in wooded areas on northern mainland

Bluebirds and Thrushes
☐ **+Eastern bluebird** (*Sialia sialis*)—local, uncommon resident; pine-oak woodland edges, northern mainland
☐ **Veery** (*Catharus fuscescens*)—variably uncommon migrant
☐ **Gray-cheeked thrush** (*Catharus minimus*)—variably uncommon migrant
☐ **Swainson's thrush** (*Catharus ustulatus*)—variably uncommon migrant
☐ **Hermit thrush** (*Catharus guttatus*)—variably rare winter visitor; woodlands, chiefly mainland
☐ **Wood thrush** (*Hylocichla mustelina*)—variably uncommon migrant, rare in winter
☐ **American robin** (*Turdus migratorius*)—variably abundant winter visitor; suburban and wooded areas, chiefly mainland and upper Keys

Mockingbirds and Thrashers
☐ **Gray catbird** (*Dumetella carolinensis*)—abundant migrant and common winter visitor; brushy areas
☐ **+Northern mockingbird** (*Mimus polyglottos*)—abundant resident; suburban and open wooded areas
☐ **Bahama mockingbird** (*Mimus gundlachii*)—rare spring and summer visitor; coastal woodlands and brush

☐ **+Brown thrasher** (*Toxostoma rufum*)—uncommon resident; brushy wooded areas, chiefly mainland and upper Keys (has nested to Key West)

Pipits
☐ **American pipit** (*Anthus rubescens*)—variably rare winter visitor; fields

Waxwings
☐ **Cedar waxwing** (*Bombycilla cedrorum*)—variably uncommon winter and spring visitor; in fruiting trees

Shrikes
☐ **+Loggerhead shrike** (*Lanius ludovicianus*)—uncommon resident; open areas with brush, mainland

Starlings and Mynas
☐ ***European starling** (*Sturnus vulgaris*)—common resident; suburbs
☐ ***Common myna** (*Acridotheres tristis*)—locally uncommon resident; chiefly shopping centers, mainland
☐ ***Hill myna** (*Gracula religiosa*)—locally uncommon resident; suburban areas with trees, chiefly Coconut Grove area

Vireos
☐ **+White-eyed vireo** (*Vireo griseus*)—common migrant and somewhat local resident; brushy woodlands
☐ **Thick-billed vireo** (*Vireo crassirostris*)—rare migrant and winter visitor; brushy coastal woodlands
☐ **Bell's vireo** (*Vireo bellii*)—rare migrant and winter visitor; brushy woodlands
☐ **Solitary vireo** (*Vireo solitarius*)—uncommon migrant and winter visitor; woodlands
☐ **Yellow-throated vireo** (*Vireo flavifrons*)—uncommon migrant and rare winter visitor; woodlands
☐ **Warbling vireo** (*Vireo gilvus*)—rare migrant, chiefly fall
☐ **Philadelphia vireo** (Vireo philadelphicus)—rare migrant, chiefly fall
☐ **+Red-eyed vireo** (*Vireo olivaceus*)—common migrant throughout, local summer breeding visitor in mesic woodlands on northern mainland
☐ **+Black-whiskered vireo** (*Vireo altiloquus*)—common summer breeding visitor; tropical woodlands, chiefly Keys and coastal mainland

Warblers
☐ **Blue-winged warbler** (*Vermivora pinus*)—variably uncommon migrant and rare winter visitor; woodlands
☐ **Golden-winged warbler** (*Vermivora chrysoptera*)—rare migrant
☐ **Tennessee warbler** (*Vermivora peregrina*)—uncommon migrant, chiefly fall
☐ **Orange-crowned warbler** (*Vermivora celata*)—fairly common winter visitor; brushy woodlands
☐ **Nashville warbler** (*Vermivora ruficapilla*)—variably uncommon migrant and

rare winter visitor; brushy woodlands

☐ **+Northern parula** (*Parula americana*)—common migrant and uncommon winter visitor throughout, local summer breeder in mesic woodlands on northern mainland

☐ **+Yellow warbler** (*Dendroica petechia*)—uncommon resident (mangroves, chiefly Keys) and uncommon migrant elsewhere

☐ **Chestnut-sided warbler** (*Dendroica pensylvanica*)—variably uncommon migrant

☐ **Magnolia warbler** (*Dendroica magnolia*)—variably common migrant and rare winter visitor; woodlands

☐ **Cape May warbler** (*Dendroica tigrina*)—common migrant and locally uncommon winter visitor; in flowering and fruiting trees

☐ **Black-throated blue warbler** (*Dendroica caerulescens*)—common migrant and rare winter visitor; woodlands

☐ **Yellow-rumped warbler** (*Dendroica coronata*)—variably abundant winter visitor; brushy and wooded areas

☐ **Black-throated gray warbler** (*Dendroica nigrescens*)—rare migrant and winter visitor

☐ **Black-throated green warbler** (*Dendroica virens*)—variably uncommon migrant and winter visitor; woodlands

☐ **Blackburnian warbler** (*Dendroica fusca*)—variably uncommon migrant

☐ **Yellow-throated warbler** (*Dendroica dominica*)—common migrant and winter visitor; woodlands and palms

☐ **+Pine warbler** (*Dendroica pinus*)—common resident; pine woodlands, mainland (also rare migrant elsewhere)

☐ **Kirtland's warbler** (*Denroica kirtlandii*)—accidental migrant; east coast **E**

☐ **+Prairie warbler** (*Dendroica discolor*)—common resident in mangroves, abundant migrant and uncommon winter visitor in brushy woodlands

☐ **Palm warbler** (*Dendroica palmarum*)—abundant migrant and winter visitor; brushy areas and lawns

☐ **Bay-breasted warbler** (*Dendroica castanea*)—variably uncommon migrant

☐ **Blackpoll warbler** (*Dendroica striata*)—variably common spring migrant and variably rare fall migrant

☐ **Cerulean warbler** (*Dendroica cerulea*)—rare migrant

☐ **Black-and-white warbler** (*Mniotilta varia*)—common migrant and fairly common winter visitor; woodlands

☐ **American redstart** (*Setophaga ruticilla*)—common migrant and fairly rare winter visitor; woodlands

☐ **+Prothonotary warbler** (*Protonotaria citrea*)—fairly common migrant and rare winter visitor throughout, local breeding visitor in cypress swamps, northern mainland

☐ **Worm-eating warbler** (*Helmitheros vermivorus*)—common migrant and fairly rare winter visitor; brushy woodlands

☐ **Swainson's warbler** (*Limnothlypis swainsonii*)—uncommon migrant; usually in woods on damp leaf litter

- [ ] **Ovenbird** (*Seiurus aurocapillus*)—common migrant and uncommon winter visitor; woodlands
- [ ] **Northern waterthrush** (*Seiurus noveboracensis*)—common migrant and uncommon winter visitor; damp margins, often in mangroves
- [ ] **Louisiana waterthrush** (*Seiurus motacilla*)—uncommon migrant and fairly rare winter visitor; slightly damp margins, usually fresh water
- [ ] **Kentucky warbler** (*Oporornis formosus*)—rare migrant
- [ ] **Connecticut warbler** (*Oporornis agilis*)—uncommon spring and fairly rare fall migrant; brushy leaf litter
- [ ] **Mourning warbler** (*Oporornis philadelphia*)—rare migrant, chiefly fall; brushy areas
- [ ] **+Common yellowthroat** (*Geothlypis trichas*)—common migrant and winter visitor throughout, fairly common resident in swampy brush on mainland
- [ ] **Hooded warbler** (*Wilsonia citrina*)—uncommon migrant and rare winter visitor; woodlands
- [ ] **Wilson's warbler** (*Wilsonia pusilla*)—variably uncommon migrant and rare winter visitor; brushy areas
- [ ] **Canada warbler** (*Wilsonia canadensis*)—variably uncommon migrant
- [ ] **Yellow-breasted chat** (*Icteria virens*)—variably uncommon migrant and rare winter visitor; brushy areas

Bananaquits and Tanagers
- [ ] **Bananaquit** (*Coereba flaveola*)—rare visitor, chiefly winter; flowering trees usually near coast
- [ ] **Stripe-headed tanager** (*Spindalis zena*)—rare winter and spring visitor; fruiting trees
- [ ] **+Summer tanager** (*Piranga rubra*)—uncommon migrant and rare winter visitor throughout; local breeding visitor in pine-oak woodlands on northern mainland
- [ ] **Scarlet tanager** (*Piranga olivacea*)—variably uncommon migrant
- [ ] **Western tanager** (*Piranga ludoviciana*)—rare winter visitor; fruiting trees

Cardinals, Grosbeaks, and Buntings
- [ ] **+Northern cardinal** (*Cardinalis cardinalis*)—common resident (rare near Key West); suburban and wooded areas
- [ ] **Rose-breasted grosbeak** (*Pheucticus ludovicianus*)—variably uncommon migrant and rare winter visitor; woodlands
- [ ] **Blue grosbeak** (*Guiraca caerulea*)—variably uncommon migrant and rare winter visitor; brushy areas
- [ ] **Indigo bunting** (*Passerina cyanea*)—common migrant and uncommon winter visitor; brushy areas
- [ ] **Painted bunting** (*Passerina ciris*)—common migrant and winter visitor; brushy areas
- [ ] **Dickcissel** (*Spiza americana*)—variably uncommon migrant and rare winter visitor; brushy areas

Towhees and Sparrows

☐ **+Eastern towhee** (*Pipilo erythrophthalmus*)—common resident; chiefly pine woodlands, mainland

☐ **+Bachman's sparrow** (*Aimophila aestivalis*)—uncommon resident; pinelands, palmettos, and scrub south to Palm Beach County, wanders occasionally to Dade County

☐ **Chipping sparrow** (*Spizella passerina*)—variably uncommon migrant and winter visitor; brushy areas and lawns

☐ **Clay-colored sparrow** (*Spizella pallida*)—variably rare migrant and winter visitor; brushy areas

☐ **Field sparrow** (*Spizella pusilla*)—rare migrant and winter visitor; brushy areas, mainland

☐ **Vesper sparrow** (*Pooecetes gramineus*)—rare migrant and winter visitor; fallow fields with brush, mainland

☐ **Lark sparrow** (*Chondestes grammacus*)—variably rare migrant and winter visitor; brushy areas

☐ **Savannah sparrow** (*Passerculus sandwichensis*)—common migrant and winter visitor; open areas, chiefly mainland

☐ **+Grasshopper sparrow** (*Ammodramus savannarum*)—uncommon migrant and winter visitor; fallow fields with brush, chiefly mainland; Florida grasshopper sparrow (A. s. floridanus) is resident, breeds central Florida to Glades County **E**

☐ **Sharp-tailed sparrow** (*Ammodramus caudacutus*)—uncommon winter visitor; salt marsh prairie

☐ **+Cape Sable seaside sparrow** (*Ammodramus maritimus mirabilis*)—rare resident; fresh-to-brackish sloughs, mostly Everglades NP **E**

☐ **Lincoln's sparrow** (*Melospiza lincolnii*)—rare winter visitor; brushy areas

☐ **Swamp sparrow** (*Melospiza georgiana*)—variably uncommon migrant and winter visitor; swampy areas, chiefly mainland

☐ **White-throated sparrow** (*Zonotrichia albicollis*)—rare migrant and winter visitor; brushy areas

☐ **White-crowned sparrow** (*Zonotrichia leucophrys*)—locally uncommon winter and spring visitor; brushy areas

☐ **Bobolink** (*Dolichonyx oryzivorus*)—common migrant; fields and agricultural areas

Blackbirds and Orioles

☐ **+Red-winged blackbird** (*Agelaius phoeniceus*)—common resident; brushy fields and swamps

☐ **+Eastern meadowlark** (*Sturnella magna*)—common resident; fields, mainland

☐ **Yellow-headed blackbird** (*Xanthocephalus xanthocephalus*)—rare migrant and winter visitor; fields and swamps

☐ **+Boat-tailed grackle** (*Quiscalus major*)—abundant resident; swamps and fields, mainland

☐ **+Common grackle** (*Quiscalus quiscula*)—common resident; suburbs and fields, absent from Keys in winter

- [ ] **+Shiny cowbird** (*Molothrus bonariensis*)—variably uncommon spring migrant, chiefly Keys and Gulf coast; local resident throughout
- [ ] **Bronzed cowbird** (*Molothrus aeneus*)—variably rare winter visitor; mainland
- [ ] **+Brown-headed cowbird** (*Molothrus ater*)—common migrant and winter visitor, some breed; fields and edges, chiefly mainland
- [ ] **Orchard oriole** (*Icterius spurius*)—variably common migrant (rarer to the east); wooded areas
- [ ] ***Spot-breasted oriole** (*Icterus pectoralis*)—uncommon resident; suburbs with fruiting trees, Miami area
- [ ] **Baltimore oriole** (*Icterus galbula*)—common migrant, fairly rare winter visitor; wooded areas

Finches
- [ ] **Pine siskin** (*Carduelis pinus*)—variably rare winter and spring visitor; wooded edges
- [ ] **American goldfinch** (*Carduelis tristis*)—variably uncommon winter and spring visitor; wooded edges

Old World Sparrows
- [ ] ***House sparrow** (*Passer domesticus*)—common resident; urban areas, local in Keys

MAMMAL CHECKLIST

Marsupials
- [ ] **Opossum** (*Didelphis virginiana pigra*)—abundant; most habitats on mainland and Keys

Insectivores
- [ ] **Short-tailed shrew** (*Blarina brevicauda peninsulae*)—uncommon; mainland
- [ ] **Least shrew** (*Cryptotis parva floridana*)—common; mainland
- [ ] **Eastern mole** (*Scalopus aquaticus porteri*)—common; mainland

Bats
- [ ] **Eastern pipistrelle** (*Pipistrellus subflavus floridanus*)—uncommon; trees and crevices (in rocks, structures) on mainland and Keys
- [ ] **Big brown bat** (*Eptesicus fuscus osceola*)—rare; buildings and trees, range unconfirmed
- [ ] **Seminole bat** (*Nycteris seminola*)—rare; trees and Spanish moss, possibly south to Miami, not southwestern Florida or Keys
- [ ] **Northern yellow bat** (*Nycteris intermedia floridana*)—uncommon; trees around Big Cypress and Atlantic coastal ridge south to Miami
- [ ] **Evening bat** (*Nycticeius humeralis subtropicalis*)—common; trees and buildings on mainland
- [ ] **Brazilian free-tailed bat** (*Tadarida brasiliensis cynocephala*)—common; buildings, trees, and crevices (in rocks, structures) near coasts

☐ **Florida mastiff bat** (*Eumops glaucinus floridanus*)—rare; buildings and trees in South Miami (the most restricted range of any Florida mammal)

Edentates
☐ ***Nine-banded armadillo** (Dasypus novemcinctus mexicanus)—uncommon; drier areas of mainland

Lagomorphs
☐ **Marsh rabbit** (*Sylvilagus palustris paludicola*)—common; most habitats (prefers marshes) on mainland; Lower Keys marsh rabbit (*S. p. hefneri*)—rare, on Lower Keys **E**

☐ **Eastern cottontail** (*Sylvilagus floridanus floridanus* and *S. f. paulsoni*)—uncommon; in pinelands and hammocks on mainland

Rodents
☐ **Gray squirrel** (*Sciurus carolinensis extimus*)—common; hammocks on mainland and Keys

☐ **Mangrove fox squirrel** (*Scuirus niger avicennia*)—uncommon; mangroves, cypress, and pinelands on western mainland; extirpated elsewhere

☐ ***Mexican red-bellied squirrel** (*Sciurus aureogaster*)—found only on Elliott Key and a few nearby keys

☐ **Southern flying squirrel** (Glaucomys volans querceti)—uncommon; pinelands on mainland

☐ **Marsh rice rat** (*Oryzomys palustris coloratus*)—common; fresh and salt water marshes on mainland; Lower Keys rice rat (*O. p. natator*) **E**

☐ **Oldfield (southeastern) beach mouse** (*Peromyscus polionotus niveiventris*)—rare (may be extirpated); coastal dunes on eastern barrier islands **T**

☐ **Cotton mouse** (*Peromyscus gossypinus allapaticola* and *P. g. telmaphilus*)—common; hammocks on mainland and upper Keys; Key Largo cotton mouse (*P. g. allapaticola*) **E**

☐ **Florida mouse** (*Podomys floridanus*)—uncommon; along coastal uplands on mainland to Dade and Sarasota counties

☐ **Hispid cotton rat** (*Sigmodon hispidus exsputus*, *S. h. floridanus* and *S. h. spadicipygus*)—abundant; ubiquitous, mainland and Keys

☐ **Key Largo woodrat** (*Neotoma floridana smalli*)—rare (almost extinct); hardwood hammocks on Key Largo **E**

☐ **Round-tailed muskrat** (*Neofiber alleni struix*)—uncommon; marshes and sloughs

☐ ***Black (Roof) rat** (*Rattus rattus*)—common; near development on mainland and Keys

☐ ***Norway rat** (*Rattus norvegicus*)—common; near development on mainland and Keys

☐ ***House mouse** (*Mus musculus*)—common; near development on mainland and Keys

Cetaceans
☐ **Atlantic bottlenose dolphin** (*Tursiops truncatus*)—common; shallow waters and estuaries of Atlantic Ocean, Gulf of Mexico, and Florida Bay

Carnivores
☐ **Gray fox** (*Urocyon cinereoargenteus floridanus*)—common; particularly eastern mainland near development

☐ **Red fox** (*Vulpes vulpes*)—status unknown, may have been introduced into Florida; local in interior mainland

☐ **Florida black bear** (*Ursus americanus floridanus*)—rare; uplands on mainland (mostly Big Cypress region in our area)

☐ **Raccoon** (*Procyon lotor auspicatus, P. l. elucus, P. l. incautus, P. l. inesperatus, P. l. marinus*)—abundant; all habitats on mainland and Keys

☐ **Long-tailed weasel** (*Mustela frenata peninsulae*)—status unknown; habitat generalist, Big Cypress region

☐ **Everglades Mink** (*Mustela vison evergladensis*)—rare; freshwater wetlands of southern Everglades

☐ **Spotted skunk** (*Spilogale putorius ambarvalis*)—uncommon; palmetto scrub and hammocks on mainland

☐ **Striped skunk** (*Mephitis mephitis elongata*)—uncommon; uplands on mainland

☐ **River otter** (*Lutra canadensis lataxina*)—common; freshwater wetlands on mainland

☐ **Florida panther** (*Puma concolor coryi*)—rare (almost extirpated); pinelands, cypress, hammocks **E**

☐ **Bobcat** (*Lynx rufus floridanus*)—common; mainland and rarely to Key Largo

Artiodactyls
☐ **White-tailed deer** (*Odocoileus virginianus seminolus*)—common; many habitats on mainland

☐ **Key deer** (*Odocoileus virginianus clavium*)—locally common; primarily pinelands, only Big Pine Key and neighboring islands **E**

☐ ***Feral hog** (*Sus scrofa*)—common; many habitats in interior of mainland; pest

Sirenians
☐ West Indian manatee (*Trichechus manatus latirostris*)—locally common in shallow marine and estuary waters around mainland and Keys **E**

REPTILE CHECKLIST

Crocodilians
☐ **American crocodile** (*Crocodylus acutus*)—rare; coastal mangroves on mainland and Keys **T**

☐ **American alligator** (*Alligator mississippiensis*)—abundant; freshwater wetlands (occasionally on coasts) on mainland and fresh water on a few lower Keys **T** (by similarity of appearance to crocodiles)

☐ ***Spectacled caiman** (*Caiman crocodilus*)—rare; fresh water in Miami area

Turtles

☐ **Florida snapping turtle** (*Chelydra serpentina osceola*)—common; fresh water on mainland

☐ **Striped mud turtle** (*Kinosternon baurii*)—common; freshwater wetlands on mainland and Keys

☐ **Florida mud turtle** (*Kinosternon subrubrum steindachneri*)—common; freshwater wetlands and salt marshes on mainland and Keys

☐ **Common musk turtle** (or stinkpot) (*Sternotherus odoratus*)—common; fresh water on mainland

☐ **Florida box turtle** (*Terrapene carolina bauri*)—common; pinelands and hammocks on mainland and some Keys (not middle Keys)

☐ **Diamondback terrapin** (*Malaclemys terrapin tequesta, M. t. rhizophorarum*, and *M. t. macrospilota*)—uncommon; mangroves and saltmarshes on coastal mainland and Keys

☐ **Peninsula cooter** (*Pseudemys floridana peninsularis*)—abundant; fresh water on mainland, except extreme southwest

☐ **Florida redbelly turtle** (*Pseudemys nelsoni*)—abundant; mostly freshwater wetlands, also mangrove borders on mainland

☐ ***Red-eared slider** (*Trachemys scripta elegans*)—established in canals in Dade County

☐ **Florida chicken turtle** (*Deirochelys reticularia chrysea*)—uncommon; freshwater marshes and ponds on mainland

☐ **Gopher tortoise** (*Gopherus polyphemus*)—uncommon and rapidly declining; pinelands and scrub of Atlantic coastal ridge, Long Pine Key (few), Middle Cape Sable, Big Cypress, and Naples

☐ **Leatherback sea turtle** (*Dermochelys coriacea*)—rare; marine waters **E**

☐ **Green sea turtle** (*Chelonia mydas*)—rare; marine waters **E**

☐ **Hawksbill sea turtle** (*Eretmochelys imbricata imbricata*)—rare; marine waters **E**

☐ **Loggerhead sea turtle** (*Caretta caretta*)—uncommon in summer; marine waters near Cape Sable and other sandy beaches, and Florida Keys **T**

☐ **Kemp's Ridley sea turtle** (*Lepidochelys kempii*)—rare; marine waters **E**

☐ **Florida softshell turtle** (*Apalone ferox*)—common; freshwater marshes on mainland (introduced to Big Pine Key)

Lizards

☐ ***Tokay gecko** (*Gekko gecko*)—locally established near development; Miami and Ft. Lauderdale area

☐ ***Mediterranean gecko** (*Hemidactylus turcicus turcicus*)—locally established; near development on Atlantic coast of mainland and Upper and Lower Keys

☐ ***Indopacific gecko** (*Hemidactylus garnotii*)—locally common, nocturnal; near development on mainland and Upper Keys

☐ ***Ashy gecko** (*Sphaerodactylus elegans elegans*)—locally established, nocturnal; Lower Keys and Miami area

☐ **Florida reef gecko** (*Sphaerodactylus notatus*)—common; pinelands and hammocks on southeast mainland and Keys

☐ ***Ocellated gecko** (*Sphaerodactylus argus argus*)—locally established; Lower Keys

☐ ***Yellowhead gecko** (*Gonatodes albogularis fuscus*)—locally established; around Miami, Ft. Lauderdale, and Lower Keys

☐ **Green anole** (*Anolis carolinensis*)—common; many habitats on mainland and Keys

☐ ***Knight anole** (*Anolis equestris*)—locally common; near development on southeast mainland and Upper Keys

☐ ***Brown anole** (*Anolis sagrei*)—abundant and increasing; many habitats on mainland and Keys

☐ ***Jamaican giant anole** (*Anolis garmani*)—locally established; Miami and Ft. Lauderdale area

☐ ***Puerto Rican crested anole** (*Anolis cristatellus cristatellus*)—locally established; Miami and Ft. Lauderdale area

☐ ***Largehead anole** (*Anolis cybotes cybotes*)—locally established; Miami and Ft. Lauderdale area

☐ ***Bark anole** (*Anolis distichus*)—locally common; Miami area

☐ ***Brown basilisk** (*Basiliscus vittatus*)—locally established; Miami and Ft. Lauderdale area

☐ ***Green iguana** (*Iguana iguana*)—locally established; developed areas

☐ ***Nile monitor** (*Varanus niloticus*)—locally established; primarily coastal developed areas

☐ ***Spinytail iguana** (*Ctenosaura pectinata*)—locally established; South Miami near Biscayne Bay

☐ **Florida scrub lizard** (*Sceloporus woodi*)—rare; pinelands and scrub along coast north from Miami and Marco

☐ ***Northern curlytail lizard** (*Leiocephalus carinatus armouri*)—locally established; around Miami and West Palm Beach

☐ ***Red-sided curlytail lizard** (*Leiocephalus schreibersii schreibersii*)—locally established; Miami and Ft. Lauderdale area

☐ **Six-lined racerunner** (*Cnemidophorus sexlineatus*)—locally common; uplands on mainland and Keys

☐ ***Giant ameiva** (*Ameiva ameiva*)—locally established; Miami area

☐ ***Rainbow whiptail** (*Cnemidophorus lemniscatus*)—locally established; Miami area

☐ **Ground skink** (*Scincella lateralis*)—common; hammocks and pinelands on mainland (except Everglades) and Keys

☐ **Southeastern five-lined skink** (*Eumeces inexpectatus*)—common; often seen on trails on mainland and Keys

☐ **Florida Keys mole skink** (*Eumeces egregius egregius*)—rare, secretive; found under debris near shore on Keys and Dry Tortugas

☐ **Peninsula mole skink** (*Eumeces egregius onocrepis*)—uncommon; sandy scrub on mainland except Everglades

☐ **Eastern glass lizard** (*Ophisaurus ventralis*)—uncommon; pinelands and hammocks on mainland

☐ **Slender glass lizard** (*Ophisaurus attenuatus*)—uncommon; dry grasslands or woods on mainland except Everglades

☐ **Island glass lizard** (*Ophisaurus compressus*)—common; marshes and pinelands on eastern mainland

Snakes

☐ ***Brahminy blind snake** (Ramphotyphlops braminus)—worm-like burrower, locally common; east coast south to Homestead, also Upper and Lower Keys

☐ **Florida green water snake** (*Nerodia floridana*)—common; fresh or brackish marshes on mainland

☐ **Brown water snake** (*Nerodia taxispilota*)—common; clear, quiet waters on mainland

☐ **Florida water snake** (*Nerodia fasciata pictiventris*)—common; marshes and canals on mainland

☐ **Mangrove salt marsh snake** (*Nerodia clarkii compressicauda*)—common; mangrove swamps and salt marshes on coastal mainland and Keys

☐ **South Florida swamp snake** (*Seminatrix pygaea cyclas*)—common; freshwater wetlands on mainland

☐ **Florida brown snake** (*Storeria dekayi victa*)—common; pinelands, hammocks, and freshwater marshes on mainland and Lower Keys

☐ **Eastern garter snake** (*Thamnophis sirtalis sirtalis*)—common; many habitats on mainland

☐ **Peninsula ribbon snake** (*Thamnophis sauritus sackenii*)—common; many habitats on mainland and Lower Keys

☐ **Striped crayfish snake** (*Regina alleni*)—locally common; very aquatic, fresh water on mainland

☐ **Eastern hognose snake** (*Heterodon platyrhinos*)—rare; sandy areas of mainland

☐ **Southern ringneck snake** (*Diadophis punctatus punctatus* and *D. p. acricus*)—common; woodlands on mainland to Upper Keys (*D. p. punctatus*), pinelands and hammocks on Lower Keys (*D. p. acricus*, uncommon)

☐ **Pine woods snake** (*Rhadinaea flavilata*)—uncommon; moist pine flatwoods in northern and central Florida to Glades County

☐ **Eastern mud snake** (*Farancia abacura abacura*)—locally common; freshwater marshes, ponds, and canals on mainland

☐ **Southern black racer** (*Coluber constrictor priapus*)—abundant; many habitats on Lower Keys

☐ **Everglades racer** (*Coluber constrictor paludicola*)—abundant; many habitats on mainland and Upper Keys

☐ **Eastern coachwhip** (*Masticophis flagellum flagellum*)—locally common; many habitats on mainland

☐ **Rough green snake** (*Opheodrys aestivus*)—abundant; many habitats on mainland and Keys

☐ **Eastern indigo snake** (*Drymarchon corais couperi*)—rare; primarily dry areas on mainland and Lower Keys **T**

- [ ] **Corn snake or red rat snake** (*Elaphe guttata guttata*)—abundant; mostly around development on mainland and Keys
- [ ] **Everglades rat snake** (*Elaphe obsoleta rossalleni*)—locally common; freshwater marshes, hammocks, and pinelands in Everglades
- [ ] **Yellow rat snake** (*Elaphe obsoleta quadrivitatta*)—uncommon; many habitats on mainland (except Everglades) and upper Keys
- [ ] **Florida pine snake** (*Pituophis melanoleucus mugitis*)—uncommon; very dry oak-pine woodlands and scrub south to Lake Okeechobee and along Atlantic coastal ridge south to Broward County
- [ ] **Florida kingsnake** (*Lampropeltis getula florida*)—uncommon; freshwater marshes, hammocks, and pinelands on mainland
- [ ] **Scarlet kingsnake** (*Lampropeltis triangulum*)—rare; pinelands and hammocks on mainland and Keys (except middle Keys)
- [ ] **Florida scarlet snake** (*Cemophora c. coccinea*)—rare; pinelands and hammocks on mainland
- [ ] **Rim rock crowned snake** (*Tantilla oolitica*)—rare, secretive; limestone areas along Atlantic coast of mainland to Upper Keys
- [ ] **Coast dunes crowned snake** (*Tantilla relicta pamlica*)—uncommon; coastal dunes and scrub of central Atlantic coast to Palm Beach County
- [ ] **Eastern coral snake** (*Micrurus fulvius*)—locally common; pinelands and hammocks on mainland and Key Largo; venomous
- [ ] **Florida cottonmouth** (or water moccasin) (*Agkistrodon piscivorus conanti*)—common; freshwater marshes and mangroves on mainland and Keys (except lower Keys); venomous
- [ ] **Dusky pygmy rattlesnake** (*Sistrurus miliarius*)—common; pinelands and freshwater marshes on mainland; venomous
- [ ] **Eastern diamondback rattlesnake** (*Crotalus adamanteus*)—locally common; many habitats on mainland and Keys (including Florida Bay); venomous
- [ ] ***Boa constrictor** (*Boa constrictor*)—local around developments; Miami and elsewhere
- [ ] ***Burmese python** (*Python molurus bivittatus*)—increasingly common; many habitats

AMPHIBIAN CHECKLIST

Salamanders
- [ ] **Two-toed amphiuma** (*Amphiuma means*)—common; freshwater marshes and sloughs on mainland
- [ ] **Greater siren** (*Siren lacertina*)—common; freshwater marshes, sloughs, and ponds on mainland
- [ ] **Everglades dwarf siren** (*Pseudobranchus striatus belli*)—common; freshwater marshes, sloughs, and ponds on mainland
- [ ] **Peninsula newt** (*Notophthalmus viridescens piaropicola*)—abundant; freshwater marshes and ponds on mainland

☐ **Dwarf salamander** (*Eurycea quadridigitata*)—secretive; wet hammocks and streams in Dade, Palm Beach, and Hendry counties

Toads and Frogs

☐ **Eastern spadefoot toad** (*Scaphiophus holbrookii holbrookii*)—uncommon, secretive; sandy, dry areas on Atlantic coastal ridge and Upper and Lower Keys

☐ **Southern toad** (*Bufo terrestris*)—abundant (uncommon in Everglades); hammocks, pinelands, and freshwater marshes on mainland and Lower Keys

☐ **Oak toad** (*Bufo quercicus*)—common; hammocks, pinelands, and freshwater marshes on mainland and Keys (except Lower Keys)

☐ ***Giant toad** (*Bufo marinus*)—common; breeds in fresh or brackish water around Miami area and Keys

☐ ***Greenhouse frog** (*Eleutherodactylus planirostris*)—may be immigrant; under leaf litter on mainland and Keys

☐ ***Puerto Rican coqui** (*Eleutherodactylus coqui*)—local, uncommon; Miami area

☐ **Florida cricket frog** (*Acris gryllus dorsalis*)—common; freshwater marshes on mainland

☐ **Green treefrog** (*Hyla cinerea*)—abundant; hammocks, pinelands, and freshwater marshes on mainland and Keys

☐ **Barking treefrog** (*Hyla gratiosa*)—uncommon; mainland except Everglades

☐ **Pine woods treefrog** (*Hyla femoralis*)—common; often around artificial lights on mainland

☐ **Squirrel treefrog** (*Hyla squirella*)—abundant; all habitats with fresh water on mainland and Keys

☐ ***Cuban treefrog** (*Osteopilus septentrionalis*)—immigrant, locally abundant; often found around buildings on Atlantic coastal ridge, Keys, and Naples

☐ **Florida chorus frog** (*Pseudacris nigrita verrucosa*)—common; freshwater swamps and marshes on mainland

☐ **Little grass frog** (*Pseudacris ocularis*)—abundant; freshwater swamps and marshes on mainland

☐ **Eastern narrowmouth toad** (*Gastrophryne carolinensis*)—common, but a secretive burrower; under leaf litter in hammocks on mainland and Keys

☐ **Pig frog** (*Rana grylio*)—abundant, commercially exploited; all fresh water habitats on mainland

☐ **Southern leopard frog** (*Rana utricularia*)—abundant; all fresh water habitats on mainland and Lower Keys

☐ **Florida gopher frog** (*Rana capito aesopus*)—uncommon; found in gopher tortoise burrows on mainland

SCIENTIFIC NAMES OF PLANTS

This is a list of the scientific names of the plants mentioned in the main text. All the plants are found in south Florida. However, the list is not intended to be a complete list of plants found in the region covered by the book. There are too many to list comfortably.

*nonnative

TREES, SHRUBS, AND WOODY PLANTS

Gymnosperms:
CYCADACEAE—Cycad family
coontie (*Zamia pumila*)

PINACEAE—Pine family
slash pine (*Pinus elliottii* var. *densa*)

TAXODIACEAE—Redwood family
bald-cypress (*Taxodium distichum*)
pond-cypress (*Taxodium ascendens* or *T. distichum* var. *nutans*)

Angiosperms:
ACERACEAE—Maple family
red maple (*Acer rubrum*)

ANACARDIACEAE—Cashew family
Brazilian pepper (*Schinus terebinthifolius*)*
poison ivy (*Toxicodendron radicans*)
poisonwood (*Metopium toxiferum*)

ANNONACEAE—Custard-apple family
pond-apple (*Annona glabra*)

AQUIFOLIACEAE—Holly family
dahoon (*Ilex cassine*)

ARECACEAE—Palm family
cabbage palm (or sabal palmetto) (*Sabal palmetto*)
coconut palm (*Cocos nucifera*)*
Florida (or Jamaica) thatch palm (*Thrinax radiata*)
Key (or brittle) thatch palm (*Thrinax morrisii*)

paurotis palm (*Acoelorrhaphe wrightii*)
royal palm (*Roystonea elata*)
saw palmetto (*Serenoa repens*)
scrub (or corkscrew) palmetto (*Sabal etonia*)
silver palm (*Coccothrinax argentata*)

AVICENNIACEAE—Black mangrove family
black mangrove (*Avicennia germinans*)

BORAGINACEAE—Forget-me-not family
Geiger-tree (*Cordia sebastena*)

BURSERACEAE—Torchwood family
gumbo-limbo (*Bursera simaruba*)

CAPPARACEAE—Caper family
Jamaica caper (*Capparis cynophallophora*)

CASUARINACEAE—Beefwood family
Australian-pine (*Casuarina litorea* and *C. glauca*)*

CHRYSOBALANACEAE—Coco-plum family
coco-plum (*Chrysobalanus icaco*)
gopher apple (*Licania michauxii*)

COMBRETACEAE—Combretum family
buttonwood (*Conocarpus erectus*)
white mangrove (*Laguncularia racemosa*)

ERICACEAE—Heath family
gallberry (*Ilex glabra*)
staggerbush (*Lyonia ferruginea*)

EUPHORBIACEAE—Spurge family
manchineel (*Hippomane mancinella*)

FABACEAE—Pea family
blackbead (*Pithecellobium guadalupense*)
catclaw (*Pithecellobium unguis-cati*)
coral bean (*Erythrina herbacea*)
Jamaica dogwood (*Piscidia piscipula*)
necklace pod (*Sophora tomentosa*)
sweet acacia (*Acacia farnesiana*)
wild-tamarind (*Lysiloma latisiliquum*)

FAGACEAE—Beech family
Chapman oak (*Quercus chapmanii*)
live oak (*Quercus virginiana*)
myrtle oak (*Quercus myrtifolia*)
sand live oak (*Quercus geminata*)
LAURACEAE—Laurel family
lancewood (*Ocotea coriacea*, formerly *Nectandra coriacea*)
redbay (*Persea borbonia*)

MAGNOLIACEAE—Magnolia family
sweet bay (*Magnolia virginiana*)

MALVACEAE—Mallow family
seaside mahoe (*Thespesia populnea*)

MELASTOMATACEAE—Melastoma family
tetrazygia (*Tetrazygia bicolor*)

MELIACEAE—Mahogany family
West Indian mahogany (*Swietenia mahagoni*)

MORACEAE—Mulberry family
banyan fig (*Ficus* spp.)
strangler fig (*Ficus aurea*)

MYRICACEAE—Bayberry family
wax myrtle (*Myrica cerifera*)

MYRSINACEAE—Myrsine family
marlberry (*Ardisia escallonioides*)
myrsine (*Myrsine floridana*)

MYRTACEAE—Myrtle family
guava (*Psidium guajava*)*
melaleuca, cajeput (*Melaleuca quinquenervia*)*
Spanish stopper (*Eugenia foetida*)
white stopper (*Eugenia axillaris*)

POLYGONACEAE—Buckwheat family
pigeon-plum (*Coccoloba diversifolia*)
sea-grape (*Coccoloba uvifera*)

RHAMNACEAE—Buckthorn family
black ironwood (*Krugiodendron ferreum*)

RHIZOPHORACEAE—Mangrove family
red mangrove (*Rhizophora mangle*)

ROSACEAE—Rose family
West-Indian cherry (*Prunus myrtifolia*)

RUBIACEAE—Madder family
black-torch (*Erithalis fruticosa*)
firebush (*Hamelia patens*)
indigo-berry (*Randia aculeata*)
rough velvetseed (*Guettarda scabra*)
seven-year apple (*Casasia clusiifolia*)
snowberry (*Chiococca alba*)
white indigo-berry (*Randia aculeata*)
wild coffee (*Psychotria nervosa*)

RUTACEAE—Citrus family
satinwood (*Zanthoxylum flavum*)
torchwood (*Amyris elemifera*)
wild-lime (*Zanthoxylum fagara*)

SALICACEAE—Willow family
coastal plain willow (*Salix caroliniana*)

SAPINDACEAE—Soapberry family
varnish-leaf (*Dodonaea viscosa*)

SAPOTACEAE—Sapodilla family
mastic (*Mastichodendron foetidissimum*)
saffron-plum (*Bumelia celastrina*)
sapodilla (*Manilkara zapota*)
satinleaf (*Chrysophyllum oliviforme*)
wild dilly (*Manilkara bahamensis*)
willow bustic (*Dipholis salicifolia*)

SIMAROUBACEAE—Quassia family
paradise-tree (*Simarouba glauca*)

SOLANACEAE—Nightshade family

Christmas berry (*Lycium carolinianum*)

SURIANACEAE—Bay-cedar family
bay-cedar (*Suriana maritima*)

ULMACEAE—Elm family
Florida trema (*Trema micranthum*)

VERBENACEAE—Verbena family
beauty berry (*Callicarpa americana*)
Florida fiddlewood (*Citharexylem fruticosum*)

ZYGOPHYLLACEAE—Caltrop family
lignum vitae (*Guaiacum sanctum*)

NON-WOODY PLANTS

AGAVACEAE—Agave family
Spanish bayonet (*Yucca aloifolia*)

AIZOACEAE—Carpetweed family
sea purslane (*Sesuvium portulacastrum*)

ARACEACE—Arum family
manatee grass (*Syringodium filiforme*)
water lettuce (*Pistia stratiodes*)

ASTERACEAE—Aster family
coreopsis (*Coreopsis* spp.)
sea ox-eye daisy (*Borrichia frutescens*)

BATACEAE—Saltwort family
saltwort (*Batis maritima*)

BROMELIACEAE—Air plant family
ballmoss (*Tillandsia recurvata*)
cardinal air plant (*Tillandsia fasciculata*)
giant wildpine (*Tillandsia utriculata*)
needle-leaved wildpine (*Tillandsia setacea*)
reddish wildpine (*Tillandsia polystachia*)

reflexed wildpine (*Tillandsia balbisiana*)
Spanish moss (*Tillandsia usneoides*)
twisted air plant (*Tillandsia flexuosa*)

CACTACEAE—Cactus family
prickly-pear (*Opuntia* spp.)

CAMPANULACEAE—Bluebell family
glades lobelia (*Lobelia glandulosa*)

CHENOPODIACEAE—Goosefoot family
glasswort (*Salicornia virginica*)

COMMELINACEAE—Spiderwort family
oyster-plant (*Rhoeo discolor*)*

CRASSULACEAE—Sedum family
kalanchoe (*Kalanchoe* spp.)*

CYPERACEAE—Sedge family
sawgrass (*Cladium jamaicense*)
spike rush (*Eleocharis cellulosa*)

DIOSCOREACEAE—Yam family
air potato (*Dioscorea bulbifera*)*

DROCERACEAE—Sundew family
round-leaved sundew (*Drocera rotundifolia*)

EMPETRACEAE—Crowberry family
rosemary (*Ceratiola ericoides*)

EUPHORBIACEAE—Spurge family
pineland (or **wooly**) **croton** (*Croton linearis*)

GENTIANACEAE—Gentian family
white sabatia (*Sabatia brevifolia*)

HYDROCHARITEAE—Frog's-bit family
hydrilla (*Hydrilla verticillata*)*
turtle grass (*Thalassia testudinum*)

IRIDACEAE—**Iris family**
celestial lily (*Nemastylis floridana*)

LENTIBULARIACEAE—Bladderwort family
bladderwort (*Utricularia* spp.)

ORCHIDACEAE—Orchid family
butterfly orchid (*Encyclia tampensis*)
cowhorn orchid (*Cyrtopodium punctatum*)
ghost orchid (*Dendrophylax lindenii*)
spider orchid (*Brassia caudata*)
worm-vine orchid (*Vanilla barbellata*)

PHYTOLACCACEAE—Pokeweed family
rouge plant (*Rivina humilis*)

POACEAE—Grass family
Florida gamagrass (*Tripsacum floridanum*)
muhly grass (*Muhlenberghia filipes*)
sea oats (*Uniola paniculata*)

POLYGALACEAE—Milkwort family
bog bachelor-button (*Polygala lutea*)

POLYPODIACEAE—Polypodium family
bracken fern (*Pteridium caudatum*)
chain fern (*Woodwardia virginica*)
giant leather fern (*Acrostichum danaeifolium*)
golden polypody fern (*Phlebodium aureum*)
resurrection fern (*Polypodium polypodioides*)
royal fern (*Osmunda regala*)
shoestring fern (*Vittaria lineata*)
strap fern (*Campyloneurum* spp.)
swamp fern (*Blechnum serrulatum*)
sword fern (*Nephrolepis biserrata*)

PONTEDERIACEAE—Pickerelweed family
pickerelweed (*Pontederia cordata*)
water hyacinth (*Eichhornia crassipes*)*

RUBIACEAE—Madder family
small-flowered lily thorn (*Catesbaea parviflora*)

SCHIZACEAE—Curly grass fern family
Old World climbing fern (*Lygodium microphyllum*)*

TYPHACEAE—Cattail family
cattail (*Typha* spp.)

ZOSTERACEAE—Pondweed family
shoal grass (*Halodule wrightii*)

SUGGESTED READING
* denotes sources used in preparation of this book.

Alden, Peter, Rick Cech, and Gil Nelson. 1998. National Audubon Society Field Guide to Florida. New York: Knopf/Chanticleer Press.

Ashton, Ray E., Jr., and Patricia Sawyer Ashton. 1981. Handbook of Reptiles and Amphibians of Florida. Part One: The Snakes. Miami: Windward Publishing. 176pp.

Ashton, Ray E., Jr., and Patricia Sawyer Ashton. 1985. Handbook of Reptiles and Amphibians of Florida. Part Two: Lizards, Turtles, and Crocodilians. Miami: Windward Publishing. 191pp.

Ashton, Ray E., Jr., and Patricia Sawyer Ashton. 1988. Handbook of Reptiles and Amphibians of Florida. Part Three: The Amphibians. Miami: Windward Publishing. 191pp.

Bell, C. Ritchie and Bryan J. Taylor. 1982. Florida Wild Flowers and Roadside Plants. Chapel Hill, NC: Laurel Hill Press. 308pp.

Brookfield, Charles M. and Oliver Griswold. 1985. They All Called It Tropical. Miami: Historical Association of Southern Florida. 77pp.*

Carmichael, Pete and Winston Williams. 1991. Florida's Fabulous Reptiles and Amphibians. Tampa, FL: World Publications. 120pp.

Carter, Elizabeth F. 1987. A Guide to the Trails of Florida. Birmingham, AL: Menasha Ridge Press. 129pp.

Cox, W. Eugene. 1989. Everglades: The Continuing Story. Las Vegas, NV: K.C. Publications. 48pp.

Davis, Steven M. and John C. Ogden (eds.). 1994. The Everglades: The Ecosystem and its Restoration. Delray, FL: St. Lucie Press. 826pp.

De Golia, Jack. 1978. Everglades: The Story Behind the Scenery. Las Vegas, NV: K.C. Publications. 64pp.

Deyrup, Mark and Richard Franz (eds.). 1994. Rare and Endangered Biota of Florida, Volume IV. Invertebrates. Gainesville, FL: Univ. Press of Florida. 798pp.

Douglas, Marjory Stoneman. 1988 (rev.). The Everglades: River of Grass. Sarasota, FL: Pineapple Press. 448pp.

FNPMA. 1991. Motorist's Guide to Everglades National Park. Homestead, FL: Florida National Parks and Monuments Association.

FNPMA. 1991. An Activity Guide for Teachers: Everglades National Park (grades 4–6). Homestead, FL: National Parks and Monuments Association.

Gato, Jeanette. 1991. The Monroe County Environmental story. Big Pine Key, FL: Seacamp Association. 368pp.

George, Jean Craighead. 1988. Everglades Wildguide. Homestead, FL: U.S. Dept. of Interior, NPS. Natural History Series, Everglades National Park. 103pp.

Gerberg, Eugene J. and Ross H. Arnett. 1989. Florida Butterflies. Baltimore, MD: Natural Science Publications. 90pp.*

Gilbert, Carter R. (ed.). 1992. Rare and Endangered Biota of Florida, Volume II. Fishes. Gainesville, FL: Univ. Press of Florida. 247pp.

Gingerich, Jerry Lee. 1994. Florida's Fabulous Mammals. Tampa, FL: World Publications. 128pp.

Greenberg, Idaz and Jerry Greenberg. 1977. Guide to Corals and Fishes of Florida, the Bahamas, and the Caribbean. Miami: Seahawk Press. 65pp. Paperback and waterproof editions.

Hammer, Roger. 2005. Everglades National Park and the Surrounding Area: A Guide to Exploring the Great Outdoors. Connecticut: Globe Pequot Press. 179 pp.

Hoffmeister, John Edward. 1982. Land from the Sea, the Geologic Story of South Florida. Coral Gables, FL: University of Miami Press. 143 pp.*

Humphrey, Stephen R. (ed.). 1992. Rare and Endangered Biota of Florida, Volume I. Mammals. Gainesville, FL: Univ. Press of Florida. 392 pp.

Kalma, Dennis. 1988. Boat and Canoe Camping in the Everglades Backcountry and Ten Thousand Islands Region. Miami: Florida Flair Books. 64 pp.

Kaplan, Eugene H. 1988. A Field Guide to Southeastern and Caribbean Seashores. Boston: Houghton Mifflin. 425 pp.*

Landrum, L. Wayne. 1990. Biscayne, the Story Behind the Scenery. Las Vegas, NV: K.C. Publications. 48 pp.

Laughlin, Maureen H., John C. Ogden, William B. Robertson, Jr., Ken Russell, and Roy Wood. 1991. Everglades National Park Bird Checklist. Homestead, FL: Florida National Parks and Monuments Association. 20 pp.*

Lazell, James D., Jr. 1989. Wildlife of the Florida Keys. Washington, DC: Island Press. 254 pp.*

Lodge, Thomas E. 2010. The Everglades Handbook: Understanding the Ecosystem. Third Edition. Boca Raton, FL: CRC Press. 422pp.

Maehr, David S. and Herbert W. Kale II. Florida's Birds, 2nd edition. 2005. Sarasota, FL: Pineapple Press. 360 pp.

McIver, Stuart. 1989. True Tales of the Everglades. Miami: Florida Flair Books. 64pp.*

Minno, Marc C. and Thomas C. Emmel. 1993. Butterflies of the Florida Keys. Gainesville, FL: Scientific Publishers. 168pp.

Moler, Paul E. (ed.). 1992. Rare and Endangered Biota of Florida, Volume III. Amphibians and Reptiles. Gainesville, FL: Univ. Press of Florida. 291pp.

Morton, Julia F. 1982. Wild Plants for Survival in South Florida. Miami: Fairchild Tropical Garden. 80pp.

Neill, Wilfred T. 1956. Florida's Seminole Indians. St. Petersburg, FL: Great Outdoors Publishing Co. 128pp.

Pranty, Bill. 1996. A Birder's Guide to Florida. Distr. by ABA Sales, P.O. Box 6599, Colorado Springs, CO 80934. 388pp.

Robertson, William B., Jr. 1989 (rev.). Everglades: The Park Story. Homestead, FL: Florida National Parks and Monuments Association. 63pp.*

Rodgers, James A., Herbert W. Kale II, and Henry T. Smith (eds.). 1996. Rare and Endangered Biota of Florida, Volume V. Birds. Gainesville, FL: Univ. Press of Florida. 736pp.

Scurlock, J. Paul. 1987. Native Trees and Shrubs of the Florida Keys. Bethel Park, PA: Laurel Press, Inc. 220pp.

SFBT. South Florida Birding Trail. Florida Fish and Game Conservation Commission. March 2007. www.floridabirdingtrail.com *

SFWMD 2009. Recreational Guide. 3rd ed. South Florida Water Management District, West Palm Beach, FL 33410. 117 pp. *

Simberloff, Daniel, Don C. Schmitz, and Tom C. Brown. 1997. Strangers in Paradise: Impact and Management of Nonindigenous Species in Florida. Island Press. 468 pp.

Stevenson, George B. 1992. Trees of the Everglades National Park and the Florida Keys. Homestead, FL: Florida Parks and National Monuments Assoc., Inc. 32pp.*

Stiling, Peter D. 1989. Florida's Butterflies and Other Insects. Sarasota, FL: Pineapple Press. 95pp.*

Stone, Calvin. 1979. Forty Years in the Everglades. Tabor City, NC: W. Horace Carter, Atlantic Publishing Co. 224pp.

Tebeau, Charleton W. 1968. Man in the Everglades. Coral Gables, FL: University of Miami Press. 192pp.*

Tomlinson, P.B. 1980. The Biology of Trees Native to Tropical Florida. Allston, MA: Harvard University Printing Office. 480pp.*

Toops, Connie M. 1988. The Alligator: Monarch of the Marsh. Homestead, FL: Florida National Parks and Monuments Assn. 58pp.

Toops, Connie M. 1989. Everglades. Stillwater, MN: Voyager Press. 96pp.

Toops, Connie and Willard E. Dilley. 1986. Birds of South Florida. Conway, AR: Conway Printing Co. 150pp.

Truesdell, William G. 1985. A Guide to the Wilderness Waterway of Everglades National Park. Coral Gables, FL: University of Miami Press. 64pp.

Voss, Gilbert L. 1988. Coral Reefs of Florida. Sarasota, FL: Pineapple Press. 80pp.*

Will, Lawrence E. 1984. A Dredgeman of Cape Sable. Belle Glade, FL: The Glades Historical Society. 158pp.*

ADDITIONAL SOURCES USED IN PREPARATION OF THIS BOOK
(Technical or not readily available)

Artman, L.P., Jr. 1974. The Overseas Railroad. [no publisher listed]. 14pp.

Clarke, Mary Helm. 1949. South Florida Treasure Trails. Tallahassee, FL: Kay Publishing Co. 103pp.

Craighead, Frank C. 1963. Orchids and Other Airplants of the Everglades National Park. Coral Gables, FL: University of Miami Press. 127pp.

Downs, Dorothy. 1982. Miccosukee Arts and Crafts. Miami: Miccosukee Indian Tribe of Florida. 21pp.

Duever, Michael J., John E. Carlson, John F. Meeder, Linda C. Duever, Lance H. Gunderson, Lawrence A. Riopelle, Taylor R. Alexander, Ronald L. Myers, and

Daniel P. Spangler. 1986. The Big Cypress National Preserve. Research Report No. 8 of the National Audubon Society, New York. 444pp. (Originally 1979, Resource inventory and analysis of the Big Cypress National Preserve, Univ. of Florida, Gainesville. 455pp.)

Everglades Natural History. March 1953 (Vol. 1, No. 1) to June 1955 (Vol. 3, No. 2). Everglades Natural History Association.

Gleason, Patrick J. (ed.) 1974. Environments of South Florida: Past and Present. Memoir 2: Miami Geological Society. Miami: Miami Geological Society. 452pp.

Griswold, Oliver. 1965. The Florida Keys and the Coral Reef. Miami: The Graywood Press. 143pp.

McGeachy, Beth. 1955. Handbook of Florida Palms. St. Petersburg, FL: Great Outdoors Publishing Co. 62pp.

Meyers, Ronald L. and John J. Ewel (eds.). 1990. 2nd pr 91. Ecosystems of Florida. Orlando, FL: University of Central Florida Press. 763pp.

MMWR. 1989. Seizures temporally associated with DEET insect repellent New York and Connecticut. Morbidity and Mortality Weekly R. 38(39):678-680.

NOAA. 2010. Climatological report. www.srh.noaa.gov/key/?n=local_climate

Parks, Pat. 1968. The Railroad that Died at Sea. Brattleboro, VT: The Stephen Greene Press. 44pp.

Stevenson, Henry M. 1976. Vertebrates of Florida (Identification and Distribution). Gainesville, FL: University Presses of Florida. 607pp.

OTHER SOURCES OF INFORMATION

Florida—General
• **Audubon of Florida**
444 Brickell Ave., Suite 850
Miami, FL 33131
305-371-6399
www.fl.audubon.org

• **Florida (official government site)**
www.myflorida.com

• **Florida State Parks Information Center**
Division of Recreation and Parks
3900 Commonwealth Blvd.
Tallahassee, FL 32399-3000
850-245-2157
www.floridastateparks.org

• **Florida Fish and Wildlife Conservation Commission**
620 South Meridian Street
Tallahassee, FL 32399-1600
850-488-4676
1-888-FISH-FLORIDA (buying a license)
South Region 561-625-5122
Southwest Region 863-648-3200
www.myfwc.com
Report wildlife violations: 888-404-FWCC (3922)

• **Florida Trail Association, Inc.**
5415 SW 13th St.
Gainesville, FL 32608
352-378-8823
www.floridatrail.org/

• **National Park Service**
1849 C Street NW
Washington, D.C. 20240
202-208-6843
www.nps.gov

- **National Weather Service**
Key West 305-295-1316 (recorded forecast)
Miami 305-229-4550 (recorded forecast)
www.weather.noaa.gov

- **U.S. Fish and Wildlife Service**
1849 C Street NW
Washington, D.C. 20240
800-344-WILD
www.fws.gov

Florida—South
- **The Conservancy of Southwest Florida**
1450 Merrihue Drive
Naples, FL 34102
239-262-0304
www.conservancy.org

- **Corkscrew Land and Water Trust**
23998 Corkscrew Road
Estero, FL 33928
239-657-2253
www.crewtrust.org

- **Florida Keys National Marine Sanctuary**
33 East Quay Road
Key West, FL 33040
305-809-4670
www.floridakeys.noaa.gov/

- **Florida Keys Visitors Bureau**
1-800-FLA-KEYS (352-5397)

- **Florida National Parks and Monuments Association**
10 Parachute Key #51
Homestead, FL 33034-6735
305-247-1216
www.evergladesassociation.org
publications on south Florida cultural and natural history

- **Friends of the Everglades**
11767 South Dixie Highway #232
Miami, Florida 33156
305-669-0858
www.everglades.org

- **Greater Homestead-Florida City Chamber of Commerce**
212 NW 1st Avenue
Homestead, FL 33030
305-247-2332
www.chamberinaction.com

- **Greater Key West Chamber of Commerce**
402 Wall Street
Key West, FL 33040
305-294-2587
www.keywestchamber.org

- **Hendry County**
County Court House
P.O. Box 1760
La Belle, FL 33935-1760
(863) 675-5217
www.hendryfla.net/

- **Monroe County**
1100 Simonton Street
Key West, FL 33040
(305) 292-4441
www.monroecounty-fl.gov/index.aspx

- **National Audubon Society**
Tavernier Science Center
115 Indian Mound Trail
Tavernier, FL 33070
305-852-5318
www.fl.audubon.org/who_Tavernier.html

- **Sierra Club**
www.florida.sierraclub.org/miami

• South Florida Water Management District
3301 Gun Club Road
West Palm Beach, FL 33406
561-686-8800
www.sfwmd.gov

• The Nature Conservancy
South Florida Office 305-445-8352
Florida Keys Office 305-745-8402
www.nature.org/wherewework/
northamerica/states/florida

• Tropical Audubon Society
5530 Sunset Drive
South Miami, FL 33143
305-666-5111 (general information)
305-667-PEEP (Birding Hotline recording
for local sightings)
www.tropicalaudubon.org

• Tropical Everglades Visitor Association
160 US 1
Florida City, FL 33034
305-245-9180
800-388-9669
www.tropicaleverglades.com/

GLOSSARY

aquifer an underground natural porous rock formation containing water; supplies water for wells or springs.

barrier island a low-lying island, usually long and narrow, that parallels the coastal shore and protects the mainland from heavy surf and winds.

bayhead a tree island in the freshwater marsh that may be submerged during the wet season; so named because it usually contains redbay or sweet bay trees.

brackish water that contains some salt and may vary considerably in salinity; usually found where a river meets the ocean.

bromeliad (pronounced "bro-me´-lee-ad") air plant; a plant from the pineapple family that is an epiphyte. Examples are Spanish moss, ballmoss, needle-leaved wildpine, giant wildpine.

coastal prairie areas along the mangrove belt lacking trees and having predominantly succulent-type, salt-tolerant plants, such as glasswort and saltwort.

coral a colony of invertebrates bound together by a limestone skeleton that forms the "backbone" of the reef off of south Florida.

cumulonimbus thunderhead; a tall, unstable cloud formation that imparts lightning and rain, common in south Florida in the summer.

Dade County pine the local name for the variety of slash pine (*Pinus elliottii* var. *densa*) that grows in Dade County and elsewhere in south Florida; historically very popular for building construction because of its resistance to insect damage and rot.

endangered species a species of plant or animal that has been declared (by a state or federal agency) in danger of becoming extinct if not protected.

endemic originating in a particular locality; indigenous.

epiphyte a plant growing upon or attached to another plant or non-living structure but is not parasitic. Florida has numerous epiphytic bromeliads, orchids, and ferns.

estuary a shallow wetland formed where a river meets an inlet of the sea; among the most productive habitats in the world.

exotic any species of plant or animal that was introduced (intentionally or unintentionally) by humans to an area it did not previously inhabit. Also called **invasive** and nonnative.

hammock a large tree island; an elevated, well-drained tract of land slightly higher than the surrounding wetlands where hardwood trees grow naturally.

hurricane a cyclone in the Atlantic Ocean having wind speeds of 74 mph or greater.

hydroperiod the length of time in any given year that an area of wetland is inundated by water.

invasive species a plant or animal species (usually not native to the area) whose introduction causes or is likely to cause economic or environmental harm or harm to human health by spreading out of control. Invasive species are undesirable in natural environments because they outcompete or deplete native species.

key a small, low-lying island; occasionally used to mean a hammock.

marl mud composed primarily of calcium carbonate, formed chiefly in short-hydroperiod freshwater wetlands; may become solidified.

midden a mound or small hill made by Indians, usually from discarding oyster, clam, or snail shells or bones.

native species of plants or animals indigenous to an area.

old growth a forest that has never been logged.

peat organic soil that accumulates under wet conditions and has great water storage capacity; the plant remains can still be identified.

pineland an area elevated on a ridge, dry most of the year and periodically swept by fires, allowing the establishment of pine trees; also called pine flatwoods.

pneumatophore pencil-like appendage rising from the root of a black mangrove tree; functions as respiratory organ at low tide.

prescribed burn an intentionally set fire on an undeveloped area, planned and controlled by fire ecologists to maintain a healthy habitat.

prop root stilt-like root that supports the trunk of a red mangrove tree.

propagule a seed that begins to germinate while still on the tree.

slough (pronounced "slew") a channel of slow-moving water, slightly deeper than the surrounding freshwater marsh.

solution hole a depression in limestone rock formed by the dissolving action of acidic water, which is created by rainwater mixing with decomposing vegetation.

strand a forest in a slough.

xeriscape (pronounced ze´-ri-scape) a landscape or garden with plants that require little water to thrive; especially useful in desert regions and in south Florida where water must be conserved.

IMAGE CREDITS

Front cover:

Alligator © William Silver, 2011/Used under license from Shutterstock.com

Roseate Spoonbill © PhotosbyElliot, 2011/Used under license from Shutterstock.com

Sunset over Everglades at Chekika © Rudy Umans, 2011/Used under license from Shutterstock.com

Bahia Honda State Park © Rebecca Connolly, 2011/ Used under license from Shutterstock.com

Porkfish on reef © Andrew Jalbert, 2011/Used under license from Shutterstock.com

Julia butterfly © Rudy Umans, 2011/Used under license from Shutterstock.com

Text:

Page 8 Fishing line © Susan D. Jewell

Page 12 Sharks © Rich Carey, 2011/Used under license from Shutterstock.com

Page17 Seven-Mile Bridge © rj lerich, 2011/ Used under license from Shutterstock.com

Page19 Walking dredge © Susan D. Jewell

Page 21 Key West © Thomas Barrat, 2011/ Used under license from Shutterstock.com

Page 24 Camping © Larsek, 2011/Used under license from Shutterstock.com

Page 25 Coral reef © Jim Lipschutz, 2011/Used under license from Shutterstock.com

Page 27 Mangroves © FloridaStock, 2011/Used under license from Shutterstock.com

Page 29 Cypress dome © Susan D. Jewell

Page 30 Slash pines © Susan D. Jewell

Page 32 Sawgrass marsh © Susan D. Jewell

Page 33 Hammock © Susan D. Jewell

Page 35 Estuary © Susan D. Jewell

Page 37 Tree snail © almondd, 2011/Used under license from Shutterstock.com

Page 40 Dolphins © Four Oaks, 2011/Used under license from Shutterstock.com

Page 43 Alligator © Rudy Umans, 2011/Used under license from Shutterstock.com

Page 44 Gopher tortoise © Susan D. Jewell

Page 48 White ibises © David Watkins, 2011/ Used under license from Shutterstock.com

Page 53 Feral hogs © Stephen Meese, 2011/ Used under license from Shutterstock.com

Page 55 Melaleuca © arnet117, 2011/Used under license from Shutterstock.com

Page 56 Old world climbing fern © Susan D. Jewell

Page 60 Loxahatchee Refuge © Susan D. Jewell

Page 64 Cape Florida © Celso Diniz, 2011/Used under license from Shutterstock.com

Page 68 Elliott Key © Jorge R. Gonzalez, 2011/ Used under license from Shutterstock.com

Page 71 Fern Forest © Susan D. Jewell

Page 77 Yellow-crowned night-heron © vilainecrevette, 2011/Used under license from Shutterstock.com

Page 79 Dupuis Reserve © Susan D. Jewell

Page 84 Marsh habitat © John A. Anderson, 2011/Used under license from Shutterstock.com

Page 91 Solution hole © William Silver, 2011/ Used under license from Shutterstock.com

Page 94 Dwarf cypress © FloridaStock, 2011/ Used under license from Shutterstock.com

Page 97 Snake Bight © William Silver, 2011/ Used under license from Shutterstock.com

Page 106 Shark Valley Tower © Rebecca Connolly, 2011/Used under license from Shutterstock.com

Page 112 Otters © lorboaz/Dreamstime.com

Page 116 Leatherback hatchling © Claudine Laabs

Page 123 Ruddy Daggerwing © Leighton Photography & Imaging 2011/Used under license from Shutterstock.com

Page 126 Navy Wells © Susan D. Jewell

Page 129 Green Cay Wetlands © Susan D. Jewell

Page 133 Loxahatchee River © William Silver, 2011/Used under license from Shutterstock.com"

Page 141 Harold A. Campbell Boat Launch in STA 3 and 4 © Susan D. Jewell

Page 145 Florida Trail in Big Cypress National Preserve © William Silver, 2011/Used under license from Shutterstock.com"

Page 152 Osprey © Randy Rimland, 2011/Used under license from Shutterstock.com

Page 156 Palmettos © pix2go, 2011/Used under license from Shutterstock.com

Page 158 Wood stork © Arto Hakola, 2011/ Used under license from Shutterstock.com

Page 159 White ibis © FloridaStock 2011/Used under license from Shutterstock.com

Page 160 Sea oats on beach © Jeff Kinsey 2011/Used under license from Shutterstock.com

Page 161 Winkler Point © Susan D. Jewell

Page 163 Ghost orchid © Leighton Photography & Imaging, 2011/ Used under license from Shutterstock.com

Page 167 Florida panther © Bephotographers/ Dreamstime.com

Page 168 Boca Grande lighthouse © jocrebbin, 2011/ Used under license from Shutterstock.com

Page 171 Snowy Egret at Ding Darling © pix2go, 2011/Used under license from Shutterstock.com

Page 174 Historic structure in Koreshan © William Silver, 2011/ Used under license from Shutterstock.com

Page 184 Picayune Strand State Forest © Susan D. Jewell

Page 189 Ten Thousand Islands NWR © Susan D. Jewell

Page 190 Bahia Honda © ActinicBlue, 2011/ Used under license from Shutterstock.com

Page 193 Bahia Honda State Park © Rebecca Connolly, 2011/ Used under license from Shutterstock.com

Page 199 Coral rock substrate © Rudy Umans, 2011/ Used under license from Shutterstock.com

Page 201 Fort Jefferson © William Silver, 2011/ Used under license from Shutterstock.com

Page 205 Florida Keys Eco-Discovery Center, Courtesy of the Florida Keys Eco-Discovery Center

Page 209 Porkfish on reef © Andrew Jalbert, 2011/Used under license from Shutterstock.com

Page 214 Buttonwood © Rudy Umans, 2011/ Used under license from Shutterstock.com

Page 216 Kayak on Long Key © William Silver, 2011/Used under license from Shutterstock.com

Page 219 Key deer © Arto Hakola, 2011/ Used under license from Shutterstock.com

Page 222 Aquatic vegetation © tonyz20, 2011/ Used under license from Shutterstock.com

Page 225 Kayaking on the Turner River © William Silver, 2011/Used under license from Shutterstock.com

Page 226 Lake Okeechobee Scenic Trail © Susan D. Jewell

Color insert:

CP 1 Lubber grasshopper © FloridaStock, 2011/ Used under license from Shutterstock.com

CP 2 Painted bunting © Claudine Laabs

CP 3 Snail Kite © Steve Byland, 2011/Used under license from Shutterstock.com

CP 4 Water hyacinth © Liquid Productions, Nikita Tiunov, 2011/Used under license from Shutterstock.com

CP 5 Beauty berry © Susan D. Jewell

CP 6 Loxahatchee observation platform © Susan D. Jewell

CP 7 Loxahatchee Marsh rainbow © FloridaStock, 2011/Used under license from Shutterstock.com

CP 8 Anhinga Trail © jeff gynane 2011/Used under license from Shutterstock.com

CP 9 Anhinga © Tony Campbell, 2011/Used under license from Shutterstock.com

CP 10 Bromeliads © iofoto, 2011/Used under license from Shutterstock.com

CP 11 Purple gallinule © FloridaStock, 2011/ Used under license from Shutterstock.com

CP 12 Green anole © Leighton Photography & Imaging, 2011/Used under license from Shutterstock.com

CP 13 Dwarf cypress © FloridaStock, 2011/ Used under license from Shutterstock.com

CP 14 Ft. Jefferson © Varina and Jay Patel, 2011/Used under license from Shutterstock.com

CP 15 Pennekamp Park © luminouslens, 2011/ Used under license from Shutterstock.com

CP 16 Gumbo Limbo Trail © Jorge R. Gonzalez, 2011/Used under license from Shutterstock.com

CP 17 West Indian manatee © Liquid Productions, LLC, 2011/Used under license from Shutterstock.com

CP 18 Paurotis palms © FloridaStock, 2011/ Used under license from Shutterstock.com

CP 19 Biscayne National Park © Henryk Sadura, 2011/Used under license from Shutterstock.com

CP 20 Aerial view of Palm Beach County © FloridaStock, 2011/Used under license from Shutterstock.com

CP 21 Hawksbill sea turtle © Andrew Jalbert, 2011/Used under license from Shutterstock.com

CP 22 Softshell turtle © gracious_tiger, 2011/ Used under license from Shutterstock.com

CP 23 Tarpon © Liquid Productions, Manda Nicholls, 2011/Used under license from Shutterstock.com

CP 24 French Angelfish © DJ Mattaar, 2011/ Used under license from Shutterstock.com

CP 25 Bahia Honda State Park © FloridaStock, 2011/Used under license from Shutterstock.com

CP 26 Sandhill Cranes © Steve Byland 2011/ Used under license from Shutterstock.com

CP 27 Key Deer © visceralimage, 2011/Used under license from Shutterstock.com

CP 28 Burrowing Owl © Ryan M. Bolton, 2011/

Used under license from Shutterstock.com

CP 29 Roseate Spoonbill © PhotosbyElliot, 2011/Used under license from Shutterstock.com

CP 30 Turner River Road in Big Cypress © William Silver, 2011/Used under license from Shutterstock.com

CP 31 Cuban treefrog © Steve Bower, 2011/ Used under license from Shutterstock.com

CP 32 Alligator eating python © 8155069152, 2011/Used under license from Shutterstock.com

CP 33 Zebra longwing butterfly © MBoe, 2011/ Used under license from Shutterstock.com

CP 34 Florida panther © jocrebbin, 2011/Used under license from Shutterstock.com

CP 35 Sunset over Everglades at Chekika © Rudy Umans, 2011/Used under license from Shutterstock.com

CP 36 Black-bellied whistling-ducks © Steve Byland, 2011/Used under license from Shutterstock.com

CP 37 Brown Pelican © pix2go, 2011/Used under license from Shutterstock.com

CP 38 Kayaker in Keys © Tree of Life, 2011/ Used under license from Shutterstock.com

CP 39 Indian Key © William Silver, 2011/Used under license from Shutterstock.com

CP 40 Limpkin © pix2go, 2011/Used under license from Shutterstock.com

CP 41 Green iguana © David Masini, 2011/ Used under license from Shutterstock.com

CP 42 Tricolored Heron © Glenn Price, 2011/ Used under license from Shutterstock.com

CP 43 Spotted eagle rays © Rebecca Connolly, 2011/Used under license from Shutterstock.com

CP 44 Sea-grape tree © Steve Carroll, 2011/ Used under license from Shutterstock.com

CP 45 Reddish egret © Glenn Price, 2011/Used under license from Shutterstock.com

Maps:
All maps by Jennifer Borresen

INDEX

Photographs are indicated by boldface. Photos on color pages are indicated by "**CP**." Map listings are indicated by "**M**." Checklists are not indexed.

153, 155, 174, 175, 176, 182, 183, 188, 192, 194, 200, 202, 203, 208, 211, 215, 225, 227

canal,
    Buttonwood, 43, 87, 99, 101, 102
    St. Lucie, 34, 226
    Tamiami, 153

canoeing, 59, 75, 85, 86, 102, 108, 110, 115, 118, 128, 134, 150, 152, 162, 170, 174, 208, **216**, 224

Cape Florida, 46, 47, 63-64, **64**

Cape Sable, 10, 17, 41, 45, 46, 47, **M83**, 97, 99, 101

caracara, crested, 47, 48, 176, 182

Card Sound Road, 23, 43

Castellow Hammock Preserve and Nature Center, **M57**, 122–23, **123**

Cayo Costa State Park, 36, 46, **M143**, 151

coastal ridge, 16, 19, 44, 50, 111

coco-plum, 33, 74, 90, 119, 130, 138

Collier County parks, 152

Collier-Seminole State Park, 28, **M143**, 153-54, 224

conch, 35, 39, 109, 192, 202, 203

conversion table, 2

coontie, 31, 71, 75, 115, 121, 127, 186

coral, 8, 21, **25**, 25–27, 38, 65, 67, 69, 192, 194, 200, 201, 202, 203, 205, 208-9, 210, 213, 215, 216, 217, 221

Corbett Wildlife Management Area (see J.W. Corbett Wildlife Management Area)

Corkscrew Marsh, 31, **M143**, 155-56, **156**

Corkscrew Swamp Sanctuary, 1, 28, 29, 43, 49, **M143**, 157-59, **158**, **159**, 164

Crane Point Hammock, 34, 195, 196

Crane Point Museum and Nature Center, **M191**, 195-96

crane, sandhill, 80, 95, 120, 137, 138, 147, **CP26**

crocodile, 6, 7, 23, 42-43, 55, 65, 84, 87, 128, 138, 139, 153, 170, 198

Crocodile Lake National Wildlife Refuge, 6, 23

Curry Hammock State Park, **M191**, 197

cypress, 18, 28–29, 47, **56**, 60, 71, 74, 78, **94**, 95, 119, 120, 130, 133, 135, 144, **145**, 146, 147, 154, 157, 158, **159**, 162, 164, 166, 178, 183, **CP13**
    bald-cypress, 28, 71, **94**, 144, 147, 157, 158
    domes, 28–29, **29**, 79, 119, 138, 155
    knees, 28
    pond-cypress, 28, 71, 95
    strand, 28, 29, 71, 72, 111, 144, 178
    swamp, 60, 61, 78, 129, 133, 148, 153, 154, 176, 181

Dade County parks, 56, 121–27

Dagny Johnson Key Largo Hammock Botanical State Park, 34, **M191**, 198-99

deer, Key, 7, 8, 22, 195, 218–19, **219**, 220, **CP27**

Deerfield Island Park, 70

Delnor-Wiggins Pass State Park, **M143**, 160

"Ding" Darling National Wildlife Refuge (see J.N. "Ding" Darling National Wildlife Refuge)

diving, scuba, 15, 38, 65, 69, 200, 201, 203, 208, 210, 217

dolphin, bottle-nose, 34, 40-41, **40**, 65, 85, 99, 102, 107, 128, 150, 175, 179, 197

Dry Tortugas National Park, 25, 27, **M191**, 200-204, **201**, **CP14**

duck, 35, 60, 96, 97, 98, 99
    American widgeon, 172
    black-bellied whistling, 129, 136, **CP36**
    blue-winged teal, 60, 97, 172
    fulvous-whistling, 60, 141
    green-winged teal, 172
    hooded merganser, 172
    mallard, 52
    mottled, 60, 75, 170, 172
    Muscovy, 52
    northern pintail, 172
    northern shoveler, 172
    redbreasted merganser, 172
    ring-necked, 60

Duck Stamp, 7, 170

Dupuis Reserve State Forest, 31, 53, **M57**, 79-81, **79**, 120

eagle, bald, 47, 80, 85, 95, 111, 128, 134, 138, 146, 153, 162, 170, 171, 176, 179, 195

Eco Pond, **48**, **83**, 87, 99–100

egret
    great, 49, 73, 9, 98, 124, 171
    reddish, 85, 48, 100, 170, 171, 179, 197, **CP45**
    snowy, 49, 97, 124, 165, 171, **171**

equestrian trail, 73, 79, 80, 81, 133, 176, 182, 183

Estero Bay, 36, 161, 175, 177, 178, 179, 224

Estero Bay Preserve State Park, **M143**, 161, **161**

Estero River, 174, 175, 224

estuary, 35, 95, 103, 117, 149, 160, 188

Everglades, 4, 5, 16, 17, 18, 19–20, 31, 32, 34, 39, 40, 42, 46, 48-49, 54, **55**, 59, 61, 73, 84, 89, 92, 93, 95, 99, 100, 105, 108, 111, 119, 121, 138, 140, 142, 208

Everglades City, 42, 49, 85, 86, 87, 88, 103, 108, 109, 110, 164, 165, 188, **M223**

Everglades National Park, 1, 7, 10, 13, 17, 18, 20, **24**, 28, **29**, **30**, 30–31, 32, 33, 34, 36, 39, 41, 42, 43, 45, 47, **48**, 49, 52, **53**, 56, **M57**, 82–110, **M83**, **84**, **91**, **93**, **97**, 126, 138, 140, 142, 144, 147, 148, 149, 162, 165, 208, **M223**, 224, **CP13**
    areas
        Chekika, **M83**, 103-4, **CP35**
        Everglades City, **M83**, 107-10
        Flamingo, **M83**, 98-103
        main, 88-98

Here are some other books from Pineapple Press on related topics. For a complete catalog, write to Pineapple Press, P.O. Box 3889, Sarasota, Florida 34230-3889, or call (800) 746-3275. Or visit our website at www.pineapplepress.com.

Easygoing Guide to Natural Florida, Volume 1: South Florida by Douglas Waitley.
Easygoing Guide to Natural Florida, Volume 2: Central Florida by Douglas Waitley.
If you love nature but want to enjoy it with minimum effort, these are the books for you. To be an easygoing nature site, it must be beautiful and easy to reach, not cost much, and require little effort. (pb)

Everglades: River of Grass, 60th Anniversary Edition by Marjory Stoneman Douglas with an update by Michael Grunwald. Before 1947, when Marjory Stoneman Douglas named the Everglades a "river of grass," most people considered the area worthless. She brought the world's attention to the need to preserve the Everglades. In the Afterword, Michael Grunwald tells us what has happened to them since then. (hb)

Florida Magnificent Wilderness: State Lands, Parks, and Natural Areas by James Valentine and D. Bruce Means. Photographer James Valentine captures environmental art images of the state's remote wilderness places. Dr. D. Bruce Means covers the wildlife and natural ecosystems of Florida. An introduction to each section is written by a highly respected Florida writer and conservationist, including Al Burt, Manley Fuller, Steve Gatewood, Victoria Tschinkel, and Bernie Yokel. (hb)

Florida's Rivers by Charles R. Boning. An overview of Florida's waterways and detailed information on 60 of Florida's rivers, covering each from its source to the end. From the Blackwater River in the western panhandle to the Miami River in the southern peninsula. (pb)

Florida's Birds, 2nd Edition by David S. Maehr and Herbert W. Kale II. Illustrated by Karl Karalus. This new edition is a major event for Florida birders. Each section of the book is updated, and 30 new species are added. Also added are range maps and color coded guides to months when the bird is present and/or breeding in Florida. Color throughout. (pb)

Myakka by Paula Benshoff. Discover the story of the land of Myakka. This book takes you into shady hammocks of twisted oaks and up into aerial gardens, down the wild and scenic river, and across a variegated canvas of prairies, piney woods, and wetlands—all located in Myakka River State Park, the largest state park in Florida. (pb)

Priceless Florida by Ellie Whitney, D. Bruce Means, and Anne Rudloe. An extensive guide (432 pages, 800 color photos) to the incomparable ecological riches of this unique region, presented in a way that will appeal to young and old, laypersons and scientists. Complete with maps, charts, and species lists. (hb, pb)

The Trees of Florida, 2nd Edition, by Gil Nelson. The only comprehensive guide to Florida's amazing variety of tree species, this book serves as both a reference and a field guide. (hb, pb)

The Springs of Florida, 2nd Edition, by Doug Stamm. Take a guided tour of Florida's fascinating springs in this beautiful book featuring detailed descriptions, maps, and rare underwater photography. Learn how to enjoy these natural wonders while swimming, diving, canoeing, and tubing. (hb, pb)

St. Johns River Guidebook by Kevin M. McCarthy. From any point of view—historical, commercial, or recreational—the St. Johns River is the most important river in Florida. This guide describes the history, major towns and cities along the way, wildlife, and personages associated with the river. (pb)

Suwannee River Guidebook by Kevin M. McCarthy. A leisurely trip down one of the best-known and most beloved rivers in the country, from the Okefenokee Swamp in Georgia to the Gulf of Mexico in Florida. (pb)

Hillsborough River Guidebook by Kevin M. McCarthy. The Hillsborough River is not long, but has played an important role in Florida commerce and history. This essential guidebook is both a history and a guide to the river. (pb)